WHAT THE
BONES
TELL US

■

JEFFREY H. SCHWARTZ

A JOHN MACRAE BOOK
HENRY HOLT AND COMPANY
NEW YORK

Library of Congress Cataloging-in-Publication Data
Schwartz, Jeffrey H.
What the bones tell us / Jeffrey H. Schwartz.—1st ed.
p. cm.
"A John Macrae book."
Includes index.
1. Physical anthropology. 2. Schwartz, Jeffrey H.
3. Anthropologists—Biography. I. Title.
GN50.6.S39A3   1993   92-12473
573—dc20   CIP
ISBN 0-8050-1056-4

Henry Holt books are available at special discounts for bulk purchases for sales
promotions, premiums, fund-raising, or educational use. Special editions or book
excerpts can also be created to specification.
For details contact: Special Sales Director,
Henry Holt and Company, Inc., 115 West 18th Street,
New York, New York 10011.

First Edition—1993

Designed by Claire Vaccaro
Endpaper illustrations: Gravemarkers from the Tophet, Carthage
Printed in the United States of America
Recognizing the importance of preserving the written word, Henry Holt and
Company, Inc., by policy, prints all of its first editions on acid-free paper. ∞

1 3 5 7 9 10 8 6 4 2

FOR MY PARENTS,
JACK AND LILLIAN

CONTENTS

PREFACE

AND

ACKNOWLEDGMENTS

I went to college thinking I was going to be a physician and ended up with a doctorate in physical anthropology, specializing in the analysis of the skeletal remains of fossil and living primates, including humans. This may have surprised my parents, but it seemed quite natural to my maternal grandmother, who pointed out to everyone that, even as a child, I had been interested in the preserved remains of long-gone animals and people. When the family had taken a trip to Niagara Falls, I spent my time pulling out pieces of shale and splitting them open in search of ancient marine fossils. And I had not endeared myself to our elderly next-door neighbor, whose garage foundation I partially exposed one summer in my quest for old bones I *knew* had to be there.

Now I study bones—or, more correctly, bony fragments—professionally. I work with fragments of bodies that have very recently lost their trappings of flesh and blood and are now represented only by their skeletal infrastructure. With fragments of the skeletons of centuries-old civilizations that had died, decayed, and had become buried until exposed by the archeologist's trowel. And with fragments of the very ancient, who lived so many hundreds of thousands, even millions, of years ago that none of their species now exist.

But these physical fragments—a bone here, a tooth there—reflect the larger picture of incompleteness, that of the evolutionary history of life. In spite of the inescapable fact of evolution, and the continuing demonstration of its processes, we will always be in the position of trying to reconstruct the evolutionary history of a group of organisms. Sometimes we know a group of organisms only as fossils, sometimes as a mixture of fossil and living forms, and, at other times, only by way of living representatives because potentially related fossils either have not yet been discovered or simply did not survive to be found. Thus, even studying the bones and teeth, and DNA and genes, for that matter, of living forms and trying to reconstruct their evolutionary relationships to one another is an endeavor in the realm of the fragmentary unknown.

It is frustrating to know, on the one hand, that every living thing on earth will have had a single, unique history—whether it be the life of an individual, of a civilization, of a species, of a diverse evolutionary group—and, on the other, to be constantly in the position of trying to discover it. But discovery is less a matter of, for example, unearthing a fossil or sequencing another species' DNA than it is interpreting data in an attempt to reconstruct the missing pieces of the puzzle.

And this brings us to the subject of this book: deciphering the unknown past from bits and pieces of what had once been whole. How do physical anthropologists, forensic osteologists, osteoarcheologists, taxonomists, and paleontologists do their work? How do or should we read their reports from the field? What may lie between the lines, or remain more completely hidden, in the pronouncements that often flood the mass media—as well as the arcane scientific journals—about the significance of one fossil find over another or the significance of skeletal remains from a long-lost civilization? Is there ever a "right" interpretation? And, if so, how would we ever know? What I hope to accomplish in this book is to provide insights into the interpretation of "evidence" and the application of the "scientific method" so that you, the reader, will be more attuned to what the scientists are saying, and why they may be saying it, and realize that the problems and issues that they are addressing are matters we can all think about critically.

Science, especially evolutionary sciences, can only proceed from learning about those theories or hypotheses that do not stand the test of time. It will stagnate when the emphasis remains on "being correct"—believing that there is only one kind of data, or only one way of interpreting data. There are always alternative interpretations of the same data. It is often the case, however, that the alternatives that are rejected are treated as if they don't exist. But they do. And we should be aware not only of their existence and potential viability, but of the possibility that the hypotheses that we might embrace so strongly today may very well be the rejects of tomorrow.

As you will notice, I have included a bibliography at the end of the text that lists all of the primary and secondary sources I used. Within the text, I have avoided technical scientific referencing, but I have left clear-cut clues to the appropriate sources in the bibliography. In some instances, though, particularly when dissecting works of Charles Darwin and Thomas Huxley, I have specified the pages from which I have extracted certain quotes and statements. I do so because my conclusions about various claims attributed to these scholars are not those that have been promulgated in the popular and professional literature. I hope that you, the reader, will not be distracted by the page numbers appended to various excerpted passages. They will help guide you, though, if you do decide to read further in the original texts.

This book contains no artists' reconstructions of what the owner of a particular fossil tooth may have looked like, or of how members of an extinct species or ancient civilization may have performed one ritual or another. Nor are there any photographs of Neandertal skulls, or those who study them, or any other items typically found in books of popular anthropology. Such illustrations rarely contribute anything fresh or original. In their stead I have done my best with verbal images.

It is difficult to know how to thank everyone who contributed in some way to the formulation of this book. I wouldn't have written about certain experiences if, for example, Ralph Solecki hadn't arranged for me to work on John Waechter's excavation at the fossil hominid site of Swanscombe, where I met Chris Stringer; or if Dexter Perkins hadn't recommended me for the position of staff osteologist for the dig at Tell Hesi, where I met Larry Stager, who later invited me to analyze the burned infant bones from his part of the multinational excavations at Carthage. And I wouldn't have been introduced to human and fossil human skeletal analysis were it not for courses with Ralph Holloway many years before. I wouldn't have become interested in other non-human primates if John Waechter hadn't convinced me to spend a year studying at the University of London, where I met Bob Martin, who directed me to Theya Molleson at the British Museum (Natural History), where Chris Stringer and then Peter Andrews eventually ended up. Bob also invited me to give a paper at his joint conference on prosimians, where I met Ian Tattersall, who was a curator at the American Museum of Natural History, and through whom I met Niles Eldredge. It's an endless chain. At the University of Pittsburgh I discussed Darwin and Huxley in depth with Jim Lennox, who graciously scrutinized the sections of this book where I deal with these scholars; likewise I was fortunate to have been able to coax Shelby Brown, who had done her dissertation on Carthaginian gravemarkers, to comment on many versions of the Carthage chapter. Terry Kaufman provided further insight into the interpretation of the Old Testament, and, in more than one chapter, Hilary Masters saved me from verbal suicide.

Alison Bond's and Amy Robbins's support throughout and Jack Macrae's mastery of nonintrusive editorial guidance, especially during those bleak periods of massive revision, were invaluable. The only other person who knew how many times I thought I'd never be able to pull everything together but who didn't have the luxury of leaving the subject behind with the hanging up of the phone was my wife, Lynn Emanuel. My thanks for the forbearance of each of you.

JHS
Pittsburgh
April 1992

PART I

■

THE
PRESENT
AND THE
RECENT
PAST

■

EVERYTHING YOU WANTED TO KNOW

ABOUT BONES (AND MORE)

Imagine a Grecian urn. It was made in a certain region of Greece, at a certain time, according to certain styles and traditions. It has a trumpetlike brim. Below the pinched neck, the body swells out but then tapers toward its expanded base. The edges of the brim and base are thickened and raised. Each of a pair of ornately curved, elongate handles arches gracefully between the neck of the urn and its belly. The yellow clay used to make this urn was taken from a known quarry. In order to give the clay stability and strength as it was being fired, and forever after, finely crushed seashells—not sand, nor the chaff of wheat, nor even finely crushed potsherds—were kneaded into the clay as temper. A uniform but fine glaze, made from a crushed mineral, bathed the urn from brim to base.

Now drop the urn down a hill and try to find the scattered pieces. You will probably find at least a few body sherds, which may, in fact, be rather large. Perhaps you'll find a piece of the brim or of the base. Perhaps one of the handles. Which, if any, are the diagnostic pieces that will tell you what kind of urn it was, where it was from, and from which time period?

Clay, types of temper, even choices of glaze offer clues to region but not to time of origin. Because urns from different periods and places have similar shapes, body sherds alone rarely allow archeologists to pinpoint their origins. In contrast, it is the details—such as twists in handles, thicknesses of rims, arcs in necks and bases—that provide the clues needed to reconstruct style and, from that, time and place. Artistic or stylistic differences, sometimes very subtle, in the details of a pot or bowl are often specific not only to different civilizations but to certain regions. And, like fashions today, they also came and went quickly. Thus a small rim sherd or a piece of a handle—called an indicator sherd—is typically more diagnostic of an urn's time and place of origin than a large body sherd. Bigger is not necessarily better.

What we might think of as indicator bones exist for human and nonhuman animals, and again it's the details that count. For example, take note of the part of the elbow joint that does not move when you raise your lower arm; it belongs to your humerus, or upper arm bone. The bump at the back of the elbow joint that does move is the hooklike upper portion of the ulna, one of the two lower arm bones. The hooklike part of the ulna rotates around the middle of the lower end of your humerus, which is spindle-shaped. As you flex your lower arm, the tip of the ulna's hook moves away from part of the lower humerus, exposing the "funny bone" on the inner side of the hook. When you straighten out your lower arm, the hook of the ulna fits into a depression at the back of the humerus, above the spindle.

On the inner side of the lower end of your humerus you can feel a prominent knob projecting toward your body. The other side—the side away from your body—is a flatter, disclike surface. The "knob" and the "disc" protrude from the spindle-shaped region of the humerus around which the ulna rotates.

As you can feel, the lower end of your humerus carries diverse, detailed anatomical, or morphological, features. Because of this, even a tiny fragment of part of the lower end of a humerus can be identified specifically. Because the knob always points toward, the disc away from, and the depression above the spindle to the back of your body, you can figure out if the fragment is from a left or a right humerus. And because of the specific shapes of the spindle, knob, and disc, a knowledgeable observer can identify a fragment of a lower end of a humerus from a human; it could not have come from a cow, or an ape; it is uniquely human.

As you "climb up" your humerus, you will feel the shaft of the bone become narrower and more tubular. If you dig into your muscles, you will feel that the shaft remains relatively consistent in shape throughout much of its length. Even with a large fragment of the shaft, you might have difficulty determining the side of the body from which it came, or you might not be able even to tell that it came from a humerus in the first place.

Only when you get to the upper part of your humerus will you again find the anatomical detail needed to identify the bone clearly. One feature is the semiglobular head of the humerus. This partially rounded surface, which faces inward when the humerus is in the correct anatomical position, rotates in a shallow socket in the end of the shoulder blade, or scapula. Toward the outer part of the upper humerus, and facing somewhat forward, you might be able to feel two bumps, between which you can feel a tendon from the biceps muscle. On the bone itself, these two bumps are very distinct; they are separated from one another by the groove in which the biceps' tendon lies.

If you had a fragment of the upper part of the humerus, you could identify it as such by the semiglobular head, two bumps, and groove. By orienting the head of the humerus inward and the two bumps to the side and slightly forward, you could determine from which side of the body the bone came. Because of the specific morphologies of these features, you could tell that it was the upper part of a human humerus, and not from some quadrupedal animal.

The upper and lower ends of a humerus are like the brim and base of an urn. The shaft of the bone is like the belly of the urn. Fragments, even minute ones, of the detailed parts of a bone are like the indicator sherds of a broken urn. Fragments, even large ones, of the shaft of a bone are like the body sherds of a broken urn. Analyzing bones, after all, is very much like analyzing pottery.

To the Field

It was 1970. I was a graduate student going on my first dig. What made this one unusual was that I was going to be in charge of the analysis of human and animal bones. One of my professors at Columbia University, Dexter Perkins, a specialist in the analysis of animal bones from archeological sites, had suggested that I go in his stead on an excavation to Tell Hesi, which is located twenty-five or so kilometers inland from the Mediterranean coast, almost due west of Jerusalem. Dexter's contact was the reigning "king" of American biblical archeologists, G. Ernest Wright, who was a distinguished professor at Harvard University's Semitic Museum.

The site of Tell Hesi holds a prominent position in the history of biblical archeology. It had been excavated first in 1890 by the renowned British archeologist Sir Flinders Petrie. Like every other tell, Tell Hesi is a mound that was created by a succession of conquerers building their cities on top of the ruins of vanquished inhabitants. Each new city level sealed beneath it the remains of the preceding civilization: architectural ruin and rubble as well as potsherds and broken bones.

Petrie chose to excavate Tell Hesi with the goal of delineating the indicator sherds that were characteristic of each successive phase of occupation. He then used this pottery chronology to unravel the histories of other sites. For instance, Petrie found that certain types of pottery were characteristic of a particular phase of the Bronze Age, whereas other styles were found only during a phase of the Iron Age, or only during the Hellenistic or Greek periods. Subsequent excavations of Tell Hesi during the early 1900s revealed a more complex history of occupation, and thus pottery chronology, than Petrie had discovered. Our reexcavation was going to focus on refining our knowledge of the site's occupational history—using more sources of input than just working out a more detailed pottery chronology or finding the foundations of more buildings.

The staff and some of the crew for the reopening of Tell Hesi met for the first time at the W. F. Albright Institute, which is one of the bases of archeological research of the American Schools of Oriental Research.

The Albright Institute is located outside of the walls of the old city of Jerusalem, near Herod's Gate. A cousin of mine, with whose family I stayed my first few days in Israel, drove me to the institute for the grand gathering of staff. Squelching first dig jitters, I walked in, under an archway between low buildings, and emerged onto the central court-yard, complete with a fountain and islands of flowers and plants. I was just in time to catch the first truckload of Hesi staff to go out to the site.

The truck circled its way down from the city of Jerusalem and headed off into the plains. A few hours later we were at Tell Hesi, which lies just on the fringe of the Negev Desert. The site thus lies in a fluctuating climatic zone. Some years the area is less arid. In other years, however, the desert expands to capture it. As the desert expands and contracts, the region's vegetation and faunal composition change. During the 1970 dig season, which lasted the full two months of June and July, I saw on various occasions small herds of desert-dwelling gazelle bounding across the fields near the tell. But whether or not the Negev was in its expanded state, it was so dehydratingly hot at the site by early after-noon that we had to get up hours before dawn in order to put in a full day's work in the field.

Tell Hesi is so massive that it towers over the fields that surround it, even though its broad base sits in a natural depression. When Petrie discovered the site, the tell's eastern face was fairly steep. This steep-ness was further emphasized by the deep erosive cut of the arroyolike Wadi Hesi that borders the site as it snakes its way across the land-scape. When we arrived at the site, the tell's eastern face was still steep—its top rose 120 feet above the wadi, which had cut its way 60 feet below natural ground level. The three other sides of the tell sloped gently to ground level. A 25-acre ancient city had once surrounded the tell on these three sides. Now the fields grudgingly produce wheat, whose roots struggle each season to take hold in the topsoil-free mixture of desert sand and rubble of dead civilizations.

Perhaps the most important effort of the 1970 expedition to Tell Hesi was an attempt to change the style of digging typically employed at biblical sites. Instead of focusing solely on the tell itself and on the buildings, pottery, and artifacts of the elite, the Hesi staff included experts in a number of areas: stratigraphy, pottery, geology, human and animal bones, seeds and pollen, clay and glaze composition, metallurgy, and even stone tools. The goal was to learn as much as possible about the people who had lived on the tell as well as those who had lived outside the fortified walls of the tell and who would not have had fine ceramics or jewelry. We wanted to learn about their culture, their habits, their physical characteristics as well as the environment in which they lived. And the only way in which this can be done is by analyzing everything that comes out of the ground. At other biblical excavations in the early 1970s, some broader analyses were also being made. But at those sites additional experts were used sparingly—for example, a geologist may have been called in to identify the sources of rocks and clays used during the different periods of occupation. The staff at Tell Hesi boasted a full-time contingent of analysts of the sort typically involved in the excavation of a prehistoric site.

Archeology and Bones

At Tell Hesi, I wore several different hats. When I wore the hat of the faunal analyst, I studied the animal bones that had ended up in the garbage dump—the leftovers of meals, the butcher's discards, the bones of overworked draft animals, and broken bone implements, such as jawbones that had been used as scythes, slices of bone that looked like napkin rings, and cosmetic applicators of various shapes and sizes. From garbage such as this you can reconstruct a lot about the animals a society depends on: the domesticated animals kept as pets; the domesticated animals kept for heavy labor, meat, milk, wool, glue, and leather; the ages at which these animals were slaughtered; the animals hunted; the way in which animals were butchered; the parts of the animal that were preferred to eat; the parts traded away; the parts used for tools and other implements. You can even extrapolate further from the data about the capacity of the land for sustaining the flocks or herds of domesticates, as well as about the areas and environments in which the wild animals would have been hunted. Even recognizing what domesticated and wild animals were potentially available to a society but that are not represented in the garbage dumps can be of importance.

Early on in our first season of excavation, a small team of British faunal analysts was making the rounds of various biblical sites, asking for permission to sink a probe into each site in order to sample the animal bones, pollen, and seeds. The idea of taking a small sample from a variety of sites was the brainchild of the late Eric Higgs, who had taught at Cambridge University. Higgs's specialty was the study of animal bones from prebiblical sites of the Mediterranean region. His grand scheme was to collect enough data to be able to reconstruct the climate and environment throughout historical times. In order to accomplish this enormous task, Higgs sent various crews around the Mediterranean to collect samples of seed, pollen, and bone from various sites—one of which was Tell Hesi.

When the Higgs crew proclaimed that they wanted to sink their probes in a few strategic spots on top of and around Tell Hesi, the directors of the dig would have nothing to do with it. It was, after all, our first season, and we were just getting acquainted with the complexities of the site. I did, however, offer to share my data with the crew. Nothing ever came of the collaboration, and the Higgs crew attached themselves for a while to the team excavating at Tell Gezer, a biblical site farther to the north.

When I wore the hat of human osteologist, I became involved in what eventually turned out to be the first systematic excavation of the bedouin burials that typically compose the uppermost layers of any tell. These burials are densely packed and centuries old. It's easy to understand why certain groups would choose to inter their dead on the tops of tells. In this part of the world, a tell is the highest elevation and thus is closer to heaven. Petrie and all tell archeologists knew about these burials. But, because they were considered too recent to be of importance, they were seen as nuisances that stood between the excavator and the important stuff. As such, they always ended up in the heap of discarded backdirt.

It took a bit of doing to convince the veterans to change their ways and excavate and save all bone with the same care they applied to walls and pots. I don't know how many burials were tossed over the side of the tell during the first week of excavations, but an urgent meeting with the directors of the dig eventually put an end to (most of) that. When the staff of Tell Hesi visited the excavations at Tell Gezer late in the 1970 field season, the director of that site chided us for taking time over these burials. He had taken care of the problem by bringing in the bulldozers. Nevertheless, in future seasons of digging at Tell Hesi, excavation of these burials—aimed at exposing and preserving them carefully for future study—became a priority. When, after the first three seasons at Tell Hesi, I decided to move on to other studies, I left a skeletal sample and an interest among the excavators in adding to it, that could be analyzed in detail by the human osteologists who took my place.

For whatever reason—competition between excavations or an attempt to learn more systematically from the garbage of earlier civilizations—osteological analysis, both human and faunal, quickly became during the 1970 archeological field season an "in" thing to do on biblical sites. On occasion I would be asked to analyze bones recovered from sites being excavated elsewhere in Israel. But even though interest in human and faunal osteological analyses grew, there was still resistance to them. For instance, I would be told, the bedouin burials had nothing to do with the important activities recorded in the layers of a tell, and who cared, anyway, what animals past societies had been hunting, herding, and eating?

Some of this resistance also came from the belief that preserved historical writings could provide all anyone needed to know about the habits of past civilizations. Thus, for instance, if you wanted to know about the plants and animals raised, eaten, or traded at, for instance, Tell Hesi, you could refer to the lists of plants and animals in the Old Testament. But historical records can be deceiving.

For instance, one season I was asked by an American crew working in the Galilee to analyze the animal bones from the floor of an early synagogue they were excavating. According to the archeologists, this site was supposed to have had an uninterrupted sequence of Israelite occupation, with all the details of Jewish orthodoxy in place. These archeologists "knew" that there had been a continual occupation of people practicing full-blown Jewish orthodoxy based on their interpretation of the preserved written records.

The floor of this synagogue was littered with hundreds of bones. The bones of domesticated sheep and goat were there, as expected. But, to the extreme surprise of the dig's staff, there were also large numbers of pig bones. In fact, approximately one-third of the bones from the floor of the synagogue were pig. Anathema! What were orthodox Jews doing with pigs?

I also had been asked to take a preliminary look at some bones that had been found directly beneath the floor of this synagogue. To the archeologists' chagrin, the first piece of bone I picked up was from the skull of a young human. Again, anathema! How could orthodox Jews build anything, much less a synagogue, over a human burial area?

The problem, of course, was that the archeologists had answered at least some of the major questions even before the start of the excavation. But maybe Jews hadn't occupied the site continuously—especially not orthodox Jews, who practiced all aspects of orthodox Jewry as we know it now. Maybe different groups—some not Jewish—came in and out during the history of this site. These are only some of the questions raised by the discovery of pig and human bones where they should not have been.

Nevertheless, the arrangement I had made with these archeologists was that they were to take my data sheets, on which I had noted the information in code. They were then supposed to have the information entered and sorted stratigraphically and taxonomically on the computers at their home institution. Perhaps they did so. However, no reports on the site including my analyses have ever seen the light of day.

Paleoanthropology and Bones

In the early 1950s, Ralph Solecki, a young prehistoric archeologist then associated with the Smithsonian Institution, went to Iraq in search of a Paleolithic site. His goal was to find the physical as well as artifactual remains of Neandertals. Solecki heard of a promising cave just outside of the town of Shanidar, which is located well north of Baghdad, near the Turkish border. Solecki sought a cave site in part because caves are relatively easy to locate. In addition, the history of periods of use and disuse of a cave site are usually well preserved stratigraphically. In contrast, open-air sites—such as a seasonal campsite along a riverbank or on a hillside—are more difficult to locate. An open-air site is also a sitting duck for landslides, floods, or other sources of erosion or destruction that can eliminate all traces of it.

In *The First Flower People*, his book on the excavations of Shanidar Cave, Solecki described the site as a Shangri-la. It was a deep, large-mouthed cave that opened high on a mountainside overlooking a verdant, rolling valley. The Greater Zab River coursed nearby. When I was a graduate student, I worked for a year as Solecki's assistant trying to edit the miles of color home movie film he had taken during the excavations. Indeed, the area of the site did look wonderful. Everything was "wild." Boars still inhabited the foothills and the vegetation was unrestrained. Even the domesticated animals looked as if they were still on the wild side. And so did their keepers, the Kurds, who prided themselves on their ferocity and propensity for warring. When Solecki first visited Shanidar Cave in the summer of 1951, he found a group of Kurds living there. The cave was so immense that these people had built a small village, complete with huts and with stables for the livestock, inside. Fortunately for Solecki, these Kurds were willing to help him excavate part of the cave.

Over the course of the succeeding excavation seasons at Shanidar Cave, Solecki identified four different occupation levels. The oldest, deepest, and thickest level he called Layer D, which was about 45,000 years old. In its upper part Solecki found the remains of his first Neandertal. This individual, catalogued as Shanidar I, was identified as a male. His death was caused by a partial collapse of the cave roof.

When T. Dale Stewart, a physical anthropologist/human osteologist from the Smithsonian Institution, studied the bones of Shanidar I, he found, to his surprise, that the Neandertal's right scapula (shoulder blade), clavicle (collar bone), and humerus (upper arm bone) were all smaller and less developed than their counterparts in the left shoulder and upper arm. From this observation, Stewart concluded that the

Neandertal had been born crippled. Curiously, the lower part of the right humerus was missing, as were all of the bones of the right arm below the elbow joint. As Shanidar I had been found lying under a huge rock that had fallen from the roof of the cave, and every other bone of his skeleton was in place, you would expect that the skeleton would have been preserved as it had been in life. As such, Stewart thought that the only reasonable explanation for the missing arm bones was that the lower part of Shanidar I's right arm had been amputated intentionally some time earlier, perhaps because of problems arising from the congenital malformation of this arm.

But not only had Shanidar I been crippled in his right shoulder and arm since birth, and sometime later had lost the lower part of this arm, he also appears to have survived other assaults on his well-being. For instance, the left side of his facial skeleton was severely scarred—which led Stewart and Solecki to speculate that the left eye of this Neandertal may have been damaged, maybe even to the point of being blinded. In addition, the top of this hapless Neandertal's skull showed signs of bone healing and scarring, which indicates that he had received a rather serious clonk on his head—perhaps from an earlier mini–cave-in. (The fact that the injury showed signs of healing and scarring indicates that the incident had happened a number of years before Shanidar I's death.) And, as if this hadn't been enough to endure, Shanidar I had had a healthy case of degenerative arthritis, which seems to have been a common affliction among Neandertals.

In spite of his ailments, Shanidar I had managed to live to the age of forty years, which, for a Neandertal, was a very old age. But Shanidar I probably couldn't have done it on his own. As Solecki pointed out, given the disability he had been born with and the afflictions that later beset him, Shanidar I must have been taken care of by his companions. Indeed, Shanidar I must have belonged to a group that had had a sense of cooperation and unity—a group with interpersonal dynamics that we, modern-day humans, could understand and to which we could relate.

When Solecki and his crew uncovered Shanidar II, it was obvious that he also had been killed by a rock fall from the cave's ceiling. His skeleton was covered with rubble and his skull had been crushed.

Interestingly, it appears he had been given a ceremonial sendoff of sorts. Solecki found a small pile of stones with some worked stone points (made out of chert, which is related mineralogically to flint) on top of Shanidar II's "grave." There also had been a large fire by the grave. In addition, Solecki found a concentration of split and broken animal bones nearby, which he thought represented the leftovers of a feast that had taken place as part of the funeral ceremony.

Shanidar III had actually been discovered before the other two Neandertals but could not be excavated until later. This male individual had been wounded, as had Shanidar I. However, Shanidar III fell victim to a rockfall before his injury had mended. But, before his demise, it seems that the wounded Shanidar III had been taken care of by his companions.

Upon returning to the site in 1960, Solecki and his crew excavated an additional four Neandertal skeletons. Instead of being the victims of rockfalls, it seems that these individuals had been buried—intentionally—by other Neandertals: A hole had been dug into the floor of the cave and the skeletons of these individuals were in it. Solecki could tell he was excavating a hole because the soil around the skeletons was softer than the soil elsewhere in the cave. Soil consistency is one of the best clues for the existence of a hole. No matter how hard you try, you cannot fill in a hole—especially a hole containing bodies that will eventually decay—to the same compactness and consistency as undug earth.

The second clue that this might be a burial came when Solecki found a series of stone blocks around the hole. The positions of the rocks around and on top of the rockfall victims were much more random than were those of these rocks. These rocks looked as if they had been purposefully arranged.

The third clue came from laboratory analyses, conducted in Paris, of soil samples taken from the general excavation layers as well as from the potential grave itself.

As is done more commonly these days, Solecki collected soil samples so that the seeds and pollen in them—and thus the plants from which they came—could be identified. The paleobotanical expert to whom Solecki sent these samples was Madame Arlette Leroi-Gourhan, who at times had collaborated with her husband, André, a French prehistoric archeologist. As expected, Madame Leroi-Gourhan found pollen of trees and grasses common to the area of Shanidar Cave. But, to everyone's surprise, she also identified the pollens of flowers in the samples from the suspected group burial. These pollens were represented in such high concentrations that it seemed extremely unlikely that they had been blown into the cave by wind or carried in on an animal's fur. A better explanation was that bunches of flowers had been placed—purposefully—in the grave with the Neandertals.

Some pollens were from plants similar to small and brightly colored wildflowers, such as grape hyacinths and bachelor's buttons. Other pollens came from larger plants, similar to hollyhock and yellow-flowering groundsel. The hollyhock, in particular, would have taken quite a bit of time to be picked, because it grows as individual plants scattered across the mountainside.

While reviewing the field data on the samples she'd analyzed, Madame Leroi-Gourhan realized that the pollen of each species of flower had come from a separate soil sample taken from the common grave. From this she concluded that individual clusters of each type of flower had been placed in the grave. Because she knew when the modern analogs of these plants flowered, and pollen is produced only when a plant flowers, Madame Leroi-Gourhan was able to calculate that the bouquets had been picked between late May and early July—which would have been when the deceased Neandertals had been laid to rest in their shared grave.

At least one of the flowers Madame Leroi-Gourhan identified, the yarrow or milfoil, was known to have been used in the recent past as a medicinal herb to promote the healing of wounds. Another flower she identified, belonging to the woody horsetail group, was still being used in Iraq as a medicinal plant. Perhaps, as Solecki would speculate, the medicinal properties of these flowers had also been known to the Neandertals of Shanidar.

Neandertals inhabited Shanidar Cave around 45,000 or 50,000 years ago. Thus, if all the evidence has been interpreted correctly, some kind of human relative—an extinct human variant or, possibly, a separate species of uncertain human affinities—had carried out purposeful, contemplated burial practices.

Older Bones

Some 70,000 years ago or more, Neandertals from what is now the site of Krapina, in Yugoslavia, may also have buried their dead. The evidence comes not from the discovery of skeletons in a potential grave but from a microscopic analysis of the bones. Through the microscope, thin scratches visible on the surfaces of these bones emerge as potential cut marks—cut marks that would have been made by a stone tool. These scratches are not randomly scattered about the surface of a bone but appear in organized patterns that are clustered in specific regions, in places where muscles, tendons, and ligaments attach. Curiously, cut marks similar in quality and in skeletal location have also been found on the bones of animals, such as reindeer, that were contemporaneous with these Neandertals.

The study of cut marks can be especially interesting. Similar to putting together a jigsaw puzzle, you can reconstruct patterns and techniques of butchering: the size, length, depth, and number of cut marks on the articular ends of bones reflect how limbs had been separated from the rest of the body, while other cuts reflect, for instance, how limbs had been reduced to roasts and rib cages to chops and tenderloins. You can tell if a joint had been hacked apart (by a cleaver or cleaverlike implement, for instance), sawn partway through and then snapped apart, or carefully dissected (by a thin metal or flint blade). Different kinds of cut marks reflect how and where large muscle masses and tough bundles of tendons had been removed from the bones. For example, cut marks on skulls and mandibles indicate butchering to get at the "jowls."

When cut marks were first noted on the bones of the Krapina Neandertals, some paleoanthropologists thought that these individuals had been cannibalized. Because it was reasonable to assume that cut marks on reindeer bones reflected the fact that reindeer had been butchered for consumption, it seemed reasonable, by extension, to assume that similar cut marks on Neandertal bones also reflected butchering for consumption. Cannibalism among the Krapina Neandertals seemed even more likely because so many of the bones were broken, "clearly" for the purpose of extracting the marrow. However, a recent series of microscopic studies of the broken bones by Mary Russell of Case Western Reserve in Cleveland has convincingly demonstrated that "cannibalism" was not the cause.

Russell's analysis revealed that breakage had resulted from various contributing factors: compression of the earth and its contents over a period of 50,000, or, perhaps, 100,000 years, pounding during rockfalls, and, in particular, shoddy excavation techniques, including trying to get a long arm or leg bone to fit into a box that's not quite long enough for it. But although the idea of breaking bones to get at the marrow could be explained without invoking cannibalism, the cut marks still had to be contended with.

Fortunately, Russell was familiar with a collection of modern human skeletons from the site of Juntunen, Michigan. The bones of these individuals bore cut marks that were virtually identical to those on the Krapina Neandertal bones. But Russell also knew that these modern bones did not represent the scraps of cannibals. Rather the Juntunen skeletons had been secondarily buried—and cut marks offer clues to the burial ritual.

Secondary burial is a common practice among various human groups. As the term suggests, an individual had to have been buried or squirreled away somewhere first. After a religiously or socially prescribed period of time, the desiccated/partially skeletonized body is retrieved from its initial resting place. With the aid of an implement, such as a knife blade, the bones are separated and cleaned of as much adherent flesh and sinew as possible. The prepared bones are then reburied or placed in a special receptacle. Depending on the culture, all of the bones may be buried together, or only some of the bones may be reburied, or the individual bones may be placed with the same bones of previous reburials. Medieval ossuaries—with separate piles of skulls, femurs, humeri, and other bones of the skeleton—represent a type of secondary burial.

When Russell studied the cut marks on the Juntunen human skeletal sample under the microscope, she found that there were more of them per bone than you typically would find on animal bones that had been butchered for meat consumption. Cleaning bone of tightly adherent, desiccated flesh and sinew requires more scraping and cutting than butchering meat does. Because the Krapina Neandertal bones were extraordinarily similar to the Juntunen skeletons not only in the location but in the profusion of cut marks, Russell felt that it was more likely that the Krapina Neandertals had had a ritualized practice of secondary burial than that they had practiced cannibalism.

Eric Trinkaus, of the University of New Mexico, has pursued another line of evidence that supports the idea that the Krapina Neandertals had buried their dead. Trinkaus is one of a handful of experts on Neandertals and has had the good fortune to study every museum collection of Neandertal bones. He pointed out that there was something odd about the kinds of bones that had been preserved in the Krapina skeletal assemblage. In particular, he thought that the collection comprised an unexpectedly large number of shoulder blades and collarbones, including collarbones of young individuals.

Because shoulder blades are flat and thin-boned and collarbones are thinly tubular, they are fragile and easily damaged. Thus archeologists lucky enough to find fossilized shoulder blades or collarbones usually find only fragments. The presence of numerous intact shoulder blades and collarbones would imply, therefore, that the Krapina skeletons had been protected in some way. Interring the remains of the dead—either permanently in a primary burial or through a process of secondary reburial—will help preserve even the most fragile bones. The fact that these shoulder blades and collarbones bore a particularly large number of cut marks, in specific locations, also indicates that the Krapina Neandertals practiced secondary burial.

And Even Older Bones

There is yet another, even older, specimen—a skull—with scratch marks. This skull was found at the site of Bodo, which is in the Awash region of Ethiopia. The age of this skull is not firmly fixed, but it may predate the Krapina Neandertals by as much as 500,000 or as few as 200,000 years.

The specimen is represented by most of the facial skeleton and large portions of the top and right side of the skull. The base of the skull is missing. To some paleoanthropologists, the specimen represents a transitional form between *Homo erectus* and *Homo sapiens,* but is neither one nor the other. To others, it is an African variant of *Homo erectus.* To yet another group of paleoanthropologists, the specimen is *Homo sapiens,* just an archaic form of it. And, as I'll also review later in chapter 7, a few of us think that it might represent an entirely different and so far unnamed species. Given the number of competing interpretations, most of us just refer to this specimen as the Bodo cranium.

In 1986 Tim White, of the University of California at Berkeley, and one of Don Johanson's collaborators on, for example, the "Lucy" skeleton, published a detailed analysis of the scratch marks on the Bodo skull. He found marks around the orbital and nasal regions, on top of the brow ridges, and along the back of the preserved skull cap. White considered every possibility he could think of to account for the marks: natural weathering of the specimen, rodent or carnivore gnawing, even abrasion or trauma before the skull became buried in the ground. After ruling out all of these possibilities, White was left with the possibility that these scratches were, indeed, cut marks. And if, he reasoned, they were cut marks, it probably meant that the skull had been defleshed. In fact, White found that the patterning and locations of these cut marks were virtually identical to cut marks taxidermists made while defleshing the chimpanzee and gorilla skulls housed in the Cleveland Museum of Natural History. White kept open the question of why the Bodo skull might have been defleshed, but it would certainly seem reasonable to assume that the defleshing had been done after the Bodo individual had died. Furthermore, we are left with the very real possibility that, whatever species of hominid the Bodo skull represents, this species' social behavior included some kind of mortuary practice.

At present, the Bodo skull represents the oldest example of any hominid giving special treatment to the body or skeleton of a comrade. Even if this was not a widespread activity for this hominid, the Bodo skull and the Krapina and Shanidar Neandertal skeletons raise the possibility that two distinct, non-*sapiens* species of *Homo* had had rituals and cultural practices that we have assumed are only within the capacity of members of our own species.

From Bodies to Bones

The processes of bone preservation are such that the farther back in time we go, the less there is. There are fewer species represented, fewer individuals representing this incomplete sampling of species, and fewer pieces of the skeleton of each of these individuals.

Various, sometimes very complex factors can affect the survival of bone—and even determine which bones are preserved and which are not. Although various scholars during the last seventy years have studied these processes, the discipline itself—called taphonomy, or "laws of burial"—has received the recognition that it should only in the past two decades.

In its broadest sense, taphonomy covers the period from the death of an individual to the fates of her or his individual bones and teeth. Although the term *taphonomy* was coined in 1940 by the Russian vertebrate paleontologist and geologist I. A. Efremov, it was the German paleontologist Johannes Weigelt who made a systematic study of the processes leading to the decay, disarticulation, and dispersal of a carcass.

About ten years ago I happened to come across a publication of Weigelt's from the 1920s. By chance, the book fell open to a series of photographs illustrating the fate and history after death of a cow's body. The first photograph pictured a cow's carcass lying in a field. This was followed by a photographic sequence that went from the desiccation of the soft tissue, through the destructive action of scavengers, microbes, and the elements, and culminated in the exposure and eventual disarticulation of the skeleton itself. By the end of the photographic sequence, parts of the skeleton were scattered all over the ground. You could tell that the entire skeleton was no longer in place. Pieces of it had been taken away by scavenging animals or dispersed by heavy rains; what remained was weakened by decalcification and weathering, or had been pulverized into fragments by the feet of other animals. The detail with which Weigelt recorded these events was astonishing.

Recently Peter Andrews, curator of paleoanthropology at the Natural History Museum in London, has been carrying out a taphonomic study in the caves of southwestern England. (Peter is probably best known for his work on the early evolution of humans and apes.) During a recent visit I unexpectedly found him tucked away in a corner of the museum, glued to a microscope, teasing apart what appeared to be a ball of tiny bones. And, indeed, he was doing just that: scrutinizing the undigestible parts of a mouse or some other small vertebrate that had been consumed by an owl. An owl swallows its victim whole—fur, skin, bones, and all. After its digestive juices have broken down the muscles and organs, the owl regurgitates the rest: a furry ball or "pellet" with the bones packed together in it. The base of a tree, or the floor of a cave, below an established owl's nest is riddled with these furry pellets. As long as the pellets survive, an owl actually helps preserve the bony record of the tinier animals. By picking apart an owl pellet, you can isolate the surviving bones to determine which animal species were in the area.

If you want to reconstruct past environments and climatic conditions—which is, in part, what Peter was ultimately up to—studying small animals can tell you certain things that studying large animals cannot. For instance, large mammals stand a better chance of enduring climatic and environmental change than smaller mammals—if conditions get too severe or different, large mammals can migrate to more suitable conditions. In contrast, the smaller the mammal, the more it is confined to smaller geographic areas. A small mammal is also more susceptible to subtle changes in climate and environment. Migration for a small mammal might be just across a road or a field, which would not remove it to a climatically more favorable locale. Consequently, species that cannot accommodate changing conditions may become extinct in the region and may, perhaps, be replaced by species that can. Thus, fluctuations in the presence or absence of certain species of small mammals—mice, for example—can reflect slight fluctuations in a region's climate and environment. On average, the absence or presence of smaller species provides more precise clues to past conditions in an area than does the information gained from study of the bone assemblages of the larger animals.

If you know how the skeletons of animals of different sizes, in different environments, and exposed to different "experiences," become disarticulated, dispersed, destroyed, or preserved, you can apply this knowledge to interpreting bones that accumulated long ago. Many taphonomic studies in paleoanthropology have focused on the carcasses and bones of animals that live in savanna and semiarid environments. These areas have been emphasized because those are the conditions in which the earliest hominids lived—hominids such as "Lucy" and other species of the genus *Australopithecus* found in East and South African deposits dating from more than three million to one or so million years ago. But not all animals, much less all hominids, inhabit or did inhabit forest fringes or dry grasslands dotted only with the occasional clustering of bushes and trees. Neandertals and *Homo erectus*, for instance, lived in much greener landscapes and more humid climatic zones. Carcasses in the more temperate European or the more tropical southeast Asian setting would decay differently and at different rates than in the drier climes of Kenya and Tanzania. The soils in which bones would end up are quite different in arid, temperate, and tropical areas. And these areas boast different kinds of predators and scavengers as well.

It turns out that Peter also has been trying to fill in some of these taphonomic blanks, at least in terms of what might happen to carcasses and bones in more temperate climes. And he's even able to carry out this study in his backyard—in the fields and pastures around the centuries-old farmhouse he and his wife own in Wales.

A few years ago, when I was back in London working with Peter on our long-term study of the evolutionary relationships of humans and apes, he invited me to Wales for the weekend. So, that Friday, there we were with everyone else trying to flee London, creeping through the late-afternoon rush-hour traffic. It was quite dark by the time we crossed into Wales. I didn't get to see the countryside until early the next morning, when I was awakened by a flock of sheep being herded past the house. My bedroom window looked out upon a sweep of rolling hills carpeted in grass and heather and dotted with sheep. Once Wales had been covered with dense forest—which the Welsh had used to their advantage in keeping invaders out of their territory. However, in 1282, the English king Edward I had the forests cut down and, consequently, was able to defeat the Welsh once and for all.

After a quick breakfast, Peter and I went up into the hills to check out the current states of decomposition, disarticulation, dispersion, and burial of the various skeletons he had been studying over the years. Near the top of one hill, we stopped at a small grassy depression in and around which were various bones, such as vertebrae, limb bones, and shoulder blades. This was all that remained of a sheep that had died the year before. During that time Peter had been observing the systematic "disappearance" of bits and pieces of this sheep.

Among the scavengers contributing to the "case of the disappearing Welsh sheep" was the fox. Although he hadn't seen foxes actually nosing around the carcass, Peter knew they had been there because they left their footprints in the damp earth and their "toothprints" on the bones. Foxes gnaw on bones, then leave them behind; they also take bones away, to gnaw on elsewhere at leisure. Some of the bones that had been gnawed on—their edges looked as if they had been "nibbled"—bore small, conical depressions made by a fox's pointed canine tooth or a sharp cusp of one of its large crushing teeth. These four multicusped, bladelike teeth—a pair in the upper jaw and a pair in the lower jaw—are called carnassial teeth and lie about halfway back in the jaws. You can easily spot similar carnassial teeth when your dog or cat, or a wolf or lion, yawns.

Some of the sheep bones also bore toothmarks left by at least one rodent. Rodents, such as mice and rats, have a pair of chisel-edged teeth at the front of the upper jaw and an opposing pair of chisel-edged teeth at the front of the lower jaw. These opposing pairs of teeth gouge and chip away at a food source. Behind the anterior gnawing teeth are rather large toothless spaces along the upper and lower jaws and then the small molar teeth. A rodent uses its front teeth to chisel off pieces of food; in so doing, the tooth marks they leave on a bone are unmistakable: They form a series of double, parallel, shallow furrows along the surface of the bone. Usually rodents gnaw at a right angle to the long axis of the bone, as we would eat a row of kernels on an ear of corn.

It is fairly common to find rodent tooth marks on bone, especially along an edge of a limb bone. Porcupines, which are large rodents, are notorious for gnawing bone into small bits. Like other rodents, they don't seem to be fussy about whose bones they gnaw on. Rodent tooth marks have been found on all sorts of mammal bones, including human bones. Bone is a major attraction to rodents because it is a good source of calcium. Ralph Solecki "discovered" many of his Neandertals by following rodent burrows, most of which went unerringly to one or another of the Shanidar skeletons.

But foxes and rodents weren't the only players responsible for the disappearance of that Welsh sheep skeleton. There were the hoofprints of sheep all around. In fact, one of the sheep of the resident flock had stepped on the small articular end of a shoulder blade—the end that articulates with the upper end of the humerus. This pushed that end of the shoulder blade into the soft earth and caused the blade portion of the bone to stand straight up.

Peter mentioned that bone fragmentation often results from animals stepping on the bones like this. On one visit, for example, he might find that one end of a bone had been pushed into the ground and that the rest of the bone was sticking up in the air. The next time he would visit the study area, he might find that bone lying horizontally while other bones would be standing upright with an end stuck in the ground. Some of the bone will become buried and perhaps be preserved. Most of the other bone will be broken into fragments that, in time, will decompose and disappear.

After leaving the diminishing pile of sheep bones, we climbed a hundred yards to the top of the hill. A mosaic of heather, exposed rock, lichens, and mosses, this was a different setting altogether. It was also cooler and breezier. Under one low bush lay a chalky-white limb bone of a small Welsh pony. The bone's surface was uneven and riddled with cracks. This limb bone was one of the few bones that remained of a pony that had died on the top of that hill ten years earlier. A few yards away a second limb bone was wedged into the top of a small bush, held by its crooked branches like an offering to nature—to the wind, rain, frost, and rays of the sun. It was in a much more advanced state of dissolution than the first. Coated in a white, powdery dust that came off on the fingers, the bone's surface was fractured and deeply cracked in places. Layers of bone had flaked off the surface in long patches, creating miniature, terraced patterns. Where the hard, outer layer of bone had disappeared entirely, the more fragile underlying spongy bone was exposed, particularly at the articulating ends of the bone. Spongy bone is composed of a myriad of tiny spaces captured within paper-thin walls of bone. Exposed to the elements, it doesn't stand a chance of surviving the battering of more than a few seasons. What still remained of this bone would have to be buried, and buried rather quickly, if it was to have any chance of surviving. This didn't seem likely because Peter was interested in gathering information on how bone fell apart under different conditions. Clearly, unless some animal happened to walk by and knock this bone to the ground, it eventually would crumble away to nothing.

On Becoming a Fossil

If a bone or, more likely, a bone fragment actually does get buried, what might its fate be? Getting buried does not guarantee that a bone will be preserved long enough for an archeologist to find it, or that it will survive that extra length of time necessary to become a fossil, which a paleontologist might then discover. Once a bone is divested of its covering of soft tissue and is exposed to the elements, water begins to leach out the minerals that give bone its rigidity. Once a bone demineralizes, it can be destroyed easily, even by the acidity of the soil and water that surrounds it. The greater the acidity, the faster the rate of decomposition.

The human skeletons I excavated at Tell Hesi were extremely delicate and friable. The soil there is sandy and acidic, and the climate is arid for much of the year. There are, however, periods of severe rainfall, during which more moisture is dropped onto the soil than it can retain. This sudden excess of water creates the gullies, or wadis, that scar the landscape. Water that does get into the soil is absorbed rapidly. When the rain stops and the soil heats up again, the water percolates up and evaporates just as quickly as it was absorbed. This moisture leaches the minerals out of bone on its way down and on its way up. The absorption and percolation of water occurs so rapidly that it virtually prevents the deposition of minerals from the surrounding soil into the leached-out matrix of bone. Even the oldest burials at Tell Hesi—which were approximately eight hundred years old—were still crumbly, unmineralized bone.

Remineralization is crucial to a bone's survival, for it is the remineralization of bone over time that resolidifies it and, eventually, fossilizes it. Bone that has been partially remineralized is called subfossil. Bone that has been turned completely to stone is a real fossil.

As long as the skeletons buried on the tell were deep in the ground, they remained intact. They were protected by the soil around them. However, as you dug away more dirt and got closer to the skeleton, you inadvertently were contributing to the destruction of the very bones you wanted to recover and analyze. By removing dirt, you were accelerating the rate at which moisture would evaporate. The 100-plus degrees Fahrenheit dry heat of the day would suck the moisture out of anything. By the time you reached the skeleton, a period of intense evaporation had already taken place. As you exposed more of the skeleton to the parching air, bones would begin to dry out completely and crack, flake, fragment, and crumble right in front of your eyes. Oddly enough, the same arid conditions can preserve flesh by desiccating it so rapidly that decay cannot set in. Bodies become mummified through various drying processes. Naturally mummified bodies have been found, for instance, in the parched, arid deserts of Egypt and the American Southwest as well as in the frigid but arid highlands of Peru.

A denser soil is not necessarily a more suitable environment for bone remineralization. Denser soil does not allow rapid transport of water in and out of it. In the Ohio Valley, for instance, around western Pennsylvania and eastern Ohio, the soils are dense and tend to be rich in clay. While burials interred there may not be flushed with flashes of rainwater, these dense soils tend to be acidic and remain moist because they drain poorly. Because of this, bones from an ancient Ohio Valley site can be even more fragile than the skeletons from the top of Tell Hesi.

Imagine that you are Peter Andrews's Welsh sheep or pony or Johannes Weigelt's cow—a carcass lying out in the elements. It is unlikely that your skeleton will be preserved even partially intact. If you had been a fish or a horseshoe crab and had died in your watery home, you would have had a better chance of remaining intact from the beginning—if the currents were not so forceful that they scattered your bones or pieces of shell, dashed them to bits on the rocks, or abraded their details in the sand.

Fortunately for the paleontologist, the corpses of water-dwelling animals often sink to the bottom and become covered with sediment. The sediment tends to protect the dead body and even at times retain an impression of its shape and external anatomical details. This environment then provides the means by which the bones of the skeleton are mineralized. The skeletons of land animals that die in or get washed into a watery haven can become preserved as completely as those of water-dwelling animals. But most land animals die and fall to the ground, without any chance of a freak flood casting them into an environment more favorable to fossilization.

Thus perhaps a handful of the hundreds of bones in an animal's body will get buried. Of these, even fewer will survive demineralization long enough to be discovered by archeologists or even longer, to be remineralized partially or even fully into rock-hard fossils. But becoming a rock does not ensure safety. Rocks, whether they have been formed in the bowels of the earth or by the transformation of bone, can be destroyed. The blasting of windblown sands, the pummeling of waves, the corrosive secretions of mosses and lichens, and even the steady rhythm of a stream can, in time, reduce a seemingly indestructible boulder to a grain of sand.

As soon as an individual dies, the clues it holds about itself begin to disappear. An osteoarcheologist, a forensic osteologist, or a paleontologist acts like a detective at different times in the taphonomic life of a corpse and its skeleton. Like Sherlock Holmes, these scientists try to sort out the viable clues from the whims that circumstance, history, and preservation place in their path to throw them off the scent. But, unlike Sherlock Holmes, they may never close the case completely.

■

INFANTS, BURNED BONES, AND

SACRIFICE AT ANCIENT CARTHAGE

Although the ancient city of Carthage had been a stronghold of four different invaders, it is probably best known as the city of Queen Dido. According to the classical Greek author Timaeus, Queen Dido (whose Phoenician name was Elissa) fled her home city, Tyre, a major Phoenician port city on the coast of what is now Lebanon, because her brother, King Pygmalion, had killed her uncle and husband, Acherbas, for the wealth he had accumulated as the high priest of the god Melqart (the Phoenician equivalent of Hercules). With a small band of faithful aristocrats, Princess Elissa escaped to the nearby island of Cyprus where she enlisted the support of the high priest of the goddess Juno as well as eighty girls who would bear children to carry on the Phoenician religion. As Queen Dido, she then continued her journey westward, eventually landing on the shores of northern Africa, where the continent swells out toward the southern Italian island of Sicily.

According to legend, when the king of the indigenous North African Berber nation told Queen Dido that she could have as much land as could be covered by an oxhide, she cut the hide into thin strips and, placing them end to end, encircled Byrsa Hill, which overlooks the

Mediterranean (*byrsa* means "oxhide" in Greek and "acropolis" in Phoenician). Queen Dido called her new home Carthage, which in Phoenician means "New City." The exact date of the founding of Carthage is, however, unknown. The oldest archeological levels at Carthage date to approximately 750 B.C.E. (before the common era). But since Pygmalion and Elissa were real historical figures, and biblical scholars date the marriage of Elissa's great-aunt Jezebel to King Ahab roughly to the period 875–850 B.C.E., Donald Harden and other experts on Phoenician history accept Timaeus's date of 814 B.C.E. Upon settling in North Africa, the Carthaginians not only carried on the Phoenician traditions of trading and seafaring but established colonies throughout the Mediterranean. Phoenician leadership soon shifted from Tyre to the new city.

Most popular histories focus on the frictions between Rome and Carthage that eventually resulted in the Punic Wars, but the Greeks were actually the first opponents the Carthaginians faced in their quest for supremacy in the Mediterranean. Although the Greeks maintained control of much of the eastern Mediterranean, the Carthaginians did successfully invade the islands of Sardinia and Sicily. They also colonized southern Spain and established a base in northern Africa that spanned from what is now Libya, beyond the Straits of Gibraltar, to the Atlantic coast. But while Carthage was preoccupied with the Greeks, it paid little attention to the new Roman republic, which, by about 350 B.C.E., had become so powerful that the Carthaginians felt it necessary to negotiate three commercial treaties—the first in 348, the second in 306, and the third in 272 B.C.E. Rome soon violated the last treaty by trying to expand into Carthaginian-held Sicily, thus setting the stage for the first Punic War. (The term *Punic* comes from the Latin *Punicus*, referring to the Phoenicians of the western Mediterranean.)

The first Punic War, which lasted from 264 to 241 B.C.E., was eventually settled by a Roman naval victory off the coast of Sicily. A result was that Carthage lost Sicily and Sardinia. The second Punic War (218–202 B.C.E.) was instigated by the thirty-three-year-old Carthaginian general Hannibal when he challenged the Romans over a Spanish border town. Hannibal did lead an army of men and elephants from southern Spain into southern France, across the Alps, and into the heartland of Roman territory, where he did defeat the Romans in a series of battles. However, it was the Roman army under the young general Pontius Cornelius Scipio Africanus that won the second Punic War by defeating Hannibal and his army at the plains of Zama, to the west of the city of Carthage. The Carthaginian empire was no longer. But, in spite of being restricted to the region of the city itself, Carthage prospered and, for the next fifty years, became the new "breadbasket" of the Mediterranean, outproducing even the Nile Valley. In 148 B.C.E., a territory-hungry Libya launched an attack on Carthage. By defending itself and retaliating, Carthage broke the ban on war imposed by Rome. Two years later the grandson of Scipio Africanus, Scipio Aemilianus, razed Carthage to the ground and brought the final Punic War to an end.

The Carthaginian Practice of Child Sacrifice: The Written Evidence

Virtually all of Carthaginian history as known to Punic Carthaginians died with the city. Surviving Carthaginian coins from Spain bearing the presumed profiles of Hannibal, his father Hamilcar, and his brother-in-law Hasdrubal give us rare glimpses of the facial features of Punic Carthaginians. Most of what we know factually about Punic Carthage, however, derives from the works of Greek and Roman historians, most of whom often borrowed from, and elaborated on, sagas composed by other historians. For instance, Appian (Greek, second century A.D.) took most of the "facts" for his famous work, *Libyca*—in which he describes the fabulous Carthaginian mercantile and naval harbors and gives the popular account of the Roman army razing the city and then salting the soil so that nothing could ever grow there—from Polybius (Greek, second century B.C.E.).

From a succession of historians we learn of a particularly gruesome component of Carthaginian daily life: the routine and ritualized sacrificing of not just animals—animal sacrifice was a common religious activity of all Mediterranean cultures—but of human infants and children. Although providing at times contradictory details of the ritual itself, Greek and Roman historians were unanimous in their abhorrence of the Carthaginian practice of child sacrifice. (This despite the fact that Greeks and Romans alike engaged openly in a variety of sanctioned atrocities, including adult human sacrifice. For example, according to the Roman author Cicero [early second-to-mid-first centuries B.C.E.], human sacrifice was not restricted to the western Phoenicians but was widely accepted among Mediterranean societies as a pious act that would please the gods.) The Carthaginians, however, were not the only Mediterranean people who regularly sacrificed children, but they did so with apparent joy.

The historical and epigraphic written evidence for the Carthaginian practice of child sacrifice has been summarized by various scholars, most notably and recently by Paul Mosca and Shelby Brown. (Those who want to pursue the classical sources further should consult Paul and Shelby's texts [cited in the bibliography] where longer passages are also quoted.) According to these scholars, the first possible classical reference to the practice consists of an enigmatic line written by the Greek philosopher Sophocles in the fifth century B.C.E.: "For among foreigners, it has been the custom, from the beginning, to require human sacrifice to Kronos." Approximately one hundred years later another Greek philosopher, Pseudo-Plato, constructed a dialogue between himself and Socrates in which the specific city is mentioned: "With us, for instance, human sacrifice is not legal, but unholy, whereas the Carthaginians perform it as a thing they account holy and legal, and that too when some of them sacrifice even their own sons to Cronos."

The first detailed picture of the Carthaginian ritual appears in the work of the Greek author Kleitarchos (third century B.C.E.):

Out of reverence for Kronos, the Phoenicians, and especially the Carthaginians, whenever they seek to obtain some great favor, vow one of their children, burning it as a sacrifice to the deity, if they are especially eager to gain success. There stands in their midst a bronze statue of Kronos, its hands extended over a bronze brazier, the flames of which engulf the child. When the flames fall upon the body, the limbs contract and the open mouth seems almost to be laughing, until the contracted [body] slips quietly into the brazier. Thus it is that the "grin" is known as "sardonic laughter," since they die laughing.

Kleitarchos was extensively paraphrased by other classical authors, but his is the only description in which the victim had not been killed before she or he was placed into the sacrificial flames. Kleitarchos also gave us the expression "sardonic grin and laughter"—the word *sardonic* referring to the island of Sardinia, on which grows a plant that not only is lethal but causes the unfortunate consumer to go into convulsions reminiscent of laughter.

The author most often cited for details of Carthaginian child sacrifice is Diodorus Siculus (Diodorus of Sicily). In *Library of History*, written in the middle of the first century B.C.E., Diodorus provides various examples. For instance, there is the act of the Carthaginian general Himilco during his 406 B.C.E. siege of the city of Acragas: ". . . then he [Himilco] supplicated the gods after the custom of his people by sacrificing a young boy to Cronus." According to Paul Mosca, the literal translation of the Greek word translated in this passage as "sacrificing" would be "cutting the throat." And then there is the oft-quoted account of what occurred in 310 B.C.E., when the Carthaginians were under siege and thought that the gods were responsible for their troubles:

They also alleged that Cronus had turned against them inasmuch as in former times they had been accustomed to sacrifice to this god the noblest of their sons, but more recently, secretly buying and nurturing children, they had sent these to the sacrifice; and when an investigation was made, some of those who had been sacrificed were discovered to have been supposititious. When they had given thought to these things and saw their enemy encamped before their walls, they were filled with superstitious dread, for they believed that they had neglected the honours of the gods that had been established by their fathers. In their zeal to make amends for their omission, they selected two hundred of the noblest children and sacrificed them publicly; and others who were under suspicion sacrificed themselves voluntarily, in number not less than three hundred. There was in their city a bronze image of Cronus, extending its hands, palms up and sloping toward the ground, so that each of the children when placed thereupon rolled down and fell into a sort of gaping pit filled with fire. Also the story passed down among the Greeks from ancient myth that Cronus did away with his own children appears to have been kept in mind among the Carthaginians through this observance.

Building upon Diodorus's description, the Roman author Plutarch (writing between A.D. 150 and 225) offered even more detail:

With full knowledge and understanding they themselves offered up their own children, and those who had no children would buy little ones from poor people and cut their throats as if they were so many lambs or young birds; meanwhile the mother stood by without a tear or moan; but should she utter a single moan or let fall a single tear, she had to forfeit the money, and her child was sacrificed nevertheless; and the whole area before the statue was filled with a loud noise of flutes and drums so that the cries of wailing should not reach the ears of the people.

Finally, there is a passage from a native North African, Tertullian (A.D. c. 160 to c. 225), who went to live in Roman Carthage:

In Africa infants used to be sacrificed to Saturn, and quite openly, down to the proconsulate of Tiberius, who took the priests themselves and on the very trees of their temple, under whose shadow their crimes had been committed, hung them alive like votive offerings on crosses; and the soldiers of my own country are witnesses to it, who served that proconsul in that very task. Yes, and to this day that holy crime persists in secret . . . Saturn did not spare his own children; so, where other people's were concerned, he naturally persisted in not sparing them; and their own parents offered them to him, were glad to respond, and fondled their children that they might not be sacrificed in tears. And between murder and sacrifice by parents—oh! the difference is great!

This passage, which postdates the fall of Punic Carthage, reveals that child sacrifice was still being practiced, although in secret. In fact, according to some authorities, child sacrifice may have been practiced in North Africa up to the third century A.D.

The impetus for sacrifice could be a crisis (such as war, siege, plague, drought), an annual or more frequently regularized ritual to a god or gods, or a request for a favor from a god or gods. A single child, or many children, could be sacrificed at one time. They could be placed or tossed into the fires, perhaps alive or, as often described, dead from a knife to the throat. The offerants were the parents, who, if they were childless but of nobility or the upper class, could purchase a child for sacrifice from a lower-class family. Sons, even firstborn sons, who would be deemed special under other circumstances, were not exempt as potential sacrificial victims. As the Italian archeologist and Phoenician expert Sabatino Moscati notes in *The World of the Phoenicians*, "the concept of offering the first fruits to the deity, whether they were human, animal, or vegetable, was typical of the ancient Near East, as is clearly proved by the Bible." During the ritual the offerants, and even the parents who had to sell a child to others for sacrifice, were supposed to supplant grief with joy.

Although the scenes of sacrifice were penned by those who were not themselves Carthaginian or participants in the ritual, the Carthaginians did leave some information on the gravemarkers they erected for their dead infants and children.

The Carthaginian Practice of Child Sacrifice: The Gravemarkers and Their Inscriptions

As summarized by Shelby Brown, sacrifice is distinguished from other forms of killing, including ritualized killing, in that it is an extraordinary act that is carried out either as a symbol of friendship with or as a gift offered to a god or gods. Inscriptions on gravemarkers associated with the interred remains of Carthaginian children indicate that the sacrificial offering was made to either one or both of the gods Tanit and Ba'al Hammon. Tanit was the western Phoenician "mother earth" whose eastern counterpart was the goddess Astarte. Tanit (Astarte) was the equivalent of the supreme female deity of the Greeks (Hera) and Romans (Juno). The icon for Tanit, according to most scholars, was usually a broad-based, triangular body. On the very top of the triangle sat a round "head," below which two short "arms" extended to the sides. The "head" could be open, like a circle, and the "arms" were often sticklike. The male deity, Ba'al Hammon, was the equivalent of the Greek god Kronos (Cronus) and the Roman god Saturn. Ba'al, the god of the sun and the heavens, and of fire, had been a major eastern Phoenician deity well before the founding of Carthage. His icon on the Carthaginian gravemarkers is most likely a crescent above a sphere or orb; a depression in the center of the sphere, which was probably made by the point of the engraver's compass, gives the icon the appearance of an eye with its upper lid floating in space. When the two gods were depicted together, the symbol of Ba'al Hammon was placed above Tanit's. Sometimes the icon for Ba'al was suspended over the image of an urn, which was the coffin in which the sacrificed infant's remains were buried.

Two types of gravemarkers have been discovered: thin, obelisklike stone ones, called stelae, as well as chunkier, thicker ones, called cippi. Cippi (the singular is "cippus"), which were hewn from sandstone, were used during the first centuries of Carthaginian history. The earliest cippi, dating from the eighth to the fifth centuries B.C.E., were L-shaped; they were inset and decorated with stucco and paint on one side. Over time, cippi became larger and squarer. Images, such as the icons of one or both of the deities, an urn, an urn on a platform, or a platform alone (perhaps a sacrificial platform), were sometimes carved on the inset surface of a cippus. Cippi did not bear engraved inscriptions, but Shelby Brown tentatively suggests that dedications similar to those inscribed on stelae may have been painted on them. Stelae (the singular is "stela"), which eventually replaced cippi as the gravemarkers of choice during the last centuries of Carthage, were carved from limestone. As with cippi, only one surface of a stela was decorated. Symbols, figures, and scenes were incised, occasionally in bas relief;

they were quite varied and sometimes elaborate. In addition to bearing the images commonly found on cippi, stelae also bore images of rosettes, palm trees, a raised hand often held palm out, an oar or part of a boat, an animal (such as an adult sheep, a lamb, a bull or cow, and even a fish or bird), or a human (usually adult). A stela could also bear an incised inscription or dedication, which, as summarized by Shelby, gave the name and genealogy of each dedicant (either a woman or a man or a male/female couple), identified the god or gods receiving the offering (Tanit or Ba'al Hammon, or both), and often associated the offering with a vow. Some inscriptions also contain terms—all based on the word transcribed as "mlk" ("mulk")—which some classical and biblical scholars interpret as specifying the type of sacrifice that took place.

The Carthaginian Practice of Child Sacrifice: Interpreting the Biblical Evidence

An additional piece of the puzzle of Carthaginian sacrifice comes from various passages in the Old Testament by way of the following association: The Phoenicians were the Canaanites. Thus Phoenicia was synonymous with the land of Canaan, which was invaded by the Israelites, who eventually pushed the Phoenicians to the coastal fringe. Subsequently, the Israelites borrowed various cultural elements from the Phoenicians (Canaanites), including the world's first alphabet. Some groups of Israelites even adopted the god Ba'al and, presumably, the practice of child sacrifice. As such, the argument goes, when we read in the Old Testament of sacrifice—whether animal or human—we are justified, according to various scholars, in making inferences about the Phoenicians.

For example, in Chronicles 27 of the Old Testament, we read that Ahaz, who "reigned sixteen years in Jerusalem . . . made molten images for the Ba'als . . . and he burned his sons as an offering, according to the abominable practices of the nations whom the Lord drove out before the people of Israel." And classical and biblical scholars often cite a passage from 29–30 Exodus 22, in which firstborn males are specified, as further evidence of the practice of child sacrifice: "Thou shalt give me the first-born of thy sons. Thou shalt do the same for thy livestock, big and small. The first-born shall be left seven days with its mother, and then, on the eighth day, thou shalt hand it over to me."

Some biblical scholars, however, suggest that the reference to "handing over" a child to a god is purely figurative and does not signify an actual sacrifice. They also interpret passages in the Old Testament, particularly in Jeremiah and Kings, in which the Israelites are portrayed as practicing a rite of "passage by fire," in this way. Rather than being sacrificed in the sense of a blood-killing, children would be "passed through" a fire as part of a symbolic offering or sacrifice to the ancient Semitic deity Molech. Thus, for example, the following passage in 2 Kings 17 would not mean that the Israelites were actually killing their children: "They rejected the commandments of the Lord . . . and served Baal. They consigned their sons and daughters to the fire."

The same interpretation would apply to this passage in 2 Kings 23, in which the place of the ritual—Tophet—is actually identified: "[King Josiah of Judah] defiled Tophet, which is in the Valley of Ben-Hinnom, so that no one might consign his son or daughter to the fire of Molech."

The word *Molech* in this passage and elsewhere in the Old Testament, which is translated from the three Hebrew letters "mlk," has traditionally been interpreted as referring to a god the Israelites may have adopted from another god—Malik—who was worshipped in lands farther to the east. Thus, when the same three Phoenician letters—"mlk"—were found in inscriptions on Carthaginian stelae, they too were interpreted as referring to the god Molech of the Old Testament. But in the 1930s an alternative interpretation of "mlk" began to emerge that relied on the fact that only consonants in Semitic languages, such as Hebrew and Phoenician, are designated by letters, while symbols for vowels are often omitted. "Mlk," the argument went, need not be a word that referred to a god Molech, but instead could be translated as a term "mulk" whose context was sacrificial. Thus, a Carthaginian stela bearing the term "mlk 'mr," which had originally been interpreted as "King of Omar," would have actually meant "mulk 'immor," which referred to a specific kind of sacrifice, the sacrifice of a lamb or kid. The clue to this interpretation of "mlk" came from the archeological discovery of a Roman stela on which a Latin inscription referred to the sacrifice of a ram to the god Saturn and in which the Phoenician term "mlk 'mr," transcribed into Latin, had been incorporated. Subsequently, a few other Roman stelae, with virtually identical inscriptions, were discovered.

If "mlk 'mr" did not refer to a god or king of a place but to the sacrifice of an animal—a ram or, as was also common among Mediterranean cultures, a lamb or kid—then, as Paul Mosca and others argued, "mlk" in conjunction with other words would refer to different kinds of sacrifice or, at least, to a promise of sacrifice. And, indeed, on some stelae from Carthage as well as from various Carthaginian colonies in Sicily, Sardinia, and northern Africa, there are references to "mlk b'al," while on stelae from the northern African colony Cirta there is reference to "mlk 'dm." Instead of following the traditional interpretation of "mlk 'dm" as "King of Men" ("Molech 'Adam"), Paul and others translate the term as "sacrifice of a human." These researchers believe references in the Old Testament to children being passed through a fire actually refer to the sacrificial burning of a real sacrificial offering. Paul suggests further that "mlk 'dm" refers to the sacrifice of a commoner, in contradistinction to "mlk b'al," which he translates as the sacrifice of a person of higher social status. In keeping with the classical written sources on Carthaginian child sacrifice, then, only the upper classes of Carthage engaged in or were allowed to engage in the ritual. But the decreasing quality of stelae during the years of the third Punic War—in carving, range of motifs, and iconographic as well as artistic embellishment—leads Shelby Brown to suspect that, if there had been a distinction between upper and lower classes in right of participation in the ritual, it became blurred during these final years. Thus, she suggests, Paul Mosca's interpretations of "mlk b'al" and "mlk 'mr" must remain provisional.

The Archeology of Carthaginian Child Sacrifice: The Early Years

In 1875 the first formal excavations of the general region of ancient Carthage unearthed thousands of stelae and cippi. Unfortunately, these gravemarkers were not in situ and thus were not associated with the remains of the infants and children implicated in the inscriptions. The first Phoenician site to provide potential archeological corroboration of activities at Carthage as attested to by classical authors was Motya, which is situated on a small island off the west coast of Sicily. There in 1919 J. I. S. Whitaker, who had begun excavations in 1906, unearthed 150 small urns containing burned bones. Analysis of the bones of 50 of the urns from this most unusual cemetery revealed that most were from domesticates (pets, such as dogs and cats, and livestock, such as lambs, kids, and calves), although some bones were from human infants; one urn even contained the remains of a monkey. Whitaker, who knew that he was excavating a Punic settlement, extrapolated from the classical writings on Carthaginian child sacrifice and concluded that the Motyans had also engaged in this ritual. The predominance of urns containing animal bones led Whitaker to suggest that the Motyans had been substituting animals for humans in the sacrificial ritual. Although Whitaker was not the first to unearth Punic urns containing burned bones— they had been excavated during the 1860s and again in 1911 at the North African site known by its Latin name Hadrumentum (its Phoenician name is unknown)—he was the first to recognize their potential significance. But, even so, until a cemetery with urns containing the burned bones of human infants and children was found at Carthage, the veracity of the classical reports would remain undocumented.

The discovery of such a cemetery finally came in 1921, during an expedition led by Count Byron Khun de Prorok, a wealthy explorer, P. Gielly, a public official of the town of Carthage, and F. Icard, the chief of police of the capital of Tunisia, Tunis. They found the exact site after Gielly bought an illegally marketed stela from an antiquities dealer and then followed the dealer, at night, as he went to rob other stelae. With funding from the Service des Antiquités, Icard and Gielly bought the land from which the stelae were being robbed and then, with Prorok, mounted an expedition that led to the discovery in 1922 of stelae and cippi that were not only in place, but associated with bone-filled urns. Icard, who referred to the cemetery as the "Sanctuary of Tanit," turned the bones over to P. Pallary, who determined that most were from human infants and children. Thus it appeared that the classical authors had been right all along: The Carthaginians had engaged in child sacrifice.

More extensive excavations of the Sanctuary of Tanit continued that year under the joint directorship of L. Poinssot and R. Lantier. After digging through layers of increasingly soggy earth (the water table had risen over the millennia), Poinssot and Lantier found that the most recent urns had been interred beneath stelae, the urns in the next level down were associated with stelae and cippi, the urns in the third level only with cippi, and the earliest urns—which were placed singly, in pairs, or in triplets in hollows in bedrock—were associated not with headstones but with piles of ordinary stone. When the bones from the urns were studied by A. Henry, he concluded, as Pallary had from his study, that most were from human infants and children. Based on that information alone, Poinssot and Lantier came to a diversity of conclusions: The Carthaginians had sacrificed their offspring often; the victims, as foretold in the Old Testament, had been firstborn males; and, of the various classical versions of the ritual, group sacrifice had not taken place.

In 1925 the successor to the excavation of the Sanctuary of Tanit, Francis W. Kelsey, a professor at the University of Michigan, uncovered more than 1,000 urns but looked at the bones of only 36 because he thought he would find just what his predecessors had found: the burned bones of human infants and children as well as of various animals. Kelsey was not, however, as convinced as his predecessors about the reality of widespread, regularized, institutionally sanctioned child sacrifice at Carthage—although he and his colleague and pottery expert, Donald Harden, allowed that the possibility did exist.

Père Lapeyre next took up the excavations of the Carthaginian sacrificial cemetery and, between 1934 and 1936, unearthed thousands of gravemarkers and more than 1,000 urns. Lapeyre thought that urns buried beneath a gravemarker as well as urns in its immediate vicinity were associated and reflected the sacrificial activities of either a single family or a few related families. Study of the burned bones yielded a picture similar to the one that had been unfolding—primarily human infants and children as well as some animals—but occasionally not only had two humans been interred in the same urn, but human and animal bones had been interred together as well. To top it off, study of the bones and teeth from a few urns indicated that the victims were not young children, but perhaps years older—which gave rise to speculation that the Carthaginians, at times, also had sacrificed adolescents.

From 1944 to 1945 G. C. Picard and P. Cintas continued expanding excavation of the Sanctuary of Tanit. In addition to confirming the results of previous expeditions, they found in the earliest level small stone shelters, some of which housed urns that sat directly on bedrock, while others housed other objects. The bones from 42 urns were eventually sent to Paris in the 1950s, to J. Richard, a doctoral candidate in forensic sciences, who unfortunately combined them into one large sample with the 138 urns from Hadrumentum he was analyzing for his dissertation project. The general picture that emerged from the total sample was that, from the oldest to the most recent urns, the frequency of human remains decreased while the frequency of animal remains increased. Approximately one-third of the urns contained human and animal bones together. Although approximately 75 percent of Richard's sample was not from Carthage, Cintas nonetheless concluded from Richard's data that not only had there been a trend toward substituting animals for humans in the sacrificial ritual as Carthage matured culturally, but that the humans who had been sacrificed had been the first-born, which is a conclusion that cannot be achieved from study of the bones.

The Archeology of Carthaginian Child Sacrifice: The Present

Cintas and Picard's excavations of the Sanctuary of Tanit would have been the last for an indeterminable period of time were it not for an escalating threat to the site and the surrounding ancient city of Carthage: the northwardly-expanding Sahara desert was forcing housing development to spread from Tunis along the seacoast, swallowing up the small towns, including the extant town of Carthage. In response to the impending destruction of the historical past, a multinational, UNESCO-sponsored archeological effort was mounted in the mid-1970s. Its goal was to recover and analyze as much as possible of the preserved history of the ancient city of Carthage. Archeological teams from Tunisia, England, Italy, Bulgaria, Poland, Denmark, Sweden, Holland, France, Germany, Canada, and the United States, under the auspices of the Tunisian government and Department of Antiquities, descended on the site and excavated for four, five, and sometimes six years of field seasons in a massive attempt to try to unravel some of the mysteries of this Phoenician stronghold.

One of the two U.S. crews was headed by Larry Stager, who was then at the Oriental Institute and is now at Harvard. After a preliminary field season at Carthage in 1975, Larry, with whom I had worked at Tell Hesi in Israel as well as at two sites in Cyprus, asked if I'd join his staff the following year to analyze the human and animal bones from the two areas of Carthage he had been allocated. One area was the dockside of one of the Punic Carthaginian harbors—the rectangular or mercantile harbor. The British team was given as one of its two areas the adjoining circular or naval harbor, in the middle of which, on a circular island, had once stood the admiral's palace. The other area assigned to our team was a portion of the Sanctuary of Tanit, or, as we called it, the tophet. These sanctuaries were now being called tophets despite the fact that the word as originally used in the Old Testament referred only to a place where children were "passed through fire," or sacrificed, not the cemetery where those who had been sacrificed were buried.

While excavating the area of the rectangular mercantile harbor, one of Larry's crews delineated an old waterway or canal that stretched from the residential, villaed section of the ancient city, across parts of what would later become the naval and mercantile harbors and docksides, to the tophet. This waterway may have been in use at least two centuries before the grand harbor system was built, or even from the very beginning of Carthage. Horses or oxen probably towed small flat-bottomed barges or rafts laden with goods along the canal. During one dig season a roughly hewn cippus was found at the bottom of the canal. It may have fallen off a raft either as it was on its way to being set in place in the tophet or as it was being taken to a site where gravemarkers periodically collected from an overcrowded tophet were relocated.

One day during the last field season, Abdelmajid Ennabli, the conservator of the site of Carthage from the National Institute of Archeology and Art, asked if I would be interested in analyzing some of the bones recovered during F. W. Kelsey's joint French-American archeological campaign of 1925. I eagerly agreed and the next day was presented with three small, shallow, obviously old, dust-covered cardboard boxes. Each box was only deep enough to hold two one-inch layers of cotton between which was sandwiched a layer of minute scraps of burned bone. One box held about a dozen of such scraps of bone, the others slightly more. Although it was immediately apparent to me that the bones in these three boxes were human in origin, because of their fragmentary nature, that was basically all I could say. The paltry fragments that had managed to survive the excavators' hands could not provide answers to any of the questions that arose from the conflicting classical reports or the enigmatic inscriptions on stelae, much less questions such as "How old were the individuals when they died?" But I could certainly understand how even getting these handfuls of bone fragments would seem like an accomplishment. By the time I was presented with these three small boxes of bony scraps, I had already processed well over four hundred urns and had learned the hard way just how difficult working on them could be.

When the Carthaginians were burying their urns in the tophet, they were digging into dry ground. By the twentieth century, however, when excavations began, the water table, which had been rising slowly over the millennia, was so high that, once you dug down a few meters, you were in mud and water. In order for Larry Stager's field crews to keep the excavated urns exposed long enough for their stratigraphic positions in the ground to be recorded, pumps had to be used nonstop to drain the water as it seeped up to the excavation surface. If, as happened with annoying regularity, a pump broke down, an excavation square would become a muddy pool within minutes. But once you got the urn out of the ground, your worries were still not over.

The urns that Larry's team had excavated before I first came to work at Carthage had been stored in and around the dig house and out on the patios with their contents in place. I picked out my first urn and, with an array of dental picks, spoons of different sizes, and brushes, tried to "excavate" its contents. It was like digging through concrete and getting your hand caught in the cookie jar at the same time. The mouth of the urn was just big enough for me to get my hand inside, but the bone and other objects in the urn had become incorporated into a solid block. As the water that had soaked the urn for centuries evaporated, the dissolved minerals crystallized and cemented together everything that happened to be in the urn. My all-but-useless attempts to scratch away the hardened mass left me with mere fragments of what had been complete bones, beads, and amulets—as must have been the case during other expeditions, including Kelsey's.

I knew there had to be a more efficient way in which to proceed, and there was: I had to prevent the urns from drying out. Because urns—each in its own bucket—were delivered to my work area at the dig house the same day they came out of the ground, I could re-create their soggy tophet environment by immediately filling up the buckets with water. If I couldn't attend to newly excavated urns as they came in from the field, they could stay in their water-filled buckets for days and their jumbled contents would remain the individual bones, teeth, beads, amulets, chunks of charcoal, and small stones they had been for centuries.

In my early trials with the "wet" technique of extracting the contents of an urn, I would submerge the urn in a plastic vat of water, carefully tip it over so that its contents would flow out into the vat, decant the water and urn contents from the vat onto a fine plastic mesh that was supported on the wire webbing of a folding metal cot, and then, with water from a garden hose, gently flush the dregs still in the vat onto the plastic mesh. Eventually I eliminated the vat phase. It was easier, less destructive, and more expedient to run water into an urn and flush the contents directly onto the plastic mesh.

After everything from inside an urn was on a mesh, I would spread the material into a single layer and gently hose everything down until the silt, clay, and—I hoped—all the water-soluble minerals had been removed. This final rinse phase also gave me the opportunity to pick over the urn contents, rough-sorting them into groups—bone, teeth, bauble, charcoal, rock, potsherd, clay, snail shell, whatever was there—and checking to see that small items were not hidden by, or inadvertently adhering to, larger items. When the bones and other objects were as clean as I thought they could be, I could let them and the now-empty urn dry safely overnight. The next day I would take brief notes on the condition and special features of the urn and its contents and then separately bag the pieces according to type of item so that each could be forwarded to the appropriate specialist for analysis. Compared to the bone fragments from the Kelsey expedition, and the fragments I created when I first tried to scrape the contents out of an urn that had been allowed to dry out, it was astonishing to see how much could be salvaged from the better-preserved urns with this simple garden-hose technique.

Clues from the Urns

Most of the urns came out of the ground in reasonably good condition— even if an urn had cracked while in the ground, it could still provide a fairly protective shell around its contents if the edges of the cracks stayed tightly together—and the mouths of many urns still had a lid in place. But I was surprised to discover that the mouths of the urns had been sealed at the time of burial with a clay stopper on top of which the lid had been placed.

The discovery came in the form of pliant lumps of clay, which, together with the expected bones and objects, I found in the bottoms of urns. In each case, the lump of clay was of the same type as that used to make the urn. When poorly fired but beautifully painted red clay urns of variable sizes were used during the earlier phases of the Carthaginian tophet, the lump of clay was red; in the latter phases of the tophet, when well-fired, but standardized, ugly pale-yellow urns just over a foot in height had been used, the lump of clay was yellow. The yellow clay was stiffer and felt more like potter's clay than the red clay, which was loose and slippery. Sometimes I found the lump of clay in the shape of a hockey puck that was the same size as the opening of the urn. On many urns patches of the same type of unfired clay clung to some part of the rim of the urn's mouth as well as to the corresponding portion of the lid's underside. Apparently, a continuous sheet of clay had spanned the mouth of the urn and had been sandwiched along its perimeter between the lid and the rim of the mouth. Over time, the unsupported clay plug came free and sank to the bottom of the urn.

Even more unexpected than finding the clay stoppers, however, was my discovery on many of them of impressions of human thumb- and fingerprints. These had to be the prints of a Carthaginian, *the* Carthaginian—priest or parent or someone else?—who had sealed the opening of the urn after the bones, beads, amulets, and whatever else had been placed inside. It was an eerie feeling to find those prints. In my mind they conjured up the image of the Carthaginian-in-charge taking a wad of clay, forming it into a thick pancake, kneading it into place across the mouth of the urn, and capping it off with a lid—sealing forever the evidence of Carthaginian sacrifice in the belly of the urn.

But this seemingly impenetrable barrier could last only so long. The weight of the increasingly soggy earth eventually cracked some of the urns. The spades of successive generations of Carthaginians using the increasingly overcrowded tophet smashed into previously interred urns. As the water table rose, and the clay that had spanned the opening of urns fell away, most urns filled up with silts and fine soils. On one occasion when I lifted the lid of an urn, I found a circular arrangement of beads lying on top of a thick layer of silt, under which the heavier bones and other objects were buried. Apparently, a necklace of beads had floated on top of the rising water. Eventually the nonmetallic cord on which the beads had been strung decayed, leaving a perfect circle of uniformly spaced beads.

The Condition of the Bones

As expected, the bones from the urns in my sample had been burned. With burning, the color of bone changes from brown, to charcoal, to steel blue, to gray, to white; gray and white burned bone is referred to as calcined bone. Beyond the white stage of calcination, bone will be completely incinerated. The surface or surfaces of the bone closest to the fire will be the most calcined. Thus a bone lying across a fire of uneven intensity will be unevenly calcined. In spite of the fact that most of the individuals from the tophet were, as I've now been discovering, extremely young—late third trimester or newborn—many of the urns contained large quantities of preserved skeletal material, albeit often fragmentary. (But even cremation using modern techniques does not turn an entire skeleton to ash. Bits and pieces of solid bone remain and must be crushed.)

Some osteologists have suggested that bone that has been defleshed prior to being burned can be distinguished from bone that has been burned with flesh still attached on the basis of the degree to which and intensity with which a bone is cracked. Burning a bone covered with flesh is supposed to create splits across the bone's surface that are deeper and more numerous than would be the case with a defleshed bone. So far, however, I have not found cracks in more than a few bones in my sample that conform to the picture of fleshy bone being cremated. But this may be due to the fact that other studies have been on adults, who would have thicker layers of muscle encasing their bones than would the perinates in my sample.

As would be predicted, the densest and hardest parts of the skeleton stand the greatest chance of surviving from sacrifice to my work area. In fetuses and infants, the two densest bones of the body lie at the base of the skull, one on the right side and one on the left. These petrosal bones—the word is derived from the Latin word for stone, *petra*—are, in an adult, almost as long as one's thumb. One end of each petrosal bone is stubby while the other tapers to a blunt tip. These bones are oriented diagonally along the base of the skull, with the stubby end lying near the ear and the other end lying farther forward and near the center of the cranial base. The upper surface of a petrosal bone contributes to the floor of the brain case while the undersurface faces into the neck. In fetuses and newborns, the stubby end of the petrosal bone lies against, but is not fused to, the flat temporal bone that forms that part of the lateral wall of the skull over which the fleshy ear lies. Within the first year of life, the petrosal and temporal bones fuse to form a larger mass. Because isolated petrosal bones dominate my sample from the Carthaginian tophet—rather than fused petrosal and temporal bones—it is obvious that most of the individuals were indeed quite young at death. In addition to petrosal bones, I also regularly find whole or partially complete bones of the face, the cranial base, the upper and lower jaws, vertebrae, pelvis, hands, feet, rib cage, and arms and legs. And I always find some tooth crowns among the bones. As with petrosal bones, the relative states of development of these bones and teeth provide clues to determining the age of an individual.

As I rummage through a pile of teeth and bones from an urn, I arrange the identifiable pieces into separate groups according to the part of the body they come from, such as skull, arm, leg, vertebral column, rib cage. In time, each skeletal region begins to fill in. For instance, I might be able to reassemble an arm, with what remains of the humerus, radius, ulna, and even hand bones laid out in their proper anatomical positions. If there's a collarbone (clavicle) and shoulder blade (scapula), I put them in place next to the top of the humerus. The same thing with any parts of the pelvis—I arrange them near the top of the femur, or, if that portion of the femur was not preserved, I put the pelvic pieces in the general vicinity of where they should go.

Sorting out ribs is a bit tricky, though. It's easy to identify the first rib and even the floating or false ribs at the very end of the rib cage. But, especially when they are in a fragmentary condition, the ribs in between cannot always be identified with such specificity. By trial and error, I keep rearranging them until I'm satisfied that I have reconstructed the shape of the rib cage accurately. Sometimes a pattern of burning across the rib cage begins to emerge, which I then can use as another source of information in arranging the ribs in their proper positions.

After sorting out the bones into skeletal regions, I try to glue together fragments from the same bone or region. For instance, in one case I was able to put together most of a child's skull cap—from the upper margins of the eye sockets almost to the base. When reconstructing bones, especially cranial bones, osteologists can tell when the pieces really go together, not just because their complementary external and internal features and contours match up, but because their edges "click in" together perfectly. It's the same thing that happens when you glue pieces of a broken plate—it not only looks right, it feels right.

The odd thing about putting together the pieces of this child's skull cap was that, while most of the fragments were calcined white, a couple of them were only charred black—even the edges of the calcined fragments were white, and the edges of the charred bone were black. At first I thought I had pieces from more than one individual's skull. But the charred pieces were not duplicates of any of the calcined ones. Rather, they represented those pieces I needed in order to complete my reconstruction. The result was a skull cap of primarily ashen bone with the odd angular island of blackened bone scattered throughout.

Skulls do not provide the only examples of this odd pairing of calcined with charred bone. I have also found this situation when reconstructing long bones.

While sorting out bones from another urn, I noticed that I had two fragments that had to have been from the same femur of the same individual, but the upper fragment was calcined white while the lower fragment was merely charred black. Because the edges of each fragment were still in good shape, I glued the two pieces together, and there it was—a miniature femur, its upper half chalky white, and its lower half charcoal black.

What do these patchwork quilts of bones of differently burned pieces mean? Could the heat of the fire have caused these bones to burst and shatter, scattering the fragments to different parts of the fire? I don't think so. Long bones in my sample that do have cracks resulting from exposure to heat have not one but a series of scallop-shape cracks along their surfaces, and cranial bones often have cracks that radiate out from a central point, like a spidery web. Cranial bones that are extremely thin also tend to buckle and even curl up at their edges, like dried leather.

The explanation, I think, is that a Carthaginian had actually broken these skulls and long bones, and that the fragments had then become lodged in different places in the fire's embers. This could have happened in two ways. Perhaps someone noticed that some bones or parts of a skull were jutting out of the fire or not burning in pace with the rest of the bones, and poked at the bones to get them deeper into the fire—breaking them in the process. Or, perhaps, when someone felt that the cremation had gone on long enough, the embers and the bones with them were poked and separated so that the fire could die out. In the process, coals and bones were broken. Unburned bones would then become charred by the last licks of the dying embers. Everything—bones, charcoal, and whatever else—was then left to cool down before being placed in an urn.

Clues to Cool Bones

One day a few months ago, Frank Houghton, my graduate research assistant on the Carthage project, came into my office with an unexpected find. He gave me what looked at first glance to be only a small, burned piece of bone. But when I turned the bone over, something with a meshlike patterning was stuck to it. With a hand lens I could clearly see that this was a small piece of cloth less than one-half inch square.

Finding even that small a piece of cloth was amazing. Certain kinds of organic substances—such as fibrous material, skin, hair, muscle, internal organs—will survive only in a watery environment that is oxygen-free and in which the pH is acidic. The oxygen-free environment prohibits the growth of microbes that feed on organic material and the acidity acts as a preservative. Raised peat bogs, in addition to being soggy, are acidic, and the compact layering of peat creates an oxygen-free environment. It is for these reasons that bodies found in bogs in England and northern Europe have been preserved. But while the acidity of the bog preserves those parts of the body that otherwise decay after burial, it tends to dissolve the bone and tooth enamel of these "bog people."

Obviously, the moist soils of the tophet were not acidic or oxygen-free enough to preserve the bulk of the nonbony, organic contents of the urns. Somehow, in one urn, one patch of a larger piece of cloth must have lodged in the one spot in which it could have survived.

But what was cloth doing in that urn in the first place?

I suppose material of some religious importance or a special item of clothing could have been placed in the urn, as the unburned amulets and beads were. Or, perhaps, the cremated remains had been wrapped in a cloth or put into a woven sack before being put into the urn. Perhaps doing so was part of the ritual. Whatever the reason, we do know that this little piece of cloth was neither burned nor singed. And because this piece of cloth was adhering to a fragment of charred bone, the bone must not have been smoldering—and probably had cooled down significantly—before the two items came into contact. After finding this piece of cloth I reviewed my slides of urns that had broken apart. I couldn't see any signs of charring on their inner surfaces, which would have occurred had charcoal and bones been transferred to the urns while still smoldering. Thus it would seem that the bones were cool when they were put into urns as well as when objects—such as cloth, beads, and amulets—were placed with them.

The Evidence of the Bones Versus the Classical Authors and the Stelae

The histories of the classical authors and the inscriptions on the stelae give rise to many questions. Some of them I can answer from study of the bones. However, as I continue to fine-tune my analyses, more questions are raised than answered.

One of the questions that I can address with some certainty is whether or not the Carthaginians were sacrificing their offspring en masse, as some of the classical authors claimed. If they had sacrificed groups of individuals at a time, I would expect to find odd associations of bones and teeth from urn to urn, because the bones of all individuals would be in a heap and then randomly distributed among urns. Thus, I might find five right humeri, twelve left petrosal bones, three left tibiae, no hand bones, one tooth, and so on in one urn, and other skeletally unrepresentative combinations of bones and teeth in other urns.

In most cases, however, it is obvious that an entire individual was represented in an urn. Each and every bone and tooth may not be there, but there would be enough—from tooth crowns to pieces of skull and jaw, vertebrae, ribs, upper and lower arm bones, upper and lower leg bones, pelvis, and hand and foot bones—to indicate convincingly that virtually everything that had gone into the crematory fire had been collected and put into an urn. Thus, from the bones in my sample, it appears that the Carthaginians were not practicing group sacrifice. But they were not always sacrificing single individuals either. Although more than 55 percent of the urns contained the remains of single individuals, another 25 percent contained the remains of two individuals, each being represented skeletally from head to toe.

Single or group sacrifices are the only options mentioned in classical sources, while inscriptions and rare engravings of priestlike figures holding infants on stelae suggest single infant sacrifice. But two individuals? Where did each come from? In 1976 my preliminary field-sorting of the first few dozen urns excavated seemed to suggest that, when two individuals were in the same urn, one was neonatal while the other was older, perhaps by two or more years. In the context of the reasons for sacrifice and the vows to Tanit and Ba'al Hammon, this potential fact led to speculation that the older individual had been a sibling who had been sacrificed to appease the gods for whatever had caused the death of the neonate and to ensure the survival of future offspring.

After many hundreds of urns, and hundreds of hours of taking the descriptive and quantitative analyses down to finer and finer levels of resolution, it now appears that this age difference, while noted on occasion, is not representative of the sample. More often than not, when one individual is demonstrably older than the other, it is only by a matter of a few months—which would imply that the two individuals were not related, at least not as siblings. Even the ages of the younger individuals are being revised down: On the basis of plotting measurements of various cranial bones and arm and leg bones against samples of individuals of known ages, it appears that many of the younger tophet individuals were late-third-trimester fetuses. In fact, the statistics at present indicate that, on the basis of cranial and long bone measurements, approximately 81 percent of all individuals in my sample—whether from single individual urns or double individual urns—were late-third-trimester fetuses. A more conservative estimate emerges when developmental criteria are combined with the measurements: As little as 54 percent but perhaps as many as 70 percent of the sample is composed of late-third-trimester individuals. These statistics imply that at least 54 percent, but possibly as many as 81 percent, of the individuals from my sample died of natural causes before they were cremated—which means, of course, that most of the individuals in this sample had not been sacrificed in the sense of being victims of a blood-killing.

But sacrifice doesn't always have to be synonymous with killing, ritualized or otherwise. If, as summarized by Shelby Brown, an element of sacrifice is that it is an extraordinary act carried out either as a symbol of friendship with or as a gift offered to a god or gods, then the cremation of these unfortunate Carthaginian perinates may itself be the ritual. The vow or oath that often appears in the inscriptions on various stelae and the invocation of Tanit and/or Ba'al Hammon need not be reflections solely of sacrifice involving ritualized killing. Such vows, oaths, and invocations may also apply to the offering, by way of burning, of the unfortunate perinate to Tanit and Ba'al.

If we continue to expand our thinking about Carthaginian sacrifice, as now we must, alternative interpretations of different apparent lines of evidence emerge. One famous stela, housed in the Bardo Museum in Tunis, often has been used to corroborate the picture of Carthaginian child sacrifice. The scene etched on one face of this stela is that of a man standing and holding a child in the crook of his left arm. Because of his headdress and robe, various scholars have identified this man as a priest. Paul Mosca and others who have discussed this stela describe the child as being or appearing to be alive. But I think there might be another way to interpret the evidence.

The first thing you have to understand about this stela is that the figures of the man and the child are merely etched outlines. They are not carved in any great detail, and, of the two outlined figures, only the man is depicted with facial features: an eye and the outline of a nose and ear. The child's face is featureless. Because the man's right arm is upraised and his eye is open, his figure appears alert and in motion. In contrast, the child—whose legs and lower arms are not figured at all—appears to be motionless: Its arm is depicted hanging down and its torso is nestled against the man's upper arm and chest and supported from below by the man's lower arm. In addition, the child's head appears to be drooping down and forward, as is sketchily indicated by the orientation of its featureless face, the downward slope of the top of its head, and the shallow curvature of the back of the neck. The dramatic contrast between the active posture of the man and the motionless attitude of the child is, I think, significant, especially when you consider that it was engraved by a Carthaginian and is, therefore, not a retold tale, but the closest we have to a photograph of two individuals who had something to do with rituals relating to the tophet. I believe there are two ways to interpret the child's apparent lack of alertness: It was either unconscious (perhaps as a result of being drugged) or dead. Given the number of fetuses in my sample that presumably had died of natural causes, it is very likely that the child depicted in this stela had met a similar fate, rather than being killed as part of a sacrificial ritual.

Obviously, not only do individual clues that have been brought to bear on Carthaginian sacrifice have to be reevaluated, the significance of the tophet at Carthage—perhaps of all tophets—needs to be rethought. How do we deal with the fact that a large number of naturally dead Carthaginian fetuses and neonates were cremated and placed in urns that were interred in the same sanctuary with the burned remains of obvious sacrificial victims, such as lambs and kids?

Taphonomy and the Tophet

If sacrifice as embodying the act of killing was not the single means by which the cremated remains of Carthaginian offspring came to be interred in the tophet, then the only universal that all tophet burials share is the youth of those who were cremated. Claude Schaeffer and Hélène Benichou-Safar made this point in their argument for rejecting the rigid linking of tophets only with human sacrifice and for suggesting, instead, that tophets were cemeteries for the very young, regardless of how a particular individual had died. To further bolster their case, Schaeffer and Benichou-Safar also cited the fact that burials of infants and young children outside of the tophet are rare at Carthage. Of the outside-of-the-tophet or nontophet burials, the youngest individuals were typically older than four years of age at death; in contrast, of the approximately two thousand nontophet burials so far excavated at Carthage, more than 95 percent were older children, juveniles, and adults. The argument that the tophet originally had been a cemetery for the very young is strengthened by the fact that most of the nontophet child burials postdate the early centuries of tophet burials—most are later than the fifth century B.C.E.

But, as those who reject Schaeffer and Benichou-Safar's hypothesis point out, the remains of children who were not interred in the tophet were simply buried in shallow graves, which would not provide long-term protection for bones and teeth. If these remains had been placed in urns or secreted, as juveniles and adults had, in chambers deep in the ground, then archeologists would presumably have found a more normal representation of this young age group. Or would they?

Drawing on the taphonomic literature on the survival of buried bone, it seems highly unlikely that all bone would be washed out of or otherwise eliminated by natural causes from a shallow grave. We know from experimental studies that, once in the ground, bones can become buried increasingly deeply just by normal processes of soil deposition and movement as well as by the inadvertent activities of burrowing rodents and earthworms. In fact, Charles Darwin was the first to publish a report on the effects earthworms have on soil movement. More recently Peter Andrews has been conducting experiments on the impact of earthworms on the redeposition of rodent bones. He has found that, as carcasses decay and fall apart, skulls and other bones tumble into earthworm channels and thus quickly become deeply buried.

If a corpse is put into the ground to begin with and then covered over, each skeletal element will have a far greater chance of staying buried than if the corpse had just been lying on the surface. Thus, even if heavy rainstorms had pummeled a child's shallow grave, I doubt that all bone would be washed away. Rather, even if most of the bones in a shallow grave were flushed out, some would be forced deeper into the ground of the grave and others would probably be reburied in the immediate vicinity. As such, it is likely archeologists would be able to find much more bony evidence of nontophet burials of newborns and children then they have.

A New Look at an Old Tophet

In sum, all interments in the Carthaginian tophet share the following features: Some or all of the bone is burned, bones of individuals are placed in urns, and these urns are buried in the same general area. In most interments individuals, whether human or animal, were extraordinarily young. Although there were few children above the age of four in my sample, metric and developmental criteria indicate that at least 90 percent of the sample is represented by individuals younger than six months of age, and, of these, at least half were late-third-trimester fetuses; adult tophet burials are so far unknown. Each category of animal and mixed human-animal interments represented only about 8 percent of the sample. Preliminary correlations of burial types with stratigraphy indicate that most of the animal burials occurred in the earlier phases of the tophet. This correlation can indicate two things: one, that human sacrifice eventually replaced animal sacrifice, or two, that, as population size increased over time, fetal-infant natural death rates increased. The latter would not be surprising.

Besides animals, individuals six months of age or older would qualify as the most likely victims of sacrifice. As such, a generous estimate from the data is that 10 percent of the individuals from the tophet could have lived long enough after birth to be sacrificed, but this still leaves approximately 90 percent that represent stillbirths, spontaneous abortions, and neonatal victims of natural deaths. This ratio may seem high, but there are modern as well as historical analogues of high rates of fetal and infant mortality. For example, Larry Angel of the Smithsonian Institution estimated from his analysis of the Middle Bronze Age cemetery at Lerna, a settlement in Greece that existed from 2000 to 1200 B.C.E., that the infant death rate alone was at least 30 percent and that the combined rate of stillbirth and premature abortion probably exceeded 60 percent. But, in spite of these high mortality rates, the adult population size actually doubled during the same period of time. I think we can safely assume that survival rates at Carthage were probably not less than those at Lerna, and that the percentages we get from the tophet do not reflect the true profile of infant mortality for the population as a whole. But whatever the precise figures, it is obvious that, at Carthage, the combined effects of natural fetal-infant death rates and child sacrifice had little detrimental effect on its success as a thriving metropolis or as a hub of expansive colonization.

The osteological evidence lends itself to the interpretation that many individuals buried in the tophet had merely died and had not been sacrificed. The tophet, then, was indeed someplace special—not just because it received the remains only of those who had been sacrificed, but because it also received the remains of the unfortunate young and unborn. And because these unfortunate unborn and neonates had met with premature deaths, they were treated differently from others who had died naturally but had done so later in life.

Their remains were cremated—which, perhaps, was seen as sending their essence back to Ba'al with the rising heat and smoke. Their charred and ashen bones were then transferred to urns in which objects were also placed—beads and amulets, perhaps clothing or religious vestments. These urns were in turn buried permanently, away from the graves of those who had lived longer lives, and in a special area dedicated to Tanit, perhaps so that she might reclaim those whose lives had failed.

We may never know what really happened at Carthage, but we certainly need to know much more than we do now before we can feel confident even in having identified all the questions still buried in the Carthaginian tophet.

■

BONES AND THE LAW

One day, not too many years ago, I received a phone call from a police captain from a nearby county. He said he had a bunch of bones but didn't know if they were human or animal. Because he had heard that I occasionally take on forensic cases, he asked if I could help him. I said I would. Later that afternoon he arrived at my office with a brown paper bag of bones, which some boys had found scattered in a field.

The officer hoped that the bones were from an animal, because, if they were human bones, and their previous owner had died within the past ten years, the departments of homicide and missing persons would have to get involved. He let on that he was a bit nervous about the discovery of these bones because he was supposed to retire in a couple of months. If, however, this situation developed into a homicide or a kidnapping, he'd have to stay on until the case was closed.

I emptied the contents of his paper bag on my desk. There wasn't much there, and, to the officer's relief, the pile became even smaller when I took away the rocks and the few scraps of bone that, although human, were very old and otherwise uninformative. But there remained a fairly complete lower jaw, a *human*'s lower jaw. It had the

heft of recent bone and it still felt greasy. It seemed highly unlikely that
the original owner of this jaw had died more than ten years ago—which
meant that the statute of limitations on this investigation had not yet
expired. In spite of the officer's repressed gasp I continued with my
verbal assessment of the mandible, pointing to various features that
indicated that its owner had most likely been male and to the relatively
unworn state of the teeth, which indicated that he had perhaps been in
his late twenties or early thirties at the latest when he died.

The police captain was not smiling. There were no outstanding missing persons reports in his jurisdiction. No unsolved murders. No suspected murders. No reports of vandalism at the local cemetery. But he
was obliged to try to track down the origin of the mandible. We put the
rocks, the unidentifiable fragments, and the offending mandible back in
the paper bag. Then he rerolled the top few inches of the bag, shook his
head as he shook my hand, turned, and left.

Sorting the Sexes by Their Bones

It's easy enough to tell the difference between females and males when
all the fleshy parts are there. It's not always that obvious when you're
dealing with bones. For instance, if I gave you the skulls of a young boy
and girl, or even a young teenage boy and girl, you'd be hard put to say
which was which. Only in the teen years will changes occur that will
make a boy's skull look different from a girl's. With young individuals,
it is also difficult to determine sex if you have the entire hip or pelvic
region—although, because females bear children and males don't,
you'd think there must be something about the pelvis that reflects these
differences. And there is. But most of these features don't become
noticeable until the teens. Up until then, a girl's pelvic region looks
pretty much like a boy's.

In general terms, young boys and girls are virtually identical in their
bones until (some) boys become male in their skulls and in the general
robusticity of the rest of the skeleton and (some) girls become female
in their pelvic regions—at least that's how it tends to be among populations of western Asian and European descent. Among eastern Asian

and especially the derivative Arctic groups, female skulls develop certain masculine features, whereas the male pelvis tends to look more feminine. Among sub-Saharan Africans, male skulls may stay more feminine-looking while the female pelvis may remain more malelike and not develop its "typical," "characteristically" female shape. This is not to say that one can't find "female" or "male" features in, respectively, any female or male's skull or pelvis. Osteologists just have to be cautious in their analysis and constantly battle against preconceptions based on stereotypes of "female" versus "male" shapes—which, as history would have it, are based on studies of the European skeleton. As such, men are usually characterized as having squarer lower jaws, more massive faces, more sloping foreheads, and even a touch of brow ridge. In contrast, women are supposed to have smaller lower jaws, slenderer faces, larger eyes, and more vertical foreheads.

When there are differences between males and females other than in organs of reproduction, the species is said to be sexually dimorphic. This means that a particular feature can be expressed in two, variably different shapes ("di" and "morph"), with a version being characteristic of each sex. Differences in body size are often cited as examples of sexual dimorphism. Among gorillas, baboons, and especially orangutans, males can be twice as heavy as females. These males are not necessarily twice as large as females in every comparable body part, but the heavier males do tend to be larger overall than females in dimensions of their skulls, jaws, teeth, and postcranial skeleton. Among human populations, males also tend to be larger than females, but not usually by more than 10 percent. Sometimes, though, size may be the only factor by which you can discriminate between young human females and males prior to their developing the shapes of bones that distinguish one sex from the other.

Measurements of teeth—usually just length and width—often are used to sort males and females. In many cases, measurements of the first and second permanent molar teeth will help separate the sexes. However, in markedly sexually dimorphic animals, such as baboons and great apes, the projecting upper canine teeth may be even better in sorting out size-related differences between males and females.

These dental measurements, as well as others on long bones or vertebrae, often cluster into two sets of data points when plotted graphically. One cluster corresponds to the smaller and the other to the larger sizes of the tooth or bone being measured; the former cluster is taken as representing the females and the latter cluster, the males. Depending on which tooth or bone is being used in the analysis, accuracy of 90 percent or more can be achieved in correctly allocating females to the female cluster and males to the male cluster. Inevitably, however, a male's tooth or bone will be clustered with the female group and vice versa, and the clusters, instead of being completely separate entities, will probably overlap a bit, because some females and some males are similar in size. The amount of overlap will be larger or smaller depending on the skeletal part measured and the degree to which sexual dimorphism is expressed in the species being analyzed. Because sexual dimorphism is not markedly expressed in humans, metric discrimination between females and males will never be 100 percent accurate.

Unfortunately, the study of sexual dimorphism in humans has been essentially restricted to adults—in spite of the fact that osteologists frequently must analyze the bones of infants, children, and juveniles. In fact, there is only one study so far—based on dental measurements—that can be applied straightforwardly to skeletal material found in an archeological or forensic context, but its results are not as reliable as one would like.

Using a skeletal sample of over three hundred individuals of known sex, Thomas Black measured the lengths and widths of all the milk teeth—on both sides of both jaws—and ran the measurements through a statistical program designed to determine the degree to which the data could be used to discriminate between groups. Black found that the teeth of females and males were classified statistically to the correct sex only about 75 percent of the time. This is a good but not a great result. A 25 percent chance of incorrectly assigning a sex to an individual is quite high, whether the analysis is for a legal case or a matter of trying to get more detail on the population dynamics of an ancient civilization.

Obviously, much more work is needed in this area of osteological research. For instance, I wish that some comparative criteria had already been worked out so that I could get at least an estimate of the sex ratio of the perinates and children from the Carthaginian tophet. More broadly, the inability to determine an individual's sex can also impact the pursuit of other types of analyses. For example, we know from various longitudinal studies that boys and girls develop at different rates. If we just look at the dentition, we know that, on average, certain teeth develop within the jaws and erupt through the gums at earlier ages in boys than in girls, while other teeth develop within the jaws and erupt through the gums at earlier ages in girls than in boys. But unless we can tell the girls from the boys in our samples, we can't even begin to think about tapping into this kind of analytical detail.

The Development of Skeletal Features of Sex

As an individual matures, bones grow larger in length, width, and breadth, but the final shape of most bones in an adult's skeleton also results from the fusion together of different parts to create a whole. For instance, take your upper leg bone, or femur. Its ball-like head, which articulates in the socket of your pelvis, remains a separate island of dome-shaped bone until the late teens. The bump of bone well below your waist that a tailor uses as a landmark when measuring your hips is one of two elevations on the upper part of the femur that do not fuse to the main bone until the late teens as well. And the lower end of your femur, which articulates with the top of the tibia, may not fuse completely with the shaft of the femur until your early twenties. So it goes throughout the skeleton. Different pieces of different sizes fuse to other pieces of other sizes in a fairly regular manner until you're about twenty-five years old. And as the skeleton grows and pieces coalesce to form fewer larger pieces, different parts of the skeleton also begin to acquire or accentuate those features related to one's biological sex.

At birth, a human's eyes are large, the forehead is high and rounded, and the back of the head bulges out. The lower face is so reduced in its size and relative proportions compared to the adult that the tooth germs developing within the neonatal upper jaw are separated from the eye sockets and the nasal cavity only by a thin layer of bone. Although a newborn's mandible typically bears one of the hallmarks of being a member of *Homo sapiens*—a well-defined chin—its general shape differs from an adult's: Each side of a mandible is essentially horizontal throughout its entire length; by adulthood, however, differential growth of different regions of the mandible cause it to flex, thereby creating the vertical and horizontal portions of the adult mandible. Growth changes transform the newborn skull and mandible into those of an adult, and it is within the framework of this common developmental scheme that sexual differences arise.

In very general terms, some of the most profound changes in the human cranium are seen in the lower face, which grows downward. As it does, the tooth-bearing portion (called the alveolar process) becomes removed from the floor of the nasal cavity and the eye sockets; at the same time and within the expanse of bone thus created beneath the eye sockets, an air space, or sinus, appears and enlarges. (Some of us are all too familiar with these sinuses—the maxillary sinuses—because their membranous linings often swell during bad allergy seasons; if these sinuses don't drain, the upper molar teeth often ache because their roots lie near or may even protrude into the floor of the maxillary sinus.)

As a rule of thumb, males tend to have deeper and bulkier lower facial skeletons and cheekbones than females. The roots of a male's teeth, especially the roots of the canines and incisors, are typically larger than a female's. These roots tend to leave larger impressions on the outer surface of the alveolar process in males than in females. (You should be able to feel, if not also see along your gums, the vertical mounds produced by the roots of your teeth.)

During their early years of childhood, males and females tend to share the same growth trajectory. But when boys mature and juvenile growth rates are supplanted by adult growth rates, changes take place that often affect the size, shape, and orientation of various facial features, such as the eye sockets, the brow or supraorbital ridge, the region just above the bridge of the nose, and the forehead. In the adult male, stereotypically, the orbits are squarer, set lower on the face, and give the appearance of being relatively smaller than in females. The male brow ridge (supraorbital ridge) tends to be more prominent than in females. Its prominence may be further accentuated by the development of a more sloping forehead. Such sexually dimorphic thickening of the brow ridge—which encompasses the upper margin of the orbit—also can affect the configuration of the upper margin of the orbit itself. In males, this superior orbital, or supraorbital, margin is typically thicker than in females. In fact, you can actually feel the difference on a skull: If you run your finger along the supraorbital margin of a male's skull, it will probably feel blunt, whereas, in a female's skull, it will usually feel quite sharp. The region between the inner ends of the eyebrows—the region above the bridge of your nose—is also often more prominent in males than in females; it may be a prominent feature even though the supraorbital ridges may not be enlarged.

Many of the other features of the skull that are used to determine the sex of an individual are based on the tendency for males to be larger than females. A male's skull often is bulkier and the bone somewhat thicker and more massive than a female's. In turn, this means that a male's skull tends to be heavier; the muscles that secure, balance, and move the skull are somewhat larger; and the scars these muscles leave where they attach to the skull are more prominent. The same applies to a male's mandible. On average, it is larger, bulkier, and heavier than a female's. This means that it requires larger muscles to move it during chewing and grinding, and thus the attachment sites of muscles on it and the skull are more pronounced.

In theory, and sometimes in practice, this kind of generalization concerning female/male differences may be valid, not only for the skull and mandible but for the rest of the skeleton as well. But in societies in which women do heavy labor of any sort—carrying heavy loads on their heads, tilling and harvesting the fields, manipulating plant fiber and sinew in their jaws—and men do not, the woman's skeleton bears "atypically" prominent muscle scars in the relevant regions. Thus, as a general rule, muscle-related features should not be used as primary sources for evaluating the sex of an individual. If, however, females can be discriminated from males on the basis of other, primarily developmental, features, muscle scarring might provide a clue to deciphering the labors each sex may have been involved in. In fact, this is a popular line of osteological investigation these days, not only in reconstructing past life-styles but also in forensic cases. One of the more straightforward analyses is determining whether an individual was right- or left-handed.

Teeth as Tools: A Lesson in Bone Remodeling

Whether or not we intend to do so, all of us modify parts of our bodies during our lifetimes. It could be just because we are right- or left-handed, engage in some form of labor-intensive activity, or use our jaws and teeth as an extra set of hands as well as in the manipulation of materials. Certainly this appears to have been the case with one of our potential fossil relatives, the Neandertals.

Characteristically, an adult Neandertal's upper and lower front teeth are worn down so far that the pulp cavities (where the nerves lie) are exposed, or at least in danger of being exposed. But instead of being worn down completely flat, these teeth often are worn so that the tops of the lower teeth tilt out and down while the tops of the upper teeth angle out and up. Thus, if the lower teeth were placed up against the upper teeth, only the tongue-side of their tops would touch. The cause of this excessive tooth wear is attributed to Neandertals' using their front teeth not just as a vise to hold something so that their hands could work on it but as a tool for processing materials. Because the kind of tooth wear we see in Neandertals is relatively uniform across the front teeth, it is more likely that they were pulling on material or objects that were broad and relatively uniform in texture rather than on narrow and stiff substances, which would tend to leave deep grooves instead of flat surfaces. The general consensus has been that Neandertals manipulated animal skin or hide with their jaws, using their front teeth to soften and stretch the material, perhaps by tucking a piece of hide in the mouth and then pulling it up and down as they drew it through their clenched teeth.

Modern analogs for Neandertals in terms of using teeth as tools have been the Inuit (Eskimos), many groups of whom still use their front teeth to manipulate skins and leather for clothing, the shells of kayaks, and snowshoes, for instance. The wear and tear on an Inuit's front teeth can be so profound that the pulp cavities may be in jeopardy even in a young individual. Despite the general similarity of wearing down the front teeth, however, I've recently discovered that Neandertals and Inuits are not similar in certain details of tooth wear. During study of a large sample of ancient western and eastern Inuits' skeletons at the American Museum of Natural History, I found that Inuits wear down their upper front teeth farther on the tongue side than on the lip side. Thus in Inuits, the plane of wear on the upper front teeth parallels the plane of wear on the lower front teeth, whereas in Neandertals, these planes of wear diverge from the tongue to the lip side of the teeth. Clearly, the kind of front tooth wear present in the Inuit teeth I studied would result from pulling material—leather and sinew to be processed or blubber on the inner surface of whale, walrus, or seal skin—past the teeth in a down-and-out motion.

Another apparent similarity pointed to between Inuits and Neandertals is an occlusal condition in which the chewing edges of the upper and lower front teeth come together in what dentists refer to as an "edge-to-edge bite." The most common occlusal relationship, seen in most humans and other primates, is a condition called "overbite," in which the upper front teeth occlude in front of the lower front teeth. A few primate species develop "underbite," in which the lower front teeth occlude in front of the upper front teeth.

In Neandertals, edge-to-edge bite occurs "naturally." When a Neandertal's mouth is closed, the edges of the upper and lower front teeth not only come together, but the articular ends of the mandible nestle in their sockets against the skull. In Inuits, however, edge-to-edge bite develops as a result of the mandible being moved forcibly so far forward that its articular ends are pulled out of their sockets in the skull and come to ride over and beyond the bony eminences that normally restrict movement of the mandible anteriorly. In time, these bony eminences are remodeled; they become flatter and often develop the look of a typical articular surface, such as in the knee joint, on the adjacent surfaces of the femur and tibia. The edges of the milk front teeth of the two youngest individuals in the sample I studied—a four-year-old and a six-year-old—were visibly worn, and the articular eminences of the skull had already begun to change shape and acquire the surface morphology of an articular joint.

The Inuit mandible also is remodeled in the course of developing and maintaining edge-to-edge bite. In females and males, the articular ends of the mandible become pulled out to the sides so severely that both ends cannot fit in their sockets in the skull at the same time. The first time I encountered this, I thought that the mandible from one individual and the skull from another had been put into the same box by mistake, but, after checking the archeologists' field notes and the American Museum's catalogs, it was clear that the skull and mandible belonged together. I eventually found that both articular ends could be placed on the skull at the same time if I put them forward along the remodeled articular surfaces. The reason this works is because the distance between right and left remodeled surfaces is wider than the distance between right and left articular sockets. Interestingly, by placing the mandible in such an unnaturally forward position, the front teeth were brought into "edge-to-edge" bite. Thus, in contrast to Neandertals, who achieved edge-to-edge bite because their mandibles were long enough to extend from the articular sockets to the upper front teeth, Inuits acquire edge-to-edge bite as a result of dislocating their mandibles from the articular sockets and changing aspects of both the mandible and the skull.

If you slide your mandible forward to produce edge-to-edge bite, you should be able to feel the articular ends of your mandible drop and move forward along your skull. If you try to hold the edge-to-edge bite and chew at the same time, you will feel how the muscles you normally use to move your mandible are being stressed, as are other muscles, which you don't use in this way. If you kept this up, though, your mandible would be remodeled to some extent by the continual action of these muscles pulling on it.

Jaw Shape: Is It Age, Disease, or Sex?

Because Inuits of both sexes subject their jaws to such degrees of stress, it is no wonder that their mandibles are similarly rugged and bear well-developed muscle scars on the outer surface and along the margin of the corner at the back of the mandible. According to the textbooks, male humans are supposed to have stouter and more muscle-scarred mandibles than female humans, but the only feature that can be used with some consistency to distinguish male from female Inuit mandibles is chin development, which tends to remain true to the stereotype: The male chin is typically more prominent and its basic triangular shape and angularity more accentuated than the female chin. I wish I could have used other features of the mandible in identifying the sex of the Inuit material I was studying, but bone remodeling had effectively obliterated what, in other human groups, would have emerged as sexually dimorphic differences.

In the case of the Inuit mandibles, the female mandible acquires male characteristics of robusticity and additional bone development where muscles attach, especially in the corner at the back of the mandible. In many human groups, the angle at this corner, which is created by the vertical and horizontal components of the mandible, typically approximates ninety degrees in males, whereas it is typically greater than ninety degrees in females. In Inuits, however, the extraordinary development of the female mandible tends to mask "female" traits.

Bone remodeling does not, however, always take the form of building up bone. Bone shape and robusticity also can be affected by bone loss, which can be brought about by the normal process of aging, by disease, and by tooth loss, which, in turn, can be a consequence of aging and disease.

As people age, the bones of the body become thin; the shoulder blade, for instance, which is basically a sheet of bone bearing various body projections, can become almost tissue-paper thin in places. The process of thinning occurs naturally because of changes in the relative contributions of those bone cells that lay down new bone and other bone cells that resorb or take away previously formed bone. In children, there is a high rate of bone resorption in areas that are still expanding, but also a generally high rate of bone deposition; after bones have reached their adult sizes and shapes, the rates of bone resorption and bone deposition are in equilibrium; with increasing age, however, bone is resorbed at a higher rate than it is deposited, which causes thinning of bone as well as shape changes in some areas. With age, the mandible becomes less robust and the angle between the horizontal and the vertical parts becomes more open and obtuse. Thus, "male" mandibles can come to look "female" and "female" mandibles "hyperfeminine."

Destruction of the gum tissues eventually can lead to tooth loss and ultimately to bone loss, which can make a "male" mandible appear to be "female." When gum tissue is lost—due, for example, to age-related recession of tissue, infectious periodontal disease, or abrasion—the blood supply to the underlying bone is cut off and bone will be lost, exposing more and more of the roots of the teeth. The phrase "long in the tooth" refers to an individual who has lived so long that his or her roots are exposed to a great degree. If the process of gum recession–bone resorption continues unabated, there may not be enough bone left in which a tooth or teeth can remain anchored. Teeth might then be lost; with tooth loss would come additional bone loss in the surrounding, now-toothless, region. Such bone loss goes all the way through the alveolar bone—which is as thick as the tooth roots are deep—to the bone of the lower face or mandible (depending on the jaw affected) upon which the alveolar bone was deposited. If a person loses enough teeth, whole stretches of tooth-bearing bone will be lost, creating no-ticeable valleys along the margins of the jaw. When all teeth are gone, the entire expanse of tooth-bearing bone will be resorbed, thereby reducing the depth of the lower face and shrinking the mandible to the thin, cordlike strut of bone that it really is. Tooth and eventual bone loss in the region of the molar series alone can modify the shape of a mandible sufficiently so as to obfuscate correct sexual identification.

Bacterial infections below the gum line, in the root socket itself, can lead to tooth loss and ultimately to loss and remodeling of bone. When such infection sets in—perhaps as a result of expansion down through the root of an infectious cavity that started on the crown of the tooth— pus collects, bone death occurs, and a pocket develops around the tip of the infected root. Similar to a boil or pustule that might develop elsewhere on the body, this pus-filled pocket or abscess enlarges. Even-tually a drainage hole, at the level of the infected root tip, might erupt through bone of the outer (cheek or lip) side of the jaw. If the infection goes unchecked, the abscess and drainage hole will enlarge to the extent that the infected tooth, which can no longer be supported, will be dropped, or exfoliated; the infection also can spread throughout the jaw and, if it is in the upper jaw, invade sinuses and destroy facial bone. Without the tooth in place, and with ongoing infection, destruction of alveolar bone continues, thinning the mandible and reducing the depth of the lower face, as the case may be. Again, tooth and bone loss in the region of the molar series alone can remodel a "male" mandible into a "female" one. In an individual in whom alveolar bone destruction not only had been extensive but had gone completely to the basilar bone of the jaw, an osteologist might not be able to tell if the cause had been periodontal disease or abscess.

Tooth and subsequent bone loss represented another complicating factor in my ability to decipher an Inuit's sex on the basis of features of the mandible. While those females who still retained a full or nearly full set of teeth in their mandibles tended to display male characteristics, males who had lost teeth and bone tended to have mandibles that looked female. As far as I could tell from the sample I studied, tooth loss was initiated by the development of abscesses, which arose as a result not of infection that started in the crown but of inflammation and subsequent infection that stemmed from the heavy wear and tear sustained by an individual's jaws and teeth. In terms of the mandible in the paper bag, it was fortunate from a forensic standpoint that it had come from a young adult with healthy teeth and mandibular bone.

The 89 Percent Solution: Accuracy in Sexing by the Pelvis

According to Wilton Krogman, one of the pioneers in forensic osteology in the United States, a well-trained osteologist can, on average, correctly identify the sex of an individual on the basis of features of the pelvic region eighty-nine times out of a hundred. This, I think, is what the ideal situation would yield—if everything fit the stereotypes. However, as with the skull, not all pelvic features are expressed to the same degree in all females or are their sexually dimorphic counterparts in all

males, and there may well be different norms of femaleness and maleness among different human populations.

You would think, however, that there should be some stable female
versus male pelvic features because only females bear children. To
some extent, this is true. However, the number of typically unequivocal
features that might fall into this category are few, and only one—a
notch in each pelvic half near its articulation with the sacrum in the
back—seems to be present in individuals of all ages. The representatives of this notch—called the greater sciatic notch—aside, it is risky
business at best to try to identify the sex of a fetus, newborn, or child
on the basis of isolated pelvic bones, which do not fuse to form the
pelvis as we know it in the adult until the teens.

In an adult, the structure referred to as the pelvic girdle is composed
of right and left pelvises that make contact in the front and, in the back,
articulate on either side of the sacrum, which is the unit at the end of
the vertebral column formed by the fusion of five or so vertebrae; the
girdle of bone thus created encircles the pelvic or birth canal. But what
we see in the adult as a single pelvic half starts out as three separate
bones—the pubis or pubic bone, the ilium, and the ischium—which, in
the teens, eventually coalesce into one structure. The region where all
three bones come together is the hip socket, in which the head of the
femur articulates.

From the hip socket, the pubic bone juts out, pointing forward and
down. The ends of right and left pubic bones meet in the midline of the
lower abdomen, underneath the fleshy pubic region; this juncture is
called the pubic symphysis and remains an unfused joint throughout
life. The ischium extends essentially straight down from the hip socket;
the two bumps you sit on are the roughened ends of the right and left
ischia (the plural of ischium). A bony strut connects the pubis and
ischium and forms the side of a roughly triangular opening bounded
above the pubic bone and, from behind, by the ischium. When right and
left pubic bones are in articulation, the struts between them and the
ischia form an upside-down V.

The third bone of the pelvis is the ilium. There are two ilia (the plural
of ilium), a right and a left. Each projects up from a hip socket. A human
ilium is broad from front to back and its upper margin is mildly arcuate.

You can see or at least feel the front end of this margin; it is the blunt point that juts out when you lie on your back and suck in your stomach. It is more difficult to feel the back end because it is tightly bound to the sacrum. But you can trace the upper edge of the ilium most of the way if you start at the front end.

When viewed from the front, the articulated pelvis looks somewhat like a mask with ears: With your head in the pelvic canal, your nose would stick out through the upside-down V, each eye would look out through the vaguely triangular opening subtended by the pubic bone, the ischium, and their connecting strut, and each ear would be in the general vicinity of a hip socket. The ilia, which are oriented from front to back, project upward like Mickey Mouse ears.

Female and male pelvises perform similar functions, such as anchoring abdominal musculature, cupping and supporting abdominal organs, and providing sockets in which the heads of the femurs can articulate. But a female pelvis must also be able to cup and support a developing fetus as well as allow for relatively unimpeded passage of the newborn through the birth canal. To varying degrees, sexual dimorphism in pelvic morphology reflects the additional roles of the female pelvic girdle.

In theory and according to the stereotype, the cupping of a developing fetus is reflected in the degree to which the ilia flare out to the sides. You can get a sense of the male/female stereotypes in this way: Hold your hands up with the palms facing each other; leave a space between your wrists that is about the length of one of your hands; with your hands flexed ever so slightly outward at the wrists, you are approximating the more vertical ilia or straight-sided pelvis generally associated with the male; with your hands flexed more severely outward at your wrists, you are approximating the ilial flare usually thought of as characteristic of the female pelvis. These differences in ilial flare are also reflected in the tendency for males to develop inguinal hernias, which result from the intestines penetrating the lower abdominal wall.

The inguinal ligament stretches between the "blunt point" at the front of the ilium and a small spit of bone on the pubic bone that lies about a centimeter in from the symphysis; there are, of course, right and left inguinal ligaments. The lower margins of the sheetlike abdominal muscles that extend down the front of your belly are tethered to the inguinal ligaments. Only skin and underlying tissue—but not muscle—span the somewhat triangular space between the inguinal ligament and the margin of the pelvis. This subinguinal space, therefore, is relatively weak compared to the muscle- and bone-strengthened areas around it. And the more vertically oriented the ilium is, as in males, the larger the subinguinal space is and the more susceptible it is to being penetrated when the space normally available for the intestines is compressed—which happens, for instance, when you crunch your stomach muscles really hard. (The intestines can also invade the scrotum, creating a scrotal hernia—but that's another story.)

After being cupped by its mother's ilia, a newborn must pass successfully through the pelvic or birth canal. Although humans have larger heads at birth relative to body size than most other mammals, the successful passage is due only in part to the compressibility of the newborn's largely unossified skull. A smooth passage during birth also is due to the typically greater breadth and depth of the female pelvic canal. The stereotypical male pelvic canal is narrower and more "heart-shaped." Of course, there will be males and females in every population who do not conform to the stereotype.

But let's stay with the stereotype a minute. In females, the typically broader and deeper pelvic canal—which is a space—results from a lengthening and deepening of the basic bones of the pelvic girdle: Compared to a typical male, the female ilia are relatively longer or deeper (from front to back), the sacrum is wider and more squatly triangular, and the pubic bones are relatively longer. The qualifier "relative" is necessary because, while the absolute length of a bone may be smaller in a female than a male, the bone would be relatively larger in the female than in the male if total body size is taken into consideration.

If, in simplistic terms, the spaciousness of the pelvic canal increases as the ilia, sacrum, and pubic bones lengthen, two other features of the greater pelvis will also change correspondingly. For one thing, the hip sockets will be farther apart. Because a female's knees still meet at the midline of her body, the effect of moving the hip sockets apart is that the angle at which the head of each femur comes into its hip socket will

be different from that in a male. The slightly different angle of articulation of a female's femur is reflected in a more downward inclination of
the hip socket and a more liplike distension of its upper rim. The typical
male hip socket faces more directly to the side, and its margin is more
uniformly rimmed; as an aside, the male hip socket is typically larger
than the female's because the male's bones, and thus the head of his
femur, are typically larger.

The other consequence of increasing the spaciousness of the pelvic
canal is that the ischia, which essentially hang down from the hip
sockets, are moved farther apart. This increases the angle between the
struts that connect to the ends of the pubic bones. In other words,
the arms of the upside-down V are pulled apart, thereby increasing the
angle they subtend beneath the pubic symphysis. As such, females tend
to have wider or more obtuse subpubic angles than males. You can
estimate the typical difference by comparing the splay between your
index finger and your thumb when it is extended to the side (the more
female subpubic angle) with the splay between the index and middle
fingers when they are spread apart (the more male subpubic angle).
Another difference between females and males involves the greater
sciatic notch, which is formed under the part of the ilium that articulates with the sacrum. In females, this notch is typically broader and
shallower than in males, in which it can be quite deep and pinched.

And, finally, some of the more subtle differences between the typical
female and male pelvis are related to keeping the pelvic canal relatively
free of intruding structures. One of the biggest potential offenders is the
sacrum, which also has a few vestigial bones—coccygeal bones—tacked
onto its tapered end. The sacrum with its tiny bony "tail" has a natural
inward curvature to it that is vaguely reminiscent of a partially flexed
lobster tail. In females, the curvature tends to be less pronounced than
in males.

There are actually a few more features that have been brought to
bear in trying to distinguish female from male pelvises. But because
they are more difficult to describe, and you can't feel them on yourself
because they're either tucked under edges of bones or buried beneath
thick layers of muscle, I think I'll stop here. However, if you asked me
which features are consistently the most reliable in determining sex, I'd

have to admit that, unless you have the entire pelvic girdle to work with—which is most often not the case—you'd have to hope that the greater sciatic notch was intact and that somehow you could reconstruct the subpubic angle.

Adding Up One's Sex

When trying to determine the sex of an individual from its bones, some osteologists identify each feature simply as female, male, or sex indeterminate. Others use a slightly more detailed scale of identification: hyperfeminine, feminine, sex indeterminate, masculine, hypermasculine. The Hungarian osteologists who proposed the latter scale also suggested coding by numbers going from -2 for hyperfeminine to $+2$ for hypermasculine. A score of $+2$ would be given, for example, to a subpubic angle that was extremely narrow or a brow ridge that jutted out farther than all other brow ridges in the study sample. A score of -2 would be given to such extremes as almost horizontally inclined ilia or to a markedly obtuse mandibular angle. Something in between— such as ilia that weren't quite vertical but weren't really flared either, or chins that weren't quite hard-edged but weren't quite soft triangles either—would be coded 0, or "who knows?"

As an osteologist became more comfortable with the sample under study, she or he might refine the analysis by using half scores. Thus a mandibular angle that was definitely masculine but not quite a $+2$ or a $+1$ might be coded as $+1.5$. Or a slight bulge in the region above the bridge of the nose might be coded as -1.5.

The ideal situation is to be able to establish comparative categories— such as hyperfeminine or even sex indeterminate—within the context of a sample of a significant number of individuals. This is important because, for instance, a $+1$ in one population might be a $+.5$ or a $+1.5$ in another. A large sample also allows an osteologist to get away from the stereotypes of female and male and isolate the demonstratively sexually dimorphic features of a particular population. Working with a large sample also allows an osteologist to begin to see the ways in which a particular population does not conform to the stereotypic "norms" of sexual dimorphism. But osteologists do not always have the luxury of working with a large sample. Oftentimes, especially in forensic cases, skeletons turn up singly—and we're actually lucky if we do get a fairly complete skeleton instead of just a mandible in a paper bag.

Whether, however, there is a number of individuals to work with, or just one, the way to determine the sex of any given individual is the same: Add up the scores and take an average. And that's the sex of the skeleton. Pretty unnerving, isn't it, to think that after having lived your life as a person of one sex, you might be recorded in the scientific literature or a court's records as having been of the other sex?

How Old?

In the early phases of life, developmental changes are reliable indicators of an individual's age. Thus teeth are most useful as age indicators from birth until the mid to late teens. The timing of fusion of bony elements to form larger bones and, eventually, the adult state of the bone can be used to deal with the period from the early teens to the early twenties. Thereafter, age-related changes often are reflected in the obliteration of the separateness of bones of the skull, in the reduction of a bone's mass, and, perhaps as a metaphor of life, in the wearing down of various articular surfaces of the pelvis.

When an infant is born, the crowns of the milk teeth and the first permanent molars are already in various states of relative development. As the youngster matures, the permanent teeth that eventually will replace milk teeth, as well as the second and then third permanent molars, begin to grow, and the milk teeth begin to erupt into the jaws. Eventually the second permanent molars erupt, other permanent teeth erupt and replace their milk tooth predecessors, and, finally, the third permanent molars or wisdom teeth come into the jaws. The timing of milk and permanent tooth development and eruption can be correlated rather consistently with an individual's age—with, however, the exception of the third permanent molars, which have been known to erupt in individuals as young as eighteen and as old as thirty-five years of age. Thus, at about the age of twelve years, after the permanent set of teeth has replaced the milk teeth and the second permanent molars have erupted into the jaws, the constant motion that had characterized tooth development and eruption comes to a standstill and the utility of this set of criteria ceases.

The variability in age at which the third permanent molars erupt has nothing whatsoever to do with the notion—the myth!—that humans are in the process of losing these teeth. True, some human populations have a slightly higher incidence of third molar absence than others. But the myth is based on much more than this curious observation alone; it is based on the assumption that modern humans are in a process of evolutionary transformation that entails a reduction of the face and jaws that will eventually interfere with third molar development. Because evolutionary transformation embodies the notion that change is constantly occurring, the occasional absence of third molars in humans, as well as the demonstration that some populations have smaller jaws than others, leads to the unjustified prediction that the continuation of this process will eventually produce humans with uniformly smaller jaws and consistently absent third molars. Interestingly, and in contradiction to the prediction, one of the human groups with the highest incidence of third molar absence—the Inuit—also has the largest jaws of any human group.

Other parts of the skeleton can provide useful age-related clues. Among these is the bony ear region or petrosal bone, which houses the inner ear bones. The three inner ear bones lie just on the inside of the eardrum, which is stretched across a bony ring that, by birth, fuses to the outer opening of the petrosal bone. After birth, a bony tube begins to grow outward from this ring of bone, forming a corridor between the opening in the fleshy ear and the eardrum. This bony tube is usually complete by the age of five years, by which time some bones elsewhere—for instance, some vertebrae—have fused and still other bones—other vertebrae—are beginning to fuse to form larger bones. The process of bony elements fusing to make larger bony units continues into the mid-twenties for tubular bones. But cranial bones keep fusing along contact points for decades.

Stages of cranial suture closure—from the meeting of sutural edges, to the elimination via fusion of all traces of their existence—have been used for decades in attempts to reconstruct age at death. However, osteologists constantly complained that the typical margin of error in the timing of cranial suture closures—twenty or as much as forty years—was too great for these analyses to be useful, especially in forensic cases. The problem, it turns out, was that osteologists had been using the wrong cranial sutures—the three, long, obvious sutures that course at or near the top of the skull. But as Owen Lovejoy and colleagues at Kent State University, Ohio, have recently pointed out, the smaller, less obvious sutural areas on the sides of the skull are the ones that should be used. As a result of the Kent State group's work, stages of closure of cranial contacts can now provide estimates of even old age with margins of error of only a few years. In fact, thanks to the work of Lovejoy and his collaborators, other areas of the skeleton also can be used reliably in osteological analyses, especially for accurately determining the ages of individuals well into their sixties and even seventies.

Two of these areas are located in the pelvic region. One is the surface of the pubic bone that contributes to the pubic symphysis, changes in which were first described in the 1920s by T. Wingate Todd. Although Todd's work was temporarily dismissed in favor of supposedly more accurate analyses, Lovejoy and colleagues demonstrated that Todd's was in fact the best approach for determining age using the pubic symphysis. Lovejoy and colleagues also went on to analyze another region of the pelvis: the surface on the side of the sacrum that articulates with the back of the ilium. It turns out that the symphyseal surface of the pubic bone and the articular surface of the sacrum change similarly in texture and topography with increasing age.

In young adults, these articular surfaces bear a series of alternating ridges and valleys and are described as being "billowy," as in rows of puffy clouds; the texture of the bone is regular. With age, the three-dimensionality breaks down and the surfaces become flatter; surface texture also becomes more granular. Eventually, in the fifty-year and older range, the margins of these surfaces break down and become arthritic; the surfaces themselves also break down further, developing patches of pitting and porosity. By using a much more detailed scale of textural and topographic changes in the pubic symphysis and articular region of the ilium, the margin of error in estimating age at death can be decreased to less than ten and sometimes as little as five years, even if an osteologist is dealing with skeletal material from very old individuals.

But what if the tried-and-true clues of skull or pelvis for determining age can't be used, because, for instance, weathering eroded the subtleties of suture closure and pubic and sacral articular surface morphology? The Lovejoy group also has addressed this problem in a number of ways, one of which involves X-raying a bone and seeing what its internal morphology—which would not be affected by weathering—looks like. Specifically, the Kent State group worked out scales of age-related change for two bones, the clavicle (collarbone) and the upper part of the femur. They point out, however, that an osteologist should be able to figure out age-related changes for virtually any bone—if the sample is complete enough.

The tubular bones (for example, a femur) of a quadrupedal mammal (for example, a cow) have thicker walls throughout the length of the bone than do those of a human; a soup bone provides a good example of this. The tubular bones of a quadrupedal mammal also have a more spacious core through the shaft than do those of a human. Only the middle third or so of a tubular bone of a human has relatively thick walls and a relatively hollow core. The upper and lower thirds, however, are thin-walled, and the core is filled with the complex network of extremely thin bony plates and spaces called spongy bone; in quadrupedal mammals, spongy bone is more restricted to the very ends of the bones. In humans, lightweight spongy bone substitutes for thick-walled bone in providing structural and weight-bearing support.

But humans pay a price for this lighter bone construction. As an animal grows older, bone is resorbed at a faster rate than it is redeposited. In humans, thin-walled bone gets thinner and the latticework of spongy bone becomes less dense and less pervasive along the length of the bone. Obviously, this diminution in bone density increases a bone's fragility. In terms of an osteological analysis, diminution in bone density also can be studied radiographically and the degree of bone thinning and spongy bone resorption correlated with age—which is what the Lovejoy group did with the clavicle and the upper part of the femur, and which anyone can do for just about any bone.

Perhaps the most important aspect of the Lovejoy group's forensic work is their demonstration that osteologists don't have to be tied to the standard areas of the skeleton for analyzing age-related changes. These changes can be delineated in any untried part of the skeleton, *if* changes in that area can be correlated with changes in at least one other skeletal region for which age-related changes are already known. Take tooth wear, for instance. You might think that patterns of tooth wear can't be used in determining the age of an individual because people in different cultures and at different time periods wear down their teeth differently because of differences in, for instance, diet and tooth use. True, a worldwide scale of age-related patterns of tooth wear can't be established. But osteologists can try to correlate age and degree of tooth wear for groups of people they have reason to believe shared common diets and other aspects of tooth use. In fact, tooth-wear patterns in groups that didn't subsist on soft, processed foods can be relatively reliable age indicators.

The first thing to do in such a study is to arrange the jaws in an order that yields a serial sequence of tooth wear, going from the least worn sets of teeth, which presumably represent the youngest individuals, to the most worn sets of teeth, which presumably represent the oldest individuals. Although this arrangement from least worn to most worn cannot provide the exact age of any individual included in the series, it does provide a perspective on the relative ages of individuals—individual Y is older than individual X (because individual Y's teeth are more worn) but younger than individual Z (because individual Y's teeth are less worn). And, of course, the larger the sample available and the greater the span of ages represented—from child to old adult—the more reliable the reconstructed scale of tooth wear will be.

If there are young individuals in the sample, one way to begin correlating relative states of tooth wear with age is by tying in to states of tooth growth, eruption, and replacement—for which general ages are already known. For instance, because the first permanent molar usually erupts at about six years of age and the second permanent molar at about twelve years of age, note can be taken of how worn down the first molar becomes during the six years it takes for the second molar to erupt. By extension, it can be predicted that the second molar will be worn down a similar amount during a six-year interval (that is, from the time it erupts to about eighteen years of age). The amount of wear the first molar acquires during the same time interval (twelve to eighteen years) also can be kept track of; the next six years of wear of the second molar (from eighteen to twenty-four) can be calibrated; and so on.

Obviously, this procedure is not limited to the molars but can be applied to any and all teeth in the sample that can be studied from eruption through wear. And if the sample is really great—with all sorts of details preserved throughout the skull and postcranial skeleton—stages of relative tooth wear can be correlated with age based on changes in, or fusions of, different parts of the skeleton. Or the focus could be on correlating tooth wear changes with age changes in spongy bone density in the first segment of the big toe, or changes in shape of the sternal end of the ribs (which a group from Florida Atlantic University has begun to do), or, on a microscopic level, changes in the relative frequency of bone cell type in the walls of tubular bones (which various groups of osteologists have been trying to do). The point is not to rely on the old standbys of determining age. If all that is left of an individual is a jaw with teeth, or a few ribs, or part of the humerus, relative tooth wear, or rib end change, or bone cell frequency can be used to estimate age.

This multiple analysis approach to estimating age—by trying to eke out age-related information from different parts of the skeleton—is limited only by the nature of the sample and the vividness of your imagination. Even as I write this, my research assistants and I are trying to devise an age scale for the Carthage human infant sample based on changes in overall shape as well as specific detail of the petrosal and other bones of the base of the skull. Because we can determine age with some accuracy using measurements of these isolated bones, we should be able to turn around and use age-related shape changes to estimate the ages of infants whose bones are damaged in the spots where measurements would be taken.

Putting a Face to the Bone: Piecing Things Together

Sometimes an osteologist's analysis is limited either by time or by circumstance of preservation to merely estimating the age and sex of an individual. If more than just a few pieces of a skeleton are represented, and especially if there is a large and well-preserved sample to work with, the analysis can expand into the details of disease and pathology and the reconstruction of stature and relative cranial and postcranial shapes and proportions. If warranted, either by the novelty of the discovery or by legal proceedings, an osteologist can go even further in reconstructing the identity of the individual or individuals.

One of the eeriest parts of working on the cremated Carthaginian infants has been the occasional piecing together of bones of the face and of the braincase to create larger portions of these regions. For some individuals, there are enough pieces preserved that I can put together almost an entire face as well as large parts of the rest of the skull. Even though these faces and skulls may be incomplete, there is enough there to think of going on to the next level, the reconstruction of soft tissue and skin to replicate the person's facial features.

One of the reasons that reconstructing soft tissue features has not been an everyday practice is that it is an extremely time-consuming proposition; computer programs that apply the same principles of reconstruction osteologists would use are not yet widely available or easily affordable. In facial reconstructions, the first thing needed is a series of little peglike pieces of plasticene, each of which represents an average thickness of skin, muscle, and fat for a specific position on the face or skull. After putting dozens of these little pegs in place, each peg must be connected to all pegs around it with strips of plasticene that reflect changes in thickness between any two pegs. And then the open spaces between strips of plasticene must be filled in so as to reflect what would have been the contours of the face—which would not be the same in different age groups because, during the aging process, an individual tends to lose fatty deposits, particularly around the cheekbones, and the skin sags in various areas, such as along the neck and below the eyes. Other soft tissue parts also change with age. For instance, the ears tend to elongate, the ear lobes become "lobier," and the tip of the nose tends to drop. But these age-related changes are even more difficult to reconstruct because these fleshy bits, like the lips and hair (or the lack of it), do not leave definite clues about their size or shape on bone.

I did, however, spend an afternoon once a few years ago with Yordan Yordanov, a Bulgarian anatomist specializing in facial reconstruction. Yordanov believed that he had figured out how to reconstruct the shape of the nose with some accuracy. After having dissected thousands of cadavers, Yordanov came to the conclusion that the shape of the fleshy nose in profile was essentially a mirror image of the margin of the bone from which the fleshy nose protrudes—the nose sticks out, the margin of the bone curves in. If, for instance, the margin of the bone was deeply invaginated, he would reconstruct an aquiline, "Roman" nose. Yordanov also could tell if the tip of the nose pointed up or down by looking at the orientation of a small spit of bone that projects from the midline of the bottom of the bony nasal region. If, for instance, this spit of bone pointed up, he would reconstruct a nose whose tip also tilted up.

You can test these claims yourself by tracing the edge of the bones of your nasal region. Start at the top of your nose, at the midline, where the nasal bones end and the cartilage (which you can move around) begins. Drag the tip of your finger down the side of your nose, pressing in so that you can follow the edge of bone; when you get near your nostril, you'll have to push in harder. It may be difficult, but you can feel the bony spit (if you want) when you move the bottom of the fleshy partition between your nostrils (in which the spit of bone is buried) from side to side. The bony outline you just traced should be a shallow mirror image of what your nose looks (or used to look) like in profile.

Sometimes a skull turns up that is believed to have come from a particular person. With a photograph or portrait of that person, an osteologist could see if the skull fit the likeness portrayed.

The way this is done is simple. A photograph is taken or a line drawing made of the skull in question with the skull in the same orientation as the head in the portrait. One of the images is then reduced or enlarged to the size of the other. Then, by photography, tracing by hand, or computer manipulation, the two images are merged. Because reduction or enlargement of one image to fit the size of the other will keep all the relative proportions of facial and cranial features at the same scale, the consistency of peculiarities of the skull—such as the disposition of the eye sockets, cheekbones, forehead, brow ridges, chin—with those of the face in the portrait or photograph can be determined. If dental records are available and if the teeth haven't fallen out of the skull in question, fillings, bridgework, artificial caps and crowns, and chipped and missing teeth can be matched up. Forensic dentistry is a highly lucrative field— and makes for great news—but it really doesn't take a whole lot of training to see if chipped incisors or fillings in the teeth of a skull are consistent with the details of the dental records.

The skulls of important people in the past—skulls that had been removed or stolen from graves—are usually identified by way of comparison with portraits, which, of course, important people often had commissioned. One of the most famous cases a few decades ago involved the purported skull of Emanuel Swedenborg, the eighteenth-century Swedish scientist, mystic, and founder of a new religious system. Swedenborg's skull had been stolen by grave robbers and, over the years, had gone from one collector to another. After a skull reputed to be Swedenborg's surfaced, its true identity was affirmed only after a series of attempts to fit the image of the skull to portraits of a small number of possible candidates whose skulls also had been stolen from their graves and kept by private collectors as curiosities.

Most recently, a skull claimed to have been Wolfgang Mozart's has been the subject of much media coverage as well as forensic analysis. Among other features, the skull has a very vertical and bulbous forehead, which, with flesh on it, would look very much like the prominent forehead of Mozart as seen in portraits. The group of French physical and forensic anthropologists that studied the skull is convinced that it is Mozart's, but the Viennese group that also studied the skull disagrees.

Looking for Murder Victims

Most of my forensic investigations begin with police officers or detectives bringing me skeletons, or parts of skeletons, for analysis. And most of the time determining the identity of the individual is either not requested or just not possible. Occasionally, however, I'm asked to go to a site where bones were found or where a body was suspected of being buried; in the first case, I'm asked to find more bones and, in the second, actually to find the buried remains. Once I was involved in a police investigation where, after the remains of one of two murder victims were found, the identity of the individual was revealed, not by any sophisticated analyses but by the murderer himself.

One hot summer day about eight years ago I found a message in my office mailbox from the police. I returned the call and found myself speaking to a person who identified herself as a detective in the homicide division. Unknown to me—because I hadn't been paying attention to the local news for a few days—a team from the homicide division had been digging up a semiwooded area in a nearby county for the bones of a suspected murder victim. Apparently they had been finding bones and wanted an expert to determine whether they were from a human or an animal. Deer hunting is popular in western Pennsylvania, and the area under police investigation was supposed to be a favorite hunting spot. Because this was a simple request, I asked if I could send one of my graduate students in my stead. The detective was insistent on my going to the site, although a student would be allowed to tag along. While police offered to send a helicopter to get me that afternoon, I asked if we could just drive there the next day.

Early the next morning I arrived at the homicide offices with one of my students. The detectives told us that they were looking for the graves of two murder victims. The confessed murderer had revealed the general area of these two graves as part of a plea bargain that sent him to jail (for yet another murder) instead of the gas chamber. But more than seven years had passed since these two murders and the murderer couldn't remember the exact locations of the graves. As a result, every police officer who did not have to be somewhere else was out at the site with a shovel or pickaxe trying to find the bodies. In the process of digging, bone had been found—and that's where I was supposed to come in. Only after we had been on the road for about half an hour did the detective driving announce that the real reason we were going out there was to *lead* the search for the victims' graves. This was a far cry from identifying a bone that had already been found. For one thing, it is not a trivial feat to locate a grave that someone has sought to hide. The only experience I had had in trying to find isolated burials that were not in "expected" places, such as cemeteries, was while on an excavation in Cyprus.

Searching for Cypriote Tombs

In 1971, a small team assembled from the crew already working at Tell Hesi, and headed by G. Ernest Wright, went to the island of Cyprus—which lies about fifty kilometers from the coast of southern Turkey and a bit farther from the western shores of Israel and Lebanon—to investigate the feasibility of excavating a major Archaic-to-Roman period site, complete with two acropolises. I was going to study the bones. The site, Idalion, was located about midway between the southern coastal city of Larnaca and the inland capital, Nicosia. The modern-day town of Dhali continues the history of occupation in that area.

The first individual to dig at Idalion was General Louis Palma di Cesnola, an amateur archeologist with an intense interest in the past. Between 1867 and 1875 Cesnola not only excavated parts of the western acropolis at Idalion, he also conducted a much larger survey of the general region. During his "survey" he looted at least 15,000 tombs, some of which were as old as the Iron Age, while others were as recent as the Roman period. Because of his successes at tomb-hunting, Cesnola accumulated a wealth of artifacts, which, in turn, prompted others to continue the search for buried treasure. The reason Cesnola and his tomb-robbers were so successful was that it was very easy to locate a tomb. And the reason for that is that the shaft of the tomb itself, although hidden underground, actually contributed to its own discovery.

In southern Cyprus, the topsoil is at best an extremely thin layer over the limestones and shales that make up bedrock. Because bedrock is always so close to the surface there, rainwater has little chance to seep into the ground and be held. Therefore, the vegetation of southern Cyprus is generally sparsely distributed and consists primarily of grasses and low shrubs. Larger vegetation—large bushes and trees— will grow only where fissures in the bedrock allow for the accumulation of looser soils and the retention of water. A tomb shaft, which can be dug relatively easily into the friable bedrock, represents a potential home for larger vegetation. Thus, all someone looking for a tomb had to do was keep an eye out for a tree or large bush in an area of otherwise low and sparse vegetation, or for any unusual arrangement of vegeta- tion—and dig. By the time I got to Cyprus, the tombsites around Idalion were thought to have been cleaned out. Nonetheless, occasionally I would take a few hours off from analyzing animal bones and seek out a likely tree or bush. My hope was to find an untouched tomb so that I could provide at least a little information about the people whose burial goods had been robbed. But the closest I ever came to realizing that desire was finding a robbed tomb—the only tree on the hillside was growing in it.

Back to the Search

Because the murderer had buried his victims in a semiwooded area, I thought that we might have a chance of finding the two graves if we kept an eye out for odd configurations of vegetation—not just trees or bushes that looked out of place, but some arrangement that would have been influenced somehow by the grave itself, perhaps its shape or the fact that it had a body in it. But I was not prepared for what greeted us when we got to the site.

The area had been untouched and semiwooded when the murderer used it for a grave site. In the intervening years, however, it had been bought by a construction company that was developing it for housing. A broad road wound its way through what remained of the woods and past houses in various states of completion. The bones of the victims, I realized, could be under the road or have been bulldozed away. The police had brought in their own bulldozer to clear unbuilt land. As the machine bullied its way through trees and underbrush, dozens of officers armed with shovels and pickaxes followed, pecking madly at the scarred ground.

I tried to explain that you don't have to dig a wide or deep hole in order to find out if someone had dug there at an earlier time, because the substance, compactness, and texture of the material thrown back into a hole always will be different from the substance, compactness, and texture of the area surrounding the hole. The dirt thrown back into a hole will not replicate the natural layering of the undisturbed earth, and it always will be softer than the soil in which the hole was dug. Therefore, in order to test for the existence of a hole that had been filled in, all we had to do was clear the surface of debris with the edge of a trowel or shovel, see if there were odd breaks in soil color, and then trowel out a small section of earth in the suspicious area to see if it had been disturbed and was soft.

Because the thirty or so police and the bulldozer seemed intent on continuing their attack, the homicide inspector in charge of the operation suggested that my student and I try our luck elsewhere. We ended up in a lone stand of pine that covered about an acre of land and was itself traversed by rambling deer trails. Instead of being layered with vines and thickets of weeds, as was the first area, the ground here was covered with years of accumulated pine needles and isolated patches of low-lying plants. We spent the early hours of the afternoon methodically walking back and forth, creeping our way down the slight slope of the landscape, making the occasional trowel test at suspicious depressions in the ground. Some of the local volunteer police and firemen's groups that had arrived during the day joined us in combing the area. One group, its members all in matching lavender jumpsuits, came to save the day with an expensively trained body-sniffing dog. We all tried to stay out of each other's way.

At about two in the afternoon, as I was scanning the ground for what seemed like the hundredth time, I looked up and noticed what, in the shifting light of the early afternoon, was clearly a long depression running parallel to a deer trail in which three saplings, not of pine, were growing side by side. My student saw the same thing from where he was standing, made a beeline for it, and started clearing away the layer of pine needles. We both felt the soil. It was soft. One more scrape, and the edge of the shovel exposed the top of a massive, human left femur. We called out. The two homicide sergeants who'd driven us out were there in a flash as was the jumpsuited volunteer group, whose body-sniffing dog stood, wagging its tail, right over the exposed femur as it tried to claim the center of attention.

Because of legal and technical matters, my student and I had to back off from the grave until the proper authority from the crime lab arrived. When he did arrive, he and the police were going to proceed as usual: dig up the entire area with a bulldozer and shovels and try to separate the bones from the dirt using a large-mesh sieving screen. Fortunately, I convinced them that we should excavate the grave as if we were on an archeological dig. Eventually we exposed not only the entire skeleton but the hole it was in.

The grave looked like a short-stemmed lollipop: The main part was relatively deep and subcircular in shape, with a shallow, narrow extension protruding from one side. Most of the skeleton lay in the subcircular part. The pelvic girdle was on its side, with the right hip deeper in the ground. From the waist up, the skeleton twisted toward its stomach, pressing its arms underneath. The lower legs were crammed into the extension, with the left leg positioned somewhat above the right. Lying near the neck vertebrae were right and left plastic collar stays, and paralleling the front of the breastbone and rib cage was a staccato of buttons, spaced as they would have been on a shirt. Near the pelvis lay a metal zipper and a patch of pubic hair, still attached to what had been skin, and the pelvic region itself cupped a stinky mass of what had once been the lower intestines, which, over the years, had turned into a dark and soaplike mass. As I lifted the pelvic region from the ground, thin threads of undecayed muscle fiber stretched between the bone of the right hip and the soil on which it had rested for at least seven years. Acidic soil, produced by the pine needles, and a fortuitous lack of oxygen must have preserved this soft tissue. I quickly forgot my reaction to these foul-smelling discoveries when I found the bullet lying near the neck vertebrae and below a hole in the back of the skull.

After exposing the entire skeleton, we measured its total length—from head to foot, taking into consideration the bends at joints—before removing it from the ground. This person, who had all the "expected" features of maleness emblazoned on his bones, had been about six feet three or four inches tall. Given the extent to which his cranial sutures had closed, the degree of fusion of the ends of his bones, and the fact that his third molars hadn't erupted, my preliminary, in-the-field estimate of his age was mid-twenties. There was a slight bit of bone resorption around the teeth, but otherwise his jaws looked healthy. The only other possible sign of pathology was the incomplete fusion of the spine of one of his neck vertebrae. His upper right first and second incisors had been replaced with gold crowns covered on their outer surfaces with ceramic; there were only a few amalgams in other teeth. We put the skeleton in a body bag, and it was carted off to the local coroner's office.

When my student and I arrived the next day to look for the second victim, the place was swarming with police—many carrying fairly heavy artillery—and the scratch of walkie-talkies filled the air. The inspector told us that the murderer himself was at the site and that the extra police and guns were to prevent a getaway. One of the sergeants also told us that there had been an anonymous phone call late the night before claiming that the second victim's grave was booby-trapped with a World War II land mine. And we were still expected to lead the search for the second victim.

We later spotted the inspector and a small group of officers near the grave from the day before, and, as we approached, heard a voice, whose owner was hidden by a pine tree, ask for a cough drop. Without thinking, I reached in my pocket to give one to the voice as an officer emerged from behind the tree with a man who was well restrained: His hands were handcuffed to one another and the chain of the handcuffs passed through a stout metal loop that projected from the front of a thick leather harness cinched around his waist. The man could pull his hands only a few inches away from his body as he reached for the cough drop. The officer introduced me to the murderer.

He was thin, in good shape, cleanly shaved, perfectly manicured and coiffed, and even wore the slightly baggy institutional pants and shirt well. His eyes looked dark and fierce and intently intelligent and thoughtful (although I allowed myself to think that there wasn't any light in them). I couldn't believe that this was someone who had not only admitted to killing three people but who, as the police told me, was suspected of having killed as many as twenty people. If this individual were sitting near me in a restaurant dressed in a suit, or even as he was minus the handcuffs and harness, I probably wouldn't even give him a second thought.

He was articulate too, talking constantly while we spent the next hour or so tromping through the woods as he tried to remember where he'd dug the second victim's grave. At one point he stopped and told me how he had poured lime into this particular grave so that the body would decompose more quickly. He wanted to know if this was the best way to go about it. "Why," one of the detectives asked, "are you planning another murder?" At least the murderer and the detectives laughed.

As the search continued, it became apparent that we weren't going to locate the second grave this way. The landscape had changed too much in the intervening years, and the murderer was getting increasingly upset because he couldn't lead us to the second body (he prided himself on remembering every detail of every crime he'd committed) as well as because, although he had remembered the grave that was in the pine grove, he had forgotten which victim he had actually put in it. Given the height, age, and dental work of the skeleton we found, the murderer knew precisely who it was. But that person was not supposed to be in that grave.

At one point, I nervously asked the murderer why he'd killed the person whose grave we did find. "To teach him a lesson," he said matter-of-factly. Well, I thought, he'll never do that (whatever "that" was) again.

The murderer went on to explain how he had taken his intended victim to the woods on the pretext of digging up and splitting the loot from a crime they had committed together. They had driven as far as they could go and then, with the murderer leading the way, made their way on foot to the supposed location of buried treasure. The murderer got his intended victim to start digging, and, when the hole seemed large enough, shot his "buddy" in the back of the head. But, because the hole was not quite large enough, the murderer had to dig an extension into which he crammed the victim's legs. He then filled in the hole and went away, not realizing that all the tamping down of the earth fill would not conceal the hole. As the body decomposed, the fill sank and three saplings took root along the length of the grave, taking sustenance from the unusual source of nutrients.

After we left the company of the murderer and had continued our unsuccessful hunt for the second grave for a few hours, I went into one of the police trailers for a can of soda. The murderer, sitting quietly between a pair of huge, heavily armed guards, was being kept in there. I bent down to get a cold can from the cooler and felt something move from my hip pocket. I turned quickly and saw one of the guards holding my trowel, slapping its blade against the palm of his other hand. I had had it in my hip pocket, where any good archeologist would put it. The guard didn't have to say anything. He just kept slapping the blade against his palm and slid his eyes in the direction of the murderer. That was all I needed to know I retrieved my trowel, forgot the soda, and fled the trailer.

We never found the second grave that day, or when we tried again the following spring. By then more houses had been put up. One of them, near a small stand of pines, even had a hole in its yard just the right size for a goldfish pond.

■

CHAPTER FOUR

FETUSGATE

The Monkey in a Jar

There are some days you should never get out of bed. But, if you do, you certainly shouldn't answer the phone. One day, a few years back, I did both.

The fateful phone call came from a nearby coroner's office, from the head coroner himself. His request was simple: to corroborate his findings and that of a pathology expert at a local hospital. Apparently, a mangled specimen—of a primate—had been found in a pile of already sanitized linens at the hospital's laundry. After having, literally, gone through the wringer, the specimen was in pretty bad shape, but it still had to go to the coroner's office for official analysis and identification. After study, the coroner was satisfied that the specimen represented what was left of the body of a monkey. The pathologist corroborated this identification. Because I was a physical anthropologist interested in primates, the coroner thought it wouldn't hurt if I took a quick look at the specimen to see if there was anything that struck me as being incompatible with their conclusions. A few hours later a young assistant from the coroner's office arrived at the anthropology department's main office with a medium-size jar in which strands of skin and associated tissue bobbed and waved in liquid that I assumed was formalin or some similar type of preservative.

The first thing I noticed was that the specimen lacked feet. The assistant said that the feet had been cut off and retained for further study. Surely, I thought, because the feet had been there and their morphology noted by those who identified the specimen as being monkey rather than human, the issue was moot. It was an open-and-shut case. There is nothing in the animal kingdom that looks like a human foot, with the occasional exception of a partially decomposed bear foot—in size and general shape, the back part of a bear's foot with the fur and skin missing superficially resembles the back part of an adult human's foot. But an expert's close look at the shapes and relationships of the bones to one another would immediately clear up the confusion, because the human foot is unmatched among mammals. In fact, taxonomists have used the distinctiveness of the human foot for more than two centuries as one of the key features in distinguishing humans in their classifications.

Typically, taxonomists set primates apart from other mammals because they have hands with thumbs and feet with big toes that are similar to thumbs in mobility and grasping ability, thus creating four functional "hands." Among primates, humans are distinguished by having feet with big toes that are large and aligned with the other toes. A human's foot is not the foot of a quadruped, primate or otherwise, but the foot of a mammal that walks in a distinctive and special way: upright and bipedally. If we had no other part of a human's body or skeleton, we still would be 100 percent certain that we had the foot of a human. And the specimen's feet were missing.

The parts of the body that were, however, still in recognizable form were the footless legs, a right arm and hand, a right ear, the lower part of the nasal region, and the upper lip. The spine or vertebral column also was still in place. The rest of what remained of the specimen was extremely macerated and mangled.

The hand was a primate hand, complete with a thumb that could be pulled away from the fingers. Another clue to the specimen's primate-ness, and general group within the primates, was that the tips of the thumb and fingers bore flattened nails. More generally among mammals, hooves or claws adorn the tips of the front and back toes. In contrast, modern-day primates are distinctive as a group in having flattened nails on the ends of at least some of their fingers and toes. Within the primate group, some anthropoid or so-called higher primates—humans, apes, and certain monkeys—have flattened nails on the tips of all fingers and toes. The hand of the defooted specimen in the jar was definitely that of an anthropoid primate.

What remained of the specimen's upper lip was also of interest: It was continuous across the midline. This is not a trivial observation, because the development of a continuous upper lip is the least common configuration among mammals, including primates. Instead, most mammals, as well as many primates, possess an upper lip that is disrupted vertically along its midline. This so-called split upper lip results in part from the extension down its midline of the moist, hairless, membranous tissue that covers the nose of most mammals. A vertical groove courses down the midline of this membranous tissue, adding further emphasis to the disruption of the continuity of the upper lip. This moist, hairless, membranous nasal tissue is called a rhinarium, and the extent to which it covers the nose and extends down the lip, and whether the downward extension is broad or thin, varies among mammals. The next time you're near a friendly dog or cat, take a look at the snout. You'll see that, if you can call them lips, there is a hairy right lip and a hairy left lip separated from one another by the grooved rhinarial extension from the animal's nose.

If you were to look even more closely—and pull up the animal's "lips" a bit—you would see that the rhinarium is connected to the membrane of the gums. In fact, the cellular distinctiveness of the rhinarium continues on through the space between the upper central front teeth of the animal and proceeds a small distance back along the midline of the palate. If you're really on good terms with this dog or cat, and it will allow you to look into its mouth, you will be able to see a small, ovoid patch of tissue on the roof of the mouth with a different texture than the surrounding palatal tissue. The rhinarium courses to this patch of distinctive tissue, which lies over two holes in the bony palate that connect the oral cavity with the nasal cavity. This connection, in turn, permits a commingling of sensory information acquired through both the oral cavity, by way of the tongue or rhinarial membrane, and the nasal cavity.

The ancestral mammal would probably have had both a pair of holes in its palate and a rhinarium. Shrews, bats, camels, cows, cats, dogs, mice, rats, and rabbits, for instance, are some of the mammals that retain a rhinarium. And so do lemurs and lorises, and bushbabies and mouse lemurs, which together constitute the nonanthropoid group of primates, the prosimians. But the anthropoid primates are different. As a group, they are distinguished by their lack of a moist, hairless rhinarium. Instead, anthropoid primates typically have a continuous upper lip, one that, like their noses, is covered with "normal," dry, hair-bearing skin. There is, of course, the occasional mammal, such as the horse, that doesn't develop a rhinarium. However, only one *group* of mammals is distinguished by its lack of a rhinarium and the development of a continuous upper lip. And that group is the anthropoid primates. The specimen in the jar had an anthropoid upper lip and nose—at least the lower part of what remained of the nose was anthropoid.

I could tell that the specimen in the jar was a primate because it had a grasping hand. I could tell further that it was an anthropoid primate, and not a prosimian primate, because all of its preserved fingertips bore nails, its upper lip was continuous across the midline, and its upper lip and the lower part of its nose bore "normal" skin. Of the anthropoid primates, the specimen didn't appear to be human because, among other things, its torso, which still had the spinal column in place, looked too long. Humans and apes are distinguished from monkeys by having fewer vertebrae in their spinal columns. It seems that lower or lumbar vertebrae were lost in humans and apes in the process of spinal column shortening.

Because the coroner and the pathologist had had the specimen's feet to study, and each had come independently to the conclusion that the specimen was monkey and not human, my going through all of these points seemed like a redundant academic exercise. Similarly, the fact that the specimen lacked a tail—which would identify it as a human or an ape—now had to be explained differently: Perhaps the tail was lost while being laundered.

About Monkeys

If this specimen was what was left of a monkey, what kind of monkey was it? Two different groups of anthropoid primates have been identified as being monkey: New World monkeys (now found in southern Mexico and on into South America) and Old World monkeys (distributed throughout sub-Saharan Africa, Indo-Pakistan, and on into southeast Asia). But even though both groups are referred to as "monkey," they really are different from one another.

The diversity of New World monkeys includes the larger organ-grinder's monkey (the capuchin), the howler monkey, and the tiny and colorful marmosets and tamarins, among other species. Many of the larger New World monkeys have prehensile tails, which, like an elephant's trunk, can wrap around objects; these monkeys use their tail as an extra limb while climbing between and hanging from branches and will wrap it around their clinging offspring to help secure them.

The colorful, almost birdlike marmosets and tamarins are specialized in unique ways. They are unusually tiny, not only compared to other anthropoid primates but to most other primates. They consistently bear twins. They are the exception among anthropoid primates in that they really don't have opposable thumbs and big toes, and the tips of their fingers and toes bear compressed and clawlike, rather than flattened nail-like, structures. They develop only two, instead of three, molar teeth in each quadrant of the jaw. And they have very simple cusp patterns on their molar teeth.

It used to be thought that most of these features reflected the fact that marmosets and tamarins were not just primitive New World monkeys but primitive anthropoid primates. But about fifteen years ago a student of mine named Susan Ford, who is now a professor at Southern Illinois University, argued compellingly that these features are specializations of marmosets and tamarins—specializations that reflect the fact that, during their evolutionary past, marmosets and tamarins had become dwarfed. Small size, fewer number of teeth in the jaws, and simplified molar tooth cusp patterns are also features of other mammals that are more obviously evolutionary dwarfs. The next time you go to a zoo or natural history museum, compare, for example, a pygmy hippopotamus with a regular hippopotamus. The pygmy hippo is obviously the evolutionary dwarf.

The second group of anthropoid primates identified as "monkey" is represented by such Old World forms as baboons, mandrills, rhesus monkeys and other macaques, langurs, and colobus monkeys. Although there appear to be many evolutionary subgroups of Old World monkeys, all are distinguished among anthropoid primates by having a very distinctive cusp arrangement on their molar teeth. In contrast to you and me, apes, New World monkeys, and all but a few prosimians, an Old World monkey's molar cusps are not discrete blips or mounds on the tooth's chewing surface, nor are the upper and lower molars morphologically different from one another. Instead, an Old World monkey's molar cusps are modified into two parallel ridges that go from side to side across the surface of the crown, with one ridge in front of the other, and upper and lower molars are mirror images of one another.

Given that these features can help us delineate between two major groups of monkeys, how could I tell if the specimen in the jar was a New World monkey or an Old World monkey?

I could have tried to rummage around what was left of the mouth and jaws to see what the tooth crowns would have looked like. If any bore two parallel ridges, the case would have been closed. It would have been an Old World monkey and nothing else. But, when I tried to go off to my lab with the specimen so I could take it out of the jar to study it more closely, the assistant, who had announced upon his arrival that this was definitely the remains of a monkey, didn't think that any further analysis was necessary and was not willing to leave the specimen. So I had to make do with an identification through the walls of the jar.

For decades, the two groups into which classifiers have subdivided anthropoid primates have been delineated on the basis of features of the nasal region. A New World monkey's nostrils are widely separated from one another, and, thus, the space between the nostrils—the internarial septum—is quite broad. The taxonomic name for New World monkeys, Platyrrhini, which means "broad nosed," reflects this broad septum and broadly separated nostrils. On the other hand, Old World monkeys, apes, and humans have long been grouped together because their internarial septum is narrow and their nostrils are, therefore, close together; in some Old World monkey species, the septum is actually quite thin. Old World monkeys, apes, and humans have thus been described as "narrow nosed," which is what their taxonomic group name, Catarrhini, means.

What about the nasal region of the specimen in the jar? From what remained intact, it was obvious that this specimen, which displayed features characteristic of an anthropoid primate, had had a broad inter-narial region. Ergo, the specimen in the jar was not an Old World monkey, or an ape, or a human. It was a New World monkey.

The ear was also of interest. It was large—broad and tall—fleshy and relatively unrolled along its edges. It looked more like the ear of various New World monkeys than the crisply rolled-at-the-edges, typically smaller, often pointed ear of many Old World monkeys. This ear also lacked an earlobe, which does develop on occasion only in humans and the African apes, the chimpanzee and the gorilla.

I briefly explained this bit of reasoning to the assistant, who asked me to put it down in writing. Never let yourself be rushed into anything, especially if it involves putting something down in writing. But, because I hadn't yet learned this lesson, I dashed off a quick note, reiterating that the specimen wasn't human and that, as a type of monkey, it appeared to be a New World monkey. With my note in hand, the assistant took off with the specimen jar.

The Monkey with Human Feet

I had completely forgotten about this episode, when, about six weeks later, I received a phone call from a pathologist from yet another hospital. He sounded very agitated and upset. He explained that the "monkey" specimen in the jar was really what was left of a stillborn human fetus that, after having been autopsied, had somehow ended up with the dirty laundry. The local newspapers also carried the story, reporting that the head coroner, a hospital pathologist, Schwartz, and some experts at the Smithsonian had identified the specimen as that of a monkey. They also carried the coroner's announcement of a missing human fetus.

I suggested to the pathologist who had autopsied the specimen that he call Larry Angel at the Smithsonian. Larry Angel, one of this country's expert forensic anthropologists, was also one of the founders of the society of forensic anthropologists and a member of the board that established national qualifying exams for forensic studies. If anyone at the Smithsonian was going to be brought in on this case, it was going to be Larry Angel. And, it turned out, Larry was one of the experts referred to in the newspapers. Another of these experts was a curator in a different department of the Smithsonian who had spent years working on Old World monkey systematics and anatomy. And the third expert was a retired physician who volunteered his efforts to assist Larry on whatever project he was working on at the time.

As I was to find out later, after meeting with Larry, he and his colleagues had been able to wrest the footless specimen away from the courier long enough to take it out of the jar, take an X ray of it, and make a few more observations than were possible through the glass container. Thus, although Larry and his collaborators did conclude, as the newspapers reported, that the specimen was a monkey, the report Larry compiled for his personal files indicated that they thought it might have been a macaque, which is a type of Old World monkey. They did take note of the broad internarial region and the large thick ear, which are not features of Old World monkeys, but were more impressed by aspects of the preserved hand: The thumb appeared relatively long compared to the length of the fingers, and it was quite divergent from the index finger. Both of these features are characteristic of the hands of Old World monkeys, such as macaques. Measurements taken from the X ray of the long bones of the arm and leg also suggested to Larry and his colleagues that the specimen could have been a macaque or macaquelike Old World monkey. Macaque arms are not excessively long compared to leg length. The X ray also revealed that there were more vertebrae in the spinal column than is typical of humans. Although this doesn't provide proof-positive that the specimen was an Old World monkey, it does go against identifying the specimen as being human. According to Larry and his colleagues, they couldn't do anything further with the specimen because the courier took it when they were out of the room and left.

The agitated pathologist did call Larry with the news of the missing human stillbirth. The newspapers soon thereafter reported that Dr. Lawrence Angel (who was now the focus of attention at the Smithsonian) had begun to question his identification of the specimen after having learned that the "monkey" could have been the missing human fetus. By this time the story took on a life of its own. Reporters called me day and night, in my office and at my home. That weekend I called Larry at his home to introduce myself as his Pittsburgh counterpart in what by now my wife and I were calling fetusgate. Larry told me that he was getting pretty fed up with the whole affair and had been trying to get the coroner to send him the missing feet for study. His efforts were finally going to be rewarded. The feet were going to be sent to the Smithsonian on Wednesday of the following week, and Larry asked if I could come to study them with him.

By the time I got to Larry's lab early Wednesday morning, the feet had arrived. They were tiny. And they were definitely human. No doubt about it. Larry and I kept saying over and over that if we had only had the feet to begin with, none of this mess could have happened. But it had, and now we had to make the best of it.

Larry and I immediately took to photographing and describing the feet. Both were severely contracted, which artificially raised the arch, which, in turn, shortened the feet. The left foot was complete but the toes were tightly clenched under, which made it even more difficult to measure foot length with any accuracy. The right foot lacked its toes— perhaps they were lost in the hospital's washer or dryer—so we had to estimate that foot's length as well.

We also tried to fit the feet to the footprints taken from the fetus before it was misplaced. We couldn't match the feet to the footprints in size. But we did notice that the second toe, which was preserved on the left foot, was longer than the first toe—the "classic" Greek foot—and this also was the size relationship of the first and second toes in the footprints. In our joint report to the coroner's office, the first part of which consisted of notes Larry had taken when he had examined the specimen the month before, we had to admit that we could not unambiguously associate the feet either with the specimen or with the footprints. Given the apparent sequence of events up to that time, we believed that the feet we now had for study did indeed belong to the specimen we had been shown weeks earlier, but we saw no way in which we could demonstrate the association with certainty.

As part of the lengthy report Larry and I submitted to the coroner's office, Larry included a paragraph in which he discussed a photocopy of a letter the coroner had sent along with the feet. This document was dated almost two weeks earlier and, although it was addressed to him, Larry had not seen it until he received the Xerox copy.

In this letter Larry was asked not to corroborate the identification of a specimen as being monkey but for his "assistance in ascertaining whether these remains are those of a human or some simian species." The letter also stated that Larry was being sent "copies of footprints of a human fetus which was misplaced at the facility where these remains were found." According to Angel, however, he had been sent a copy of footprints labeled "Newborn Identification with 2 small footprints." Toward the bottom of that document was a note referring to a human fetus that had been sent to the morgue, not one that had been misplaced and then found. Only when Larry and I got the feet did we realize the significance of this document and its inclusion among the other letters and documents that had been sent, not all of which related to the case of the missing fetus.

What makes this case even more extraordinary is that Larry's health had been deteriorating due to some complications arising from a blood transfusion he'd received while undergoing an operation not too long before. Years before "fetusgate" I had observed him in action at a national society meeting. Physically, he was a little on the plump side. In his presentation and interactions, he was spunky and cantankerous. When I spoke to him over the phone about the missing fetus case, I thought his voice sounded tired and weak. When I walked into his lab to examine the fetal feet with him, I was actually shocked to see how wasted and wan he looked, and how every movement seemed to be an effort. If I hadn't known I was going to spend the day with Larry Angel, and if he hadn't kept the muttonchop sideburns that were part of his physical calling card, I wouldn't have known who this person was. He was like one of the Smithsonian's skeletons, but with skin stretched across it.

One of the worst parts of this case, he confided to me after our long day of examining the feet and writing up the report in longhand, was that he felt he had been taken advantage of, and he was embarrassed. We were all embarrassed, and angry. But Larry was particularly upset because he felt that he should have known better. I tried to point out that, given the condition of the specimen, the fact that it had been shown to each of us for a limited amount of time and then without its feet, and all the other details of the case, he had done the best that he or anyone could have done. When I finally had to leave to catch my return flight home, I left him in his office, his head low and resting wearily on one hand while the other kept jotting down notes.

About two weeks later I received a final version of a long, typed copy of the report. There were more than a few typographical errors, which Larry's secretary admitted were due to her grief at his being in the hospital in critical condition. Within a week Larry Angel was dead. I never was able to tell him that I had found out that a particular developmental disorder, called Apert's Syndrome, is known to lead to a fetus being stillborn and to its having, among other things, extra vertebrae, a broad nasal region, and large fleshy ears. Finding this out didn't make me feel any better about the case, but at least it put some closure on it. I felt a great loss with Larry Angel's death.

Making Monkeys out of Humans

One of the most frustrating aspects of this case was that I could not get the point across to any reporter who called that not only was the specimen incomplete and in very bad shape, but, with the feet missing, it was not at all obvious that the specimen was human. The difficulty in comprehending this fact lies, I think, in people's general belief that being human is so special that partial, and even pathological, remains of a human would obviously appear human. But obviously—and this is the only obvious part of the whole affair—this was not the situation at all.

If this had not been a forensic case, especially one that was so charged with emotion and confounded by complexity, it would never have received any media hype. Fossilized skeletal and dental remains are misidentified as to species and even to major group of mammal on occasion, often because the "right" parts—those parts that demonstrate the specifically unique features of a species or a group—are not preserved. As much as we would like to think otherwise, not every bit of what makes you or me a complete, functioning organism is unique to you and me as *Homo sapiens*.

The very fact that Larry Angel and his Smithsonian colleagues and I could come to the conclusions we did about which type of monkey the specimen might represent demonstrates this fact of nature. One of the reasons that I thought the specimen was not an Old World monkey, an ape, or a human was because its nostrils were not closely approximated and separated by a narrow septum. However, the specimen's broad internarial region did not specifically indicate that it could be a New World monkey. Rather, its broad internarial region meant that the specimen *was not* a member of the group that includes Old World monkeys, apes, and humans.

How could a human fetus end up with a broad internarial region? In general terms, the explanation is straightforward. The developing embryos and early-stage fetuses of all mammals have the equivalent of a broad internarial region because the indentations—called nasal pits— that foreshadow the development of the nasal region are widely separated from one another. It is only later on—farther on in fetal development—that changes away from this broad internarial configuration will occur, if they are going to occur at all. Then there will be a remodeling of the nasal region, with the acquisition of features specific to the animal's larger evolutionary group, if not also to the animal's species. With regard to the "human-monkey" fetus, the simplest explanation is that something interfered with the developmental and genetic cues that would have caused a normal human fetus to veer ontogenetically away from the broad internarial condition common not just among mammals but vertebrates in general and to develop the catarrhine primate type of nose.

As long ago as the 1820s, the German embryologist Karl Ernst von Baer broke away from embryological dogma and suggested that animals paralleled each other during their development, or ontogeny, in recapitulating only the very young stages of development. At that time, and even for some decades thereafter, the prevailing dogma among embryologists was that the ontogenetic stages through which an animal passed represented the adult stages of those animals lower down on the scale of nature—that, for instance, the gill slit stage one sees variably expressed during embryonic development in mammals represents the fish stage, as expressed in an adult fish, of an ascending scale of nature's perfection.

Von Baer disagreed. He argued that, when animals did share common ontogenetic stages, the stages they were sharing were only those of the developing embryo and/or fetus. Thus, for instance, the gill slit stage that a fish and a mammal went through had nothing to do with an adult fish with gills. Instead, this embryonic gill slit stage was a normal consequence of development. In fact, there would be nothing truly fish or mammal about the ontogenetic stages that a developing fish and mammal had in common. It was only when the fish veered from— or, to use von Baer's terminology, deviated from—the common ontogenetic pathway that it would proceed to develop the specific attributes that one sees in the adult fish. The ontogenetic phases a mammal goes through that are similar to those of a fish or reptile, or any other animal, are similar only insofar as they represent shared embryonic or fetal similarities. Only after a developing mammal passes through, so to speak, the embryonic and fetal stages it shares with a hierarchy of other groups of animals does it enter into the phases of ontogeny that are specific first to its being a mammal, then to its being a member of a particular group of mammals, and, ultimately, to its being the kind of mammal that it is.

Von Baer's suggestion sounds a bit evolutionary, but it was not meant to be. Von Baer differed from his contemporaries only in how he interpreted the significance of an animal's course through a succession of ontogenetic stages. For him, and for virtually all scientists of the first half of the nineteenth century, life on earth was the act of a divine creator. It was the role of the naturalist, the comparative anatomist, or the embryologist, for example, to try to decipher the hierarchical arrangement of this life, this scale of nature. Embryology, so it seemed, might provide a glimpse at how that life was arranged. These scientists believed that, by studying the development of the most complex forms, the whole picture would unfold, revealing a sequence from the simple to the complex.

When, however, during the latter half of the nineteenth century, the reality of evolution became more widely accepted, the science of embryology took on a different significance. Through the study of an organism's sequence of ontogenetic stages, it seemed that the evolutionary history of an organism could actually be seen unfolding. The most famous scientist to write about the interrelation of an organism's development—ontogeny—and its evolutionary history—phylogeny—was the German evolutionist Ernst Haeckel. It was Haeckel who formulated the so-called biogenetic law that states: Ontogeny recapitulates phylogeny. More simply, the biogenetic law asserts that as an individual develops from embryo to fetus, it repeats the stages of evolution that preceded the emergence of its own species.

But Haeckel did not translate von Baer's ontogenetic scale of nature into an evolutionary one. The evolutionary stages revealed in ontogeny were not, according to the biogenetic law, the embryonic or fetal stages of an animal's ancestors. For Haeckel, each ontogenetic stage represented the adult form of an ancestor or ancestral stage. When you or I, in the course of our development, passed through the "gill slit stage," we were, as far as Haeckel was concerned, passing through the fish stage of mammal evolution—but a fish stage that would be mirrored in the body of an adult fish. According to Haeckel's biogenetic law, "evolution" usually occurred by going through the stages of the animal's adult ancestors and then adding on a new stage. (I put quotation marks around the word *evolution* because it was originally an embryological term, meaning an unfolding, and did not until later come to mean change, as you and I are accustomed to using it.) The twentieth century had little use, however, for Haeckel's biogenetic law.

With the acceptance during the twentieth century of von Baer's interpretation of ontogenetic stages—that stages shared by different species represent common embryonic, not adult, stages—all formulations that, either specifically or in part, equated phylogeny with ontogenetic stages were rejected. It's too bad, in a way, because, as a few evolutionary biologists have pointed out more recently, there can be a correlation between ontogeny and phylogeny, but not with adult forms as part of the equation. If we translate a von Baerian view of ontogeny into evolutionary terms, then things make sense.

An ontogenetic stage held in common by a diverse array of species— such as among amphibians, reptiles, birds, and mammals—would represent an ancestral or primitive condition if retained in any particular amphibian, reptile, bird, or mammal. An ontogenetic stage that is not broadly represented but is present in a restricted group of species— such as among mammals—would be a derived or unique condition for the group involved. As such, this more restricted condition might reflect the evolutionary unity of that particular group of species.

Because an ontogenetic stage refers to something embryonic, and individuals do develop into adults, two other possibilities must be taken into consideration. An individual may retain a juvenile condition or stage into adulthood. Or an individual may, during development into adulthood, grow away, or become different, from an earlier ontogenetic or juvenile condition.

For instance, let's take broad internarial regions. All living mammals start off embryonically with a broad, fleshy internarial region. If we look at the noses of adults, we see that most adult mammals possess a broad, fleshy internarium that separates the two nostrils. This, then, is presumably a primitive condition for mammals—retention of the embryonically broad internarium into the adult. But some mammals do not retain the embryonically broad internarium into the adult. Instead, in these mammals, the cartilaginous nasal septum advances forward and assumes the role of separating the nostrils. One of these groups of mammals is the "narrow-nosed" group of anthropoid primates, the catarrhine primates—Old World monkeys, apes, and humans; in humans, the cartilaginous nasal septum advances so far forward that the nose protrudes from the face. According to the German embryologist and comparative anatomist Helmut Hofer, the development of the "narrow-nosed" condition of catarrhine primates involves an alteration of—or, as von Baer would have described it, a deviation away from—the embryonic or fetal condition common to mammals. As Hofer put it in a recent article: "Probably not only an involution of the fetal nasal cartilages took place, but also new elements of cartilage originated in the connective tissue." The development of the narrow-nosed condition in catarrhine primates, therefore, would appear to be derived or unique for that group and presumably would reflect the evolutionary unity of that group.

The catarrhine nasal configuration thus starts off like the nasal configuration of any other mammal. However, unlike many other mammals, catarrhine primates do not as adults retain the embryonic organization of the nasal region. Sometime during the ontogeny of a catarrhine primate, the nasal region changes. It becomes something distinctive and different. Because the basic plan of the nasal region is similar in all catarrhine primates, we can hypothesize that they inherited this novel developmental sequence from the last common ancestor they shared, that this developmental sequence had been an evolutionary novelty of the last common ancestor of all catarrhine primates. Or, to state it more simply, the last common ancestor of all catarrhine primates had evolved the catarrhine nose. Thus, if we have things in the correct sequence, there would appear to be a parallel between phylogeny and ontogeny, as evidenced, for example, in the development of the catarrhine nose.

I have relied heavily on an ontogenetic component in my own evolutionary studies, but I wasn't the first, by a long shot, to do so. As I will go into in more detail in the next chapter, Thomas Huxley, Charles Darwin's sometime defender, used not only an ontogenetic argument for grouping humans within the order Primates but a von Baerian approach in his argumentation. As Huxley saw it, the more similar species are to one another, the more of their ontogenies they share before going off on their own developmental courses. Thus a dog or a cat—being a mammal, and a particular kind of mammal, a carnivore—shares only a short period of similar ontogeny with a bird. But a dog and a cat share a long period of ontogeny because they are both not only mammals, but mammals of a particular kind—carnivores. Humans,

Huxley argued, had to be mammals, because they, like monkeys, shared a similar course of ontogeny with dogs and cats. Humans had to be primates because they continued to share with a monkey the developmental course that transforms a monkey in detail from a generalized mammal to a specific kind of mammal, a primate. Thus, with regard to "Man's place in Nature," Huxley argued that, as demonstrated by the study of ontogeny, "without a doubt, in these respects, he is far nearer the Apes, than the Apes are to the Dog."

Looking at the development of morphological features can provide insight into the potential evolutionary significance of features you see in the adult. It seems obvious—at least about as obvious as things can be in evolutionary studies—that the catarrhine nose is a special or evolutionarily derived feature because catarrhine primates constitute the only group of primates in which the cartilaginous nasal septum comes to separate the nostrils. On the basis of this comparison, it could be argued that this uniqueness, this evolutionary novelty, also would have characterized the last common ancestor of catarrhine primates, and that catarrhine primates are united as an evolutionary group by their possession of this evolutionary novelty. I would accept this argument, based as it is on a broad comparison among mammals. But I feel more comfortable about the identification of uniqueness by being able to see from a developmental perspective that the catarrhine nose deviates from the common mammalian embryonic configuration.

Obviously, the "human-monkey" fetus did not develop away from the common vertebrate embryonic nasal configuration. But what about the extra vertebra in its spinal column? How can this be explained?

The spinal or vertebral column has a different developmental history from the face and nasal region. The face develops from a series of paired, almost balloonlike, prominences through or in which, loosely speaking, separate areas or structures, such as the nasal region, arise. The vertebral column, on the other hand, is linear and segmented into individual units, similar to beads on a string. The bony parts that come to make up the facial skeleton are irregular in shape; neighboring bones are dissimilar from one another in shape and size. In contrast, the vertebrae are arranged in a pattern or gradient of size and shape. Although vertebrae are separate bony units, there is no major morphological disjuncture between two adjacent vertebrae—with the exception of the first and second vertebrae in the neck, but that's because the second vertebra captures and incorporates part of the first, making the first vertebra incomplete and the second more than it should be.

In spite of the fact that it is a linear gradient, the vertebral column does not arise ontogenetically in the same way throughout its entire length. In the embryo, the upper segments of the presumptive vertebral column differentiate almost simultaneously. As the end of the embryonic trunk elongates into a tail segment, presumptive vertebral units differentiate, adding to what looks like a series of buttons extending down an increasingly elongate coat-front. Roughly, the way this happens is that a groove forms in the midline of what will be the back of the animal. The groove develops and deepens as the embryo lengthens. Coincident with the invagination of the groove, the edges that border it become segmented. Meanwhile, farther up along the embryo, the right and left edges of the deepened groove come together and form a roof over it, which brings together opposing segments. The final product is a tube, the neural tube, which eventually will develop into the spinal cord; the string of segments eventually will contribute to the formation of vertebrae.

The picture of the embryonic development of the neural tube reminds me of a zipper, but one that closes as you pull it down—away from the presumptive head—not up. The opposing segments are represented by the right and left opposing bits of the zipper, which are brought together as you pull the zipper down, which, in turn, forms the top of the tube. The only part of this vertebral zipper that isn't like a real zipper is that the opposing presumptive vertebral segments meet head-on at the midline instead of overlapping to form an interlocking chain.

If you've ever looked closely at a skeleton of a tailed animal, such as a dog or cat, or even a dinosaur at a natural history museum, you've noticed that there is a size and shape gradient of the vertebral column that continues from the first neck vertebra all the way to the tip of the tail. This gradient is not, however, uniform from one end to the other. Rather, like the undulations of rolling hills, the vertebrae increase in size up to a point and then reverse the process and decrease in size. You can follow the increase in size from the neck vertebrae on down to vertebrae in the region of the pelvis. There, in mammals, the vertebrae fuse to form the sacrum. It is along the sacrum that the vertebrae begin to diminish noticeably in size, creating the triangular shape typical of a sacrum. Extending from the end of the sacrum, the tail or caudal vertebrae form a gradient of decreasing size, eventually terminating in the last caudal vertebra, which tapers at its end.

The length or shortness of an animal's tail is related to the strength, if you will, of the proliferating cellular mass that began its march down the embryo and on into what would become the tail segment. As long as cells keep proliferating and extending the tail segment, more units representing presumptive vertebrae will be generated. How much potential there is in the cellular mass that governs a tail's lengthening and segmentation into presumptive vertebrae—and, thus, how long the tail will be—depends on the species in question. Because most mammals, like the reptiles, develop a reasonably long tail, it would seem that reduction of the tail—that is, reduction of vertebrae by way of inhibition of the proliferating cell mass of the embryonic tail segment—would be the more unique condition. Thus short tails, and even no tails, would represent the evolutionary novelties among mammals.

One group of prosimian primates—the lorises of sub-Saharan Africa, Sri Lanka, and southeast Asia—is distinguished by having a very reduced tail. And the hominoid primates—humans, orangs, gorillas, chimps, and gibbons—are distinct among all living primates in their lack of a tail altogether. The only vestige of tail growth that persists in a hominoid is represented by three to five rudimentary and morphologically simple coccygeal vertebrae that are tacked on to the end of the sacrum. In keeping with the picture of a gradient—but, in this case, a severely truncated and diminished one—these coccygeal vertebrae taper down to the bluntly pointed last coccygeal vertebra.

One of the basic facts learned in biology class is that all mammals have seven neck or cervical vertebrae, regardless of whether the mammal is a giraffe or a human. On the other end of the scale, the most variable portions of the vertebral column, if we don't count the tail, are the sacral and lumbar regions. The lumbar vertebrae come after the thoracic vertebrae, which are the vertebrae that come after the neck vertebrae and that are associated with ribs. The last lumbar vertebra articulates with the sacrum. Hominoid primates typically do not develop more than five lumbar vertebrae. Humans have five lumbar vertebrae. The great apes typically have fewer than five vertebrae. Old World monkeys, on the other hand, develop, on average, seven lumbar vertebrae. In fact, most primates develop more than five lumbar vertebrae. Thus hominoids are distinguished among primates in having a reduced lumbar region.

There are also differences among primates in the number of segments that become incorporated into the sacrum. Most primates do not have a very long sacrum. For instance, Old World monkeys typically have three sacral vertebrae. Hominoids, on the other hand, are distinctive in having a longer sacrum. The lesser apes—the gibbons—have four, but sometimes five, sacral vertebrae. Humans typically have five and the great apes typically have six sacral vertebrae. If you don't think of the sacrum as the solid triangular block of bone it is in the adult, but as the separate segments or vertebrae that eventually fuse together to make an adult's sacrum, the differences among primates in number of lumbar and sacral vertebrae become understandable.

Every once in a while, while analyzing an assemblage of human skeletons, I've come across a specimen in which the sacrum appears to be longer and to have more vertebrae or segments to it than is normal. At the same time I've found, when counting up the rest of the vertebrae, that the individual involved had only four, instead of five, lumbar vertebrae. In these cases the last lumbar vertebra has fused to the top of the sacrum and has developed articulations with the ilium on each side. But this occurs only occasionally in humans. Gorillas and chimps, however, according to the Swiss primatologist Adolph Schultz, typically have one less lumbar vertebra and one more sacral vertebra than humans—which is actually one of the uniquenesses cited in arguments for the close evolutionary relationship of gorillas and chimps.

What seems to have happened in individuals with reduced lumbar regions and elongated sacral regions is that the pelvis has captured, so to speak, the last lumbar vertebra. More figuratively, Schultz characterized the reduction of the lumbar region among primates as the result of the pelvis marching up the vertebral column, incorporating lumbar vertebrae into the sacrum. If we tag a bit of developmental biology onto this image, we can envision the reduction of the vertebral column as a repositioning of the pelvis farther up the vertebral column and a truncation of segmentation at the tail or coccygeal end.

But reduction of vertebral number is not the only way in which developmental alterations can proceed. Schultz found in his study of vertebral number that two out of the one hundred human skeletons he studied had an extra lumbar vertebra. Unfortunately, it cannot be determined from Schultz's data whether these two individuals also had abbreviated sacra (the plural of sacrum). However, in terms of segmental development, it is not uncommon to find the occasional development of an extra, or supernumerary, segment. This also happens with molar teeth, which, on a gross level, mirror the lower vertebrae in the way they proliferate backward in the jaw and form separate units.

You probably know someone who never did develop a third molar or wisdom tooth. You might also know someone who developed an extra or fourth molar tooth. In fact, supernumerary tooth development is not uncommon in mammals; in some mammals it is even the rule. For instance, orang-utans are notorious for developing fourth and even fifth molars, and a kangaroo-related marsupial, the Little Rock Wallaby, develops up to eight molars in each quadrant of the jaw, which is twice the number of molars most marsupials develop. The mammal that pushes the development of supernumerary molars to the extreme is the manatee, or sea cow. The manatee, which has molar teeth located only along the back portions of its jaws, keeps adding new molars to the back of the series as the worn-out and used-up molars at the front are shed. It's comparable to a conveyor belt, with old molars moving forward to make room for the new molars at the rear.

If a developing vertebral column were to continue to elongate and create segments in excess of the normal number of vertebrae, it would end up with at least one extra vertebra. If this extra vertebra were in the right place for the pelvis to "capture" it, the sacrum would be longer. If, however, the pelvis captured only the normal number of sacral vertebrae, the lumbar region would be longer.

The lesson to be learned from supernumerary structures, especially segmental units such as teeth and vertebrae, is that control of segmental proliferation, as well as the number of segments differentiated, appears to be a matter of developmental timing, cellular competence, and inhibition at the appropriate time. If the proliferating cell mass that will give rise to a series of teeth or vertebrae is inhibited, or just plain runs out of developmental steam, the number of segments will be reduced accordingly. If, on the other hand, there is a release of inhibition on a proliferating cell mass, or if the proliferating cell mass has the competence to continue to produce segments beyond the number that is normal for the species, supernumerary structures will result.

The "human-monkey" fetus had a long back. It turns out that there was an extra or supernumerary vertebra in the lumbar region; unfortunately, the pelvic and sacral regions were crushed and uninformative. But now we merely say that the vertebral count was atypical for a human. When the specimen was thought to be a monkey, the vertebral count was acceptable and corroborated the monkey identification. Now that we are talking about a human, however, we are confronted with a supernumerary vertebra, the presence of which we can at least understand in developmental terms. Apparently, something about the syndrome that may have affected this fetus and may have been in part responsible for the retention of the embryonic mammalian nasal region may also have been involved with the development of extra segmentation of the vertebral column. The thick, fleshy, flat ear that goes along with the syndrome appears to be a straightforward developmental anomaly, unconnected to the fetus's mammalian heritage or to the developmental miscues that resulted in the retention of the embryonic nasal region as well as the development of a supernumerary vertebra.

But as baffling and as upsetting as fetusgate was, it should serve as a lesson larger than just the incident itself. No matter whether we are analyzing a fossil, a bone from an archeological site, or the remains of the recently deceased, the specter of error always looms in the background. Sometimes the error is a simple matter of misidentification. Other times it may be due to incomplete information—either the "right" pieces of a known entity are missing, or the entity itself had previously been unknown to science. Error can derive from any number of sources, including the intellectual environment in which we find ourselves.

PART II

THE

EVOLUTIONARY

PAST

AND

PRESENT

HUMAN EVOLUTION:

DART, HUXLEY, AND DARWIN

The Skull from Taung

On November 28, 1924, Raymond Dart, a young professor of anatomy at the University of Witwatersrand in Johannesburg, South Africa, was presented with a partial fossil skull that would forever change the course of human evolutionary studies. The actual events of discovery of this skull, however, were not the usual. Instead of being found by a paleontologist crawling over fossil outcrops on hands and knees or picking away at a fossil-bearing deposit, this partial skull was exposed by dynamite used by the limestone mining company working the site of Taung. Fortunately, one of the quarryman, a Mr. M. de Bruyn, not only salvaged the limestone-encrusted specimen but was able to recognize that it was not one of the fossil baboon skulls that were typically unearthed while blasting away at the limestone. De Bruyn took this find, which he thought might be a fossil Bushman, as well as two other specimens, to his boss, Mr. A. E. Spiers, who turned them over to Dr. R. B. Young, a geologist at the University of the Witwatersrand, who in turn gave them to Raymond Dart.

The two other specimens were not fossilized bones or incomplete skulls. Rather they were limestone casts of part of the inside of the braincases of two individuals. The casts were formed when water bearing dissolved limestone seeped inside the skulls. The outer surface of such a brain cast, which is called an endocranial cast or endocast, picks up the shape and surface topography of the individual's brain—at least insofar as the surface details of the brain have impressed themselves upon the inner surface of the skull. De Bruyn also figured out that one of these limestone endocasts—of the right half of the brain—actually went with the partial skull he had salvaged from the blast.

Dart realized immediately that the smaller of the two endocasts had come from some kind of baboon and that the larger endocast was from something else entirely. For one thing, there was the obvious size difference. The "new" endocast was larger. But, more important, Dart thought that the pattern of grooves preserved on the larger endocast's surface was more similar to that found on the brains of apes (such as the African chimpanzee and gorilla) than on monkeys (such as baboons).

Dart knew that the limestone endocast had come from the limestone-encrusted partial skull. It must have been an amazing experience for him to clean off the matrix from the skull and watch the face of something previously unknown emerge: two large, ovoid bony orbits filled with limestone where eyes had once sat; the sweep of the smoothly accurate bony forehead, abruptly broken off before it reached its peak but still able to cup the front part of the large endocast; the portion of the base of the skull, on which the brain had rested and through which the spinal cord had exited; the slender face, barely dished out in the nasal region and minimally extended forward toward the mouth; the lightly built lower jaw; a full set of milk teeth, with the upper and lower milk canines surprisingly short and barely projecting beyond the level of the teeth on either side; and, behind the last milk tooth, in all four quadrants of the mouth, a first permanent, adult molar tooth, which had begun to erupt.

Rather than keep this discovery to himself for decades to come—which was a tendency among paleontologists—Dart quickly prepared a manuscript on the partial skull and its endocast and, on January 6, 1925, sent it to the British journal *Nature*, where it was published on February 7. Not only would the scientific community be astonished at the relative completeness of this specimen, but it would be stunned to read Dart's interpretation of its evolutionary significance.

This specimen "is of importance," Dart wrote in the opening paragraphs of his article, "because it exhibits an extinct race of apes *intermediate between living anthropoids and man.*" For one thing, Dart asserted, "the whole cranium displays *humanoid* rather than anthropoid lineaments." Specifically, the Taung individual was not at all like the African apes in any of their particular characteristics of skull, brow ridge, nasal bone, cheek bone, orbit, or upper and lower jaw. Instead, Dart concluded, the shapes and configurations of the Taung individual's skull and jaw "all betray a delicate and humanoid character." In the morphology of its teeth, the majority of which belonged to the milk set, Dart also felt that the Taung individual was anatomically *"humanoid rather than anthropoid."* Thus, because the only adult teeth visible were the incompletely erupted first permanent molars, and modern humans erupt their first permanent molars at about the age of six years, Dart concluded that this now-fossilized "humanoid" had been approximately this old when it died.

Dart then launched into a line of speculation about the Taung child's posture that began with the following observation: "That hominid characters were not restricted to the face in this extinct primate group is borne out by the relatively forward situation of the foramen magnum."

The foramen magnum is (literally) the great big hole in the occipital bone at the base of the skull through which the spinal cord passes after it leaves the brain. On each side of the foramen magnum lies a raised, somewhat lima bean–shape elevation of bone. These two, small bony platforms—called occipital condyles—articulate with the first vertebra of the bony spinal column. Because an animal's eyes point forward, the position of the vertebral column relative to the skull can be reconstructed by looking at the direction in which the foramen magnum and its attendant occipital condyles are pointing when the skull is oriented as if the animal were staring straight ahead.

In typical quadrupedal animals—such as horses, cows, and even most primates—the vertebral column is oriented horizontally and the skull is essentially an extension of it. As such, the foramen magnum and occipital condyles are located at the most posterior portion of the skull and point virtually straight back. Although the great apes—the chimpanzee, gorilla, and orang-utan—are technically quadrupeds, they do not carry their heads and trunks in a typically quadrupedal manner when traveling on the ground because their arms are so much longer than their legs. An ape's long arms angle its torso up so that the vertebral column slopes down and back, from the head to the hips. Correspondingly, an ape's foramen magnum and occipital condyles face not straight back or straight down, but somewhere in between. However, compared to a typical quadruped, a great ape's foramen magnum and occipital condyles are situated in a more forward position—more toward the base of the skull. Humans, as erect bipeds, are different yet again in that the head is held atop a vertical vertebral column and thus the occipital condyles and foramen magnum face down and are positioned well forward on the cranial base.

Dart described the foramen magnum of the Taung skull as being in a relatively forward position, which he interpreted as indicating "an attitude appreciably more erect than that of modern anthropoids." From this simple deduction, Dart went on to speculate about the possible consequences:

The improved poise of the head, and the better posture of the whole body framework which accompanied this alteration in the angle at which its dominant member was supported, is of great significance. It means that a greater reliance was being placed by this group upon the feet as organs of progression, and that the hands were being freed from their more primitive function of accessory organs of locomotion. Bipedal animals, their hands were assuming a higher evolutionary role not only as delicate tactual, examining organs which were adding copiously to the animal's knowledge of its physical environment, but also as instruments of the growing intelligence in carrying out more elaborate, purposeful, and skilled movements, and as organs of offence and defence. The latter is rendered the more probable, in view, first of their failure to develop massive canines and hideous features, and, secondly, of the fact that even living baboons and anthropoid apes can and do use sticks and stones as implements and as weapons of offence.

(At the very end of this passage, Dart cites Charles Darwin's opus, *The Descent of Man.* As I will argue later in this chapter, much of Dart's discussion of the Taung child is predicated on the predictions Darwin advanced in that work about human origins and evolution.)

From the consequences of bipedalism, Dart went on to discuss the anatomy of the Taung child's brain, which he felt justified in comparing favorably with the human brain. Citing the work of Sir Richard Owen, the dominant British anatomist of the first half of the nineteenth century, Dart pointed out that the modern human brain, although large at birth and almost adult size by about the tenth year, has a long period of growth and does not reach its full size until twenty or even thirty years of age. Because measurements of the Taung child's brain demonstrated that it was larger than an adult chimp's and only a bit smaller than an adult gorilla's, Dart concluded that the brain of this "humanoid" would, like ours, have continued to grow had the individual lived. As such, it would have probably equaled, if not exceeded, the size of a gorilla's brain.

But there were other ways in which the Taung child's brain appeared to be more human- than apelike. For one thing, it would not have been flattened, as in an ape, but high and rounded, as in ourselves, which thus would have meant, according to Dart, that the Taung individual had had a "balanced development of the faculties of associative memory and intelligent activity." The side of the fossil brain, in the parietal region, was also expanded, and a particular groove, the lunate sulcus, was in "the posterior *humanoid* situation." Neuroanatomists use these two features as indicators of the extent to which the thinking portion of the brain is developed. Humans are characterized by both a greater expansion of the parietal region and a more posterior position of the lunate sulcus.

Dart derived further evidence of the inner workings of the Taung individual's brain from the observation that its orbits were large, faced forward, and closely approximated at the midline, being separated from one another only by a narrow expanse of bone. Dart put together his thoughts on the Taung child's brain and eyes and concluded that this individual represented a "group of beings," which, "having acquired the faculty of stereoscopic vision, had profited beyond living anthropoids by setting aside a relatively much larger area of the cerebral cortex to serve as a storehouse of information concerning their objective environment as its details were simultaneously revealed to the senses of vision and touch, and also of hearing." But the potential evolutionary significance of the Taung "group of beings" was, for Dart, even more profound:

> They possessed to a degree unappreciated by living anthropoids the use of their hands and ears and the consequent faculty of associating with the colour, form, and general appearance of objects, their weight, texture, resilience, and flexibility, as well as the significance of sounds emitted by them. In other words, their eyes saw, their ears heard, and their hands handled objects with greater meaning and to fuller purpose than the corresponding organs in recent apes. They had laid down the foundations of that discriminative knowledge of the appearance, feeling, and sound of things that was a necessary milestone in the acquisition of articulate speech.

The Taung child, therefore, displayed not only "dominantly human characters" in its face and teeth but an "improved quality of the brain." Thus, whoever the Taung "humanoid" was, it was not an ape. It was a "pre-human," a "man-like ape"—the ancestor of all hominids, living and extinct—and not "a caricature of precocious hominid failure," which is how Dart referred to the well-known specimens of "Java Man" that had been discovered nearly thirty-five years earlier by the Dutch physician and self-proclaimed ancestor-hunter, Eugène Dubois. But Dart's "man-like ape," while presumably distinguished from true apes by its erect posture and enlarged and enlightened brain, was not a true human—at least in terms of one of the longstanding criteria imposed by taxonomists: the possession of language or speech. In fact, this criterion was critical to the taxonomy of the genus *Homo*, as it was defined by one of the most important taxonomists of all time, Karl von Linné.

The Swedish botanist and naturalist Karl von Linné, or Linnaeus, was the first taxonomist to classify humans in a group with other animals. In 1735, in the first edition of his classic *Systema Naturae*, or system of nature, Linnaeus placed humans together with monkeys and sloths in the order Anthropomorpha, (meaning "man-shaped"). By the tenth edition of the *Systema*, which was published in 1758, lemurs had been added and sloths had been replaced by bats, which, in turn, would not be properly allocated by another taxonomist to their own order for another fifty-one years. It was also in the tenth edition of the *Systema* that Linnaeus changed the name of the order Anthropomorpha to Primates, which is the ordinal name we continue to use.

From our perspective, however, it is important to understand that, in spite of his unorthodox, even heretical, classification of *Homo* within Primates, Linnaeus was not an evolutionist. His taxonomic investigations of any group were ultimately motivated by the same desire as his predecessors, contemporaries, and many who followed: to demonstrate the workings of a divine creator by discovering the trail of organisms of increasing perfection, leading to humans, left by such a divine being, and then translating this supposed order into a classification. Linnaeus stood apart from his colleagues only in the degree to which he separated humans taxonomically—in a written classification—from other animals. He nonetheless still thought of humans, and especially the "highest" of humans, as being distinct from other animals in various telling ways.

Linnaeus placed an animal in his genus *Homo* if it was (or he believed it to be) capable of emotions. On these grounds, the orang-utan, which had been thought of for centuries as something more human than animal, qualified as a member of the genus *Homo*. However, as for admittance to our own species, *Homo sapiens*, the orang-utan lacked that crucial quality: the ability to speak. In this regard, Dart believed that his Taung "humanoid" had been incapable of speech ("a creature with anthropoid brain capacity, and lacking the distinctive, localised temporal expansions which appear to be concomitant with and necessary to articulate man, is no true man"), and thus identified it as a "man-like ape."

In trying to deal with his "humanoid" taxonomically, Dart tentatively proposed that it might be placed in a new family, which he called

Homo-simiadae. But it was essential that this proclaimed "link between man and his simian ancestor" should be recognized taxonomically by way of new genus and species names, for which Dart created *Australopithecus africanus*; "australo-" refers to the extremely southern occurrence of this apelike creature ("-pithecus") from Africa ("africanus"). In keeping with the tradition in which taxonomic names often reflect ideas that are important to the classifier, Dart specified Africa in the species name *africanus* because he believed that his discovery "vindicat[ed] the Darwinian claim that Africa would prove to be the cradle of mankind."

As history would have it, Dart's *Australopithecus africanus* fell by the scientific wayside for more than twenty years. Two of England's most eminent anatomists, Sir Grafton Elliot Smith and Sir Arthur Keith, ridiculed Dart in public lectures and in letters to the journal *Nature*. Many of the world's leading anatomists and paleontologists followed suit. A common response was that Dart's "man-like ape" was a fossil ape, perhaps related to the chimpanzee. Even Dart's sometime defender Robert Broom, a South African physician and amateur (but professionally respected) paleontologist—who was himself responsible during the 1930s and '40s for adding significantly to our knowledge of early, *Australopithecus*-like hominids—did not see eye to eye with Dart's assessment of the evolutionary significance of *Australopithecus*. The reasons for this essentially universal rejection of Dart's suggestions are complex and tightly intertwined. However, I believe that a major, underlying factor behind the scientific community's virtually unanimous dismissal of Dart was that he had allied himself with Darwin. Indeed, as is obvious from his arguments and from his claims of vindicating Darwin, Dart predicated much of his interpretation of the Taung "humanoid" on Darwin's ideas on natural selection and human origins and, in particular, on the region of the world in which evidence of human ancestry should be sought: Africa. The problem, however, was that Darwin's writings, especially on these subjects, were not popular at the time.

For example, many human paleontologists and even some of the leading geneticists of the 1920s were unconvinced of the reality of evolution as championed by Darwin. In fact, as Broom put it as recently as 1951, Darwin undermined his own theorizing specifically because he had too many theories:

> Darwin had placed himself in an awkward position by having two theories, and even a third. If a character is of manifest advantage to an animal, like the powerful canine teeth or the claws of the tiger, then manifestly it arose by Natural Selection. If a character, like a peacock's tail, is a manifest disadvantage it arose by Sexual Selection. And if a character is neither an advantage nor a disadvantage, like the loss of the power of flight in the Dodo, then we have always Lamarckism to fall back on. It makes one feel that none of these theories is the true one [p. 101].

For Broom and others, evolution by natural selection, or any form of Darwinian selection, was too problematic a process to explain not only the diversity of life on earth but the perceived evolutionary history of groups, as seemingly played out in the fossil record. This sentiment was particularly prevalent among those who pondered human evolution. There had to be, it seemed to them, a "plan." Evolution had to be directed, or orthogenetic. Evolution had to have a goal, especially when it came to humans.

In terms of the details of human evolution, there were two major elements to contend with. One had to do with the question of who among the apes was or were most closely related to humans. The other addressed the question of where, geographically, humans actually originated. With regard to place of origin, the prevailing theory (of which there had been and were various subtheories) focused not on Africa, especially Southern Africa, with all of its attendant dangers and where Darwin argued such evolutionary events had occurred, but on Asia, with its long-lived, sophisticated civilizations and lush tropical landscapes. In terms of ape-human relatedness, the dominant theory, as championed in the twentieth century by the Swiss primatologist Adolph Schultz, was that all three great apes—the orang-utan and the two African apes, the chimpanzee and the gorilla—constituted a group to which, albeit somewhat distantly, humans were somehow related. Darwin, however, had argued that humans were most closely related to the African apes—but it would not be until the early 1970s that this alternative theory of human-ape relatedness would become the favored one. Thus, when Dart concluded his *Nature* article with the following Darwinian notions of natural selection and human origins, he was inadvertently undermining his own case:

> In anticipating the discovery of the true links between the apes and man in tropical countries, there has been a tendency to overlook the fact that, in the luxuriant forests of the tropical belts, Nature was supplying with profligate and lavish hand an easy and sluggish solution, by adaptive specialisation, of the problem of existence in creatures so well equipped mentally as living anthropoids are. For the production of man a different apprenticeship was needed to sharpen the wits and quicken the higher manifestations of intellect—a more open veldt country where competition was keener between swiftness and stealth, and where adroitness of thinking and movement played a preponderating role in the preservation of the species. Darwin has said, "no country in the world abounds in a greater degree with dangerous beasts than Southern Africa," and, in my opinion, Southern Africa, by providing a vast open country with occasional wooded belts and a relative scarcity of water, together with a fierce and bitter mammalian competition, furnished a laboratory such as was essential to this penultimate phase of human evolution.

It might seem surprising that there was a time when aligning oneself with Darwin was not a popular or careerwise thing to do. Today Darwin is lauded for promulgating notions of human origins and the evolutionary relationships of humans and apes. But it is of historical and scientific significance to see just what that role was and on what these ideas were predicated—especially because a large part of the folklore surrounding Darwin's contribution points to Thomas Henry Huxley as being the first to suggest that humans are most closely related to the African apes.

Dart's Predecessors: Evolving Human Evolution

Although Darwin published his theory of evolution by natural selection in 1859, in *On the Origin of Species*, he did not undertake a public discourse on human evolution until twelve years later, in *The Descent of Man*. In fact, the only reference in the *Origin* to human evolution comes two pages before the end of the book, in a passage on the positive effects the acceptance of evolution and natural selection as fact would have on a diversity of scientific disciplines: "In the distant future I see open fields for far more important researches. Psychology will be based on a new foundation, that of the necessary acquirement of each mental power and capacity by gradation. Light will be thrown on the origin of man and his history."

When Darwin addressed the subject of human origins in *The Descent of Man*, he deferred to his younger colleague, Thomas Henry Huxley, who in one of three essays published in 1863 argued for the first time on the basis of comparative embryology and somewhat detailed anatomy that humans should not only be grouped with primates, but specifically with apes and monkeys. In fact, as Huxley wrote in 1896 (when his original essays of 1863 were reprinted), Darwin may never have been able to tackle the subject of human origins if he, Huxley, had not made the effort first and provided him with the necessary details:

The weighty sentence "Light will be thrown on the origin of man and his history" [1st ed. p. 488] was not only in full harmony with the conclusions at which I had arrived, respecting the structural relations of apes and men, but was strongly supported by them. And inasmuch as Development and Vertebrate Anatomy were not among Mr. Darwin's many specialties, it appeared to me that I should not be intruding on the ground he had made his own, if I discussed this part of the general question. In fact, I thought that I might probably serve the course of evolution by doing so.

And, indeed, Huxley did just that.

In the historic essay "On the Relations of Man to the Lower Animals," Huxley argued that, in broad aspects of the development of the embryo, its fetal membranes, and the placenta that links it to its mother, humans are, in fundamental and incontrovertible design, similar to a diversity of other mammals, such as a dog, or an ape, or a gorilla. But in certain specific, less commonly developed features, humans are most similar to apes—in spite of the fact, which is obvious to any human, that humans appear to be quite different from all apes, including the gorilla—and should therefore be grouped most closely among mammals with apes. In order to drive the point home, Huxley drew on examples from other seemingly incompatible pairs of related animals: "No one doubts that the Sloth and the Ant-eater, the Kangaroo and the Opossum, the Tiger and the Badger, the Tapir and the Rhinoceros, are respectively members of the same orders," even though "these successive pairs of animals may, and some do, differ from one another immensely." Nevertheless, Huxley continued, "with all these differences," these pairs of animals "are so closely connected in all the more important and fundamental characters of their organization, and so distinctly separated by these same characters from other animals, that zoologists find it necessary to group them together as members of one order." If it is reasonable on embryological grounds to group together, for example, tigers and badgers, then it is equally valid to do so for humans and apes ("apes" to Huxley, Darwin, and others included what you and I would distinguish as monkeys and apes). Although he anticipated an audience that would require more than an embryological demonstration of "man's place in nature," Huxley at least was convinced that embryology "alone appears . . . sufficient to place beyond all doubt the structural unity of man with the rest of the animal world, and more particularly and closely with the apes."

Huxley sought to fend off his potential critics by providing, by way of comparative anatomy, answers to the following two questions. First, Huxley asked, "Is Man so different from any of these Apes that he must form an order by himself? . . . Or does he differ less from them than they differ from one another, and hence must take his place in the same order with them?" Huxley followed these questions with a summary of how he was going to answer them:

> Being happily free from all real, or imaginary, personal interest in the results of the inquiry thus set afoot, we should proceed to weigh the arguments on one side and on the other, with as much judicial calmness as if the question related to a new Opossum. We should endeavour to ascertain, without seeking either to magnify or diminish them, all the characters by which our new Mammal differed from the Apes; and if we found that these were of less structural value than those which distinguish certain members of the Ape order from others universally admitted to be of the same order, we should undoubtedly place the newly discovered tellurian genus with them [p. 96].

He then tells the reader exactly what the answer is going to be: "I now proceed to detail the facts which seem to me to leave us no choice but to adopt the last-mentioned course"—which will result in placing "Man" in the same order as, but not in the same family with, the "Apes." And the way in which Huxley is going to demonstrate this is by focusing on one of the "Man-like Apes" in particular as his primary source of comparison with "Man."

> It is quite certain that the Ape which most nearly approaches man, in the totality of its organisation, is either the Chimpanzee or the Gorilla; and as it makes no practical difference, for the purposes of my present argument, which is selected for comparison, on the one hand, with Man, and on the other hand, with the rest of the Primates, I shall select the latter (so far as its organisation is known)—as a brute now so celebrated in prose and verse, that all must have heard of him, and have formed some conception of his appearance. I shall take up as many of the most important points of difference between man and this remarkable creature, as the space at my disposal will allow me to discuss, and the necessities of the argument demand; and I shall inquire into the value and

magnitude of these differences, when placed side by side with those which separate the Gorilla from other animals of the same order [p. 97].

Huxley chose the gorilla as his major source of comparison with "Man" because it was the most well known, publicly and even scientifically, of the "Man-like Apes." His argument as to "Man's Place in Nature" was thus based primarily on anatomical comparisons between the gorilla and "Man" and then between the gorilla and the "lower Apes," the Old and New World monkeys, which, in turn, were used to demonstrate that the differences between "Man" and the gorilla were less than those between the gorilla and the "lower Apes." However, throughout his essay, Huxley also made comparisons between humans and the other "Man-like Apes," the chimp, the orang, and the gibbon. His goal here was the same as it was when comparing humans and gorillas: to encapsulate humans within the order Primates. By "encapsulate" I do not mean to imply that Huxley demonstrated, or even thought that he had, the evolutionary relationships of humans to one or more of the great apes.

Readers of Huxley's essay must be cognizant of when he was writing, who his audience was, and also what the language was that he was using—in short, the historical significance of what he was trying to do must be recognized. He was arguing on the basis of somewhat detailed comparative embryology and anatomy that, because humans are so similar morphologically to other primates, they should be *classified* with these particular mammals, not apart from them. I emphasize *classified* because Huxley used the word *relation* to refer to a taxonomic relationship; modern-day systematists typically misinterpret his language and intentions as arguing for a close evolutionary relationship. That Huxley's intent is taxonomic rather than evolutionary is obvious in his concluding comments on what he thinks he has demonstrated by way of comparative anatomy:

There is no existing link between Man and the Gorilla, but do not forget that there is a no less sharp line of demarcation, a no less complete absence of any transitional form, between the Gorilla and the Orang, or the Orang and the Gibbon. I say, not less sharp, though it is somewhat narrower. The structural differences between Man and the Man-like Apes certainly justify our regarding him as constituting a family apart from them; though, inasmuch as he differs less from them than they do from other families of the same order, there can be no justification for placing him in a distinct order [pp. 144–145].

Having thus convinced himself that humans should indeed be regarded as constituting a family within the order Primates, Huxley reminds the reader, and skeptic, of "the sagacious foresight of the great lawgiver of systematic zoology, Linnaeus," whom he feels he has vindicated. Thus Huxley becomes the second systematist, after Linnaeus, in placing "Man" in the order Primates. But by 1863 this had become taxonomically more diverse than it was a century earlier. In contrast to the handful of genera (the plural of genus) in Linnaeus's primate order, Huxley's contained seven family groups "of about equal systematic value." For our purposes, it is sufficient to note that, as Huxley arranged the different types of primates within the groups he set up, "the first, the Anthropini, contains Man alone" and "the second, the Catarhini, embraces the Old World apes," which, in turn, embraced both the "Man-like Apes" and the Old World "lower apes," the Old World monkeys. I find it odd, though, that Huxley lumped the "Man-like Apes" in the same family with the Old World "lower apes" because, as he clearly states in the quotes earlier in this section, he considers humans to differ less from the "Man-like Apes" "than they do from other families of the same order."

Regardless, however, of this apparent taxonomic inconsistency, obviously the thrust of Huxley's enterprise in "Man's Place in Nature" was to *classify* humans within the order Primates—not to suggest that humans are specifically related to one or some number of the apes. Nevertheless, from time to time it is claimed in the scientific literature that Huxley sought to, and did, demonstrate that humans are closely related evolutionarily to the chimpanzee and the gorilla. The quote from Huxley used to substantiate this claim is only part of a quote I cited earlier—"It is quite certain that the Ape which most nearly approaches man, in the totality of its organisation, is either the Chimpanzee or the Gorilla"—in which he consciously selected the gorilla as his primary ape of comparison with humans (because it is "so celebrated in prose and verse").

But while Huxley chose the gorilla purposefully—not only because its general anatomy was the best known of the apes, but because in specific body proportions as well as overall appearance it was the most similar among the apes to a human—he occasionally did make comparisons between humans and other apes. In fact, he had to use the chimpanzee and the orang-utan in his discussion of the brain because comparably detailed information on the brain of the gorilla was lacking. And, as we would expect in hindsight, Huxley concluded from this comparison that chimpanzee and orang-utan brains differed only slightly from a human's:

> The surface of the brain of a monkey exhibits a sort of skeleton map of man's, and in the man-like apes the details become more and more filled in, until it is only in minor characters, such as the greater excavation of the anterior lobes, the constant presence of fissures usually absent in man, and the different disposition and proportions of convolutions, that the Chimpanzee's or the Orang's brain can be structurally distinguished from Man's [p. 139].
>
> So far as cerebral structure goes, therefore, it is clear that Man differs less from the Chimpanzee or the Orang, than these do even from the Monkeys, and that the difference between the brains of the Chimpanzee and of Man is almost insignificant, when compared with that between the Chimpanzee brain and that of a Lemur [p. 140].

In fact, Huxley considered the differences in brain morphology to be significant taxonomically only at the level of the genus. Only because of apparently greater difference in other features did he distinguish humans from apes by putting them in a separate family: "Regarded systematically, the cerebral differences of man and apes, are not of more than generic value; his Family distinction resting chiefly on his dentition, his pelvis, and his lower limbs" (p. 143). In 1869, however (only six years later), Huxley rethought his taxonomic assessment of humans and placed them alone in one of the three suborders into which he then subdivided the order Primates. Clearly, although Huxley sought to demonstrate degrees of greater similarity between humans and apes than between humans and monkeys, he was *not* advocating a close evolutionary relationship either between humans and apes as a group or, specifically, between humans and the African apes. Rather, it seems that twentieth-century minds took Huxley's suggestion that humans could be compared favorably anatomically with gorillas and chimpanzees and translated it into a statement of evolutionary relatedness. In fact, to be true to the popular assumption that "overall similarity equates with evolutionary closeness," we would have to conclude from Huxley's essay that the gorilla is our closest living relative—because it was with this ape in particular that Huxley found and made the most favorable comparisons with humans.

If I were to presume to put words into Huxley's mouth (a bold proposition, even these many decades after his death) and tease a statement of evolutionary relatedness out of his essay, I would conclude that his argument lends itself to uniting humans in some way with a group composed of the "Man-like Apes." In this regard, it is important to remember that Adolph Schultz, who was from the 1920s through the 1960s one of the most universally influential of comparative primate anatomists, continually cited Huxley as the source of the suggestion that the chimp, gorilla, and orang constituted a great ape group to which humans were ultimately, but distantly, related. In fact, Schultz made a career of defending and consequently convincing most other primatologists to embrace this theory of human-ape relatedness above all others, including the human–African ape scheme proposed by Darwin. If we follow Schultz and credit Huxley with being the first (albeit inadvertent) creator of human–great ape theory of relatedness, then, clearly, this theory was popular for well over a century.

The taxonomic thrust of his essay aside, did Huxley ever broach the subject of the evolutionary relatedness of humans and apes? Yes, but only toward the very end of the essay and in such a way that he actually sidestepped the issue of specific relationships by questioning a larger issue, that of the validity of Darwinian evolution:

But if Man be separated by no greater structural barrier from the brutes than they are from one another—then it seems to follow that if any process of physical causation can be discovered by which the genera and families of ordinary animals have been produced, that process of causation is amply sufficient to account for the origin of Man. In other words, if it could be shown that the Marmosets [small New World monkeys], for example, have arisen by gradual modification of the ordinary Platyrhini [large New World monkeys], or that both Marmosets and Platyrhini are modified ramifications of a primitive stock—then, there would be no rational ground for doubting that man might have originated, in the one case, by the gradual modification of a man-like ape; or, in the other case, as a ramification of the same primitive stock as those apes.

At the present moment, but one such process of physical causation has any evidence in its favour; or, in other words, there is but one hypothesis regarding the origin of species of animals in general which has any scientific existence—that propounded by Mr. Darwin.

At the present moment, therefore, the question of the relation of man to the lower animals resolves itself, in the end, into the larger question of the tenability, or untenability, of Mr. Darwin's views [pp. 146–47; author's notes appear in brackets].

If we read further, we begin to realize that, at least while he was composing this essay, Huxley was not fully convinced of Darwin's views on the origin of species and evolution by natural selection—especially because Darwin often invoked the selective breeding of domesticated animals as an analog of the natural process of selection as he saw it. Huxley was skeptical:

Our acceptance of the Darwinian hypothesis must be provisional so long as one link in the chain of evidence is wanting; and so long as all the animals and plants certainly produced by selective breeding from a common stock are fertile, and their progeny are fertile with one another, that link will be wanting. For, so long, selective

breeding will not be proved to be competent to do all that is
required of it to produce natural species. . . . I adopt Mr. Darwin's
hypothesis, therefore, subject to the production of proof that physi-
ological species may be produced by selective breeding.

Perhaps Huxley did not discuss the evolutionary relatedness of humans to one or more of the apes because he could not reconcile human
evolution with a Darwinian model of evolution. And perhaps his own
brand of evolutionary change—saltationism, which postulated the ad-
vent of novel species not through a long period of a gradual accumulation of small changes but more rapidly by way of a major organismal
reorganization—seemed inappropriate to apply to humans. Regardless,
however, of why he did so, Huxley left the task of reconstructing
schemes of human evolution to other systematists.

Enter Darwin

If Huxley, the inveterate anatomist, did not advocate a close evolutionary relationship between humans and the two African apes, how did
Darwin come to argue it? In terms of the specifics of humans to other
primates, Darwin referred specifically to Huxley in *The Descent of
Man* only insofar as "our great anatomist and philosopher, Prof. Huxley
has fully discussed this subject, and concludes that man in all parts of
his organization differs less from the higher apes, than these do from the
lower members of the same group . . . Consequently there is 'no justification for placing man in a distinct order' " (p. 146). Darwin takes issue
with Huxley's 1869 classification of animals, in which he had subdivided
the order Primates into three suborders, with humans alone in one (the
Anthropidae), New and Old World monkeys, gibbons, and the great
apes in another (the Simiadae), and various prosimians in the third (the
Lemuridae). In reaction to Huxley's classification, Darwin echoed an
earlier Huxley by suggesting that "man ought to form merely a Family,
or possibly even only a Sub-family."

Huxley's Simiadae of 1869 came to embrace the families "Catarhini"
and "Platyrhini" in his essay of 1863. And it is with the former

group, the "Catarhine" or Old World monkey–ape group, and not the "Platyrhine" or New World monkey group, that Darwin saw a connection to "man": "man unquestionably belongs in his dentition, in the structure of his nostrils, and some other respects, to the Catarhine or Old World division . . . There can, consequently, hardly be a doubt that man is an off-shoot from the Old World Simian stem; and that under a genealogical point of view, he must be classed with the Catarhine division" (p. 149). In contrast to Huxley, Darwin based his taxonomic decision on "man" ("classed with the Catarhine division") in some part on the evolutionary context in which he perceived "man" ("an off-shoot of the Old World Simian stem"). Thus Darwin was the first to recognize that classification might or should reflect something evolutionary about the group being classified.

Almost in passing, Darwin accepted Huxley's suggestion that the "anthropomorphous apes"—the chimp, gorilla, orang, and gibbon—form a natural group apart from Old World monkeys. He then went on to conclude that "as man agrees with them, not only in all those characters which he possesses in common with the whole Catarhine group, but in other peculiar characters, such as the absence of a tail and of callosities, and in general appearance, we may infer that some ancient member of the anthropomorphous sub-group gave birth to man" (p. 150). And if "man from a genealogical point of view belongs to the Catarhine or Old World stock, we must conclude, however much the conclusion may revolt our pride, that our early progenitors would have been properly thus designated" (p. 151). Thus, not only should humans be classified in a group with the "anthropomorphous apes" because of potential evolutionary relatedness, but the common ancestor of humans and the "anthropomorphous apes" would also have been a member of the same group.

In the few pages in which he theorizes about the relatedness of humans and apes, and the derivation of human ancestors from an Old World stock, Darwin is oddly—and atypically—brief, both in speculation and in diversity of detail brought to bear on the argument. He provides very little discussion of morphology—just enough about noses, hair patterns, or tails, for example, to give a sense that a broader range of comparative anatomy exists to support the stated conclusions. In terms of the larger subgroupings of Primates, this "sense" was bolstered by the work not only of Thomas Huxley but of such other nineteenth-century notables as St. George Mivart and Ernst Haeckel. Mivart, Lecturer on Comparative Anatomy at St. Mary's Hospital, London, attempted the first in-depth definition of the order Primates, among other things. Haeckel, a professor at the University of Jena, was the author of the biogenetic law as well as of treatises on human evolution. And he also preceded Darwin by three years in suggesting that humans had evolved from a "Catarhine" ancestor. In general, however, Darwin went through his arguments on the evolutionary relationships of humans quickly and with little supporting detail, reaching a climax in his totally unsubstantiated conclusion that humans are related closely to only the African great apes. Because he believed that the evolution of closely related species is played out in the geographic region in which one finds the present-day species, he was then free to speculate about Africa being the seat of human origins:

> In each great region of the world the living mammals are closely related to the extinct species of the same region. It is therefore probable that Africa was formerly inhabited by extinct apes closely allied to the gorilla and chimpanzee; and as these two species are now man's nearest allies, it is somewhat more probable that our early progenitors lived on the African continent than elsewhere [p. 151].

Surprisingly, given Darwin's penchant for anatomical detail, his argument in *The Descent of Man* for human–African ape relatedness is devoid of comparative anatomy. Instead, the passage just cited, plus his belief that the forces of natural selection necessary to produce a species with human attributes are to be found in Africa, and not in Asia, constitute a large part of the argument for human–African ape relatedness.

Darwin's notebooks of 1836 to 1844 also reveal nothing from a comparative anatomical perspective as to how he reached the conclusion that the gorilla and chimpanzee "are now man's nearest allies." On pages 68–69 of Darwin's Notebook E, we find notes, most of which are choppy and in shorthand, that were written sometime between December 2 and December 16, 1838:

> The Value of a group does not depend on the number of species.: therefore Man & monkeys have equal chance that progenitor was bimanous, or quadrumanous.—What a chance it, has been, (with what attendant organization, Hand & throat) that has made Man.—[any monkey probably might, with
> (next page)
> such chances be made intellectual, but almost certainly not made into man.—It is one thing to prove that a thing has been so, & another to show how it came to be so.

In the first part of this quote Darwin suggests that it is equally probable that the ancestor of humans was either bimanous (having feet like ours and only one pair of handlike extremities) or quadrumanous (being like monkeys and apes, in which the feet are functionally like hands). He eventually solved the question to his satisfaction, as is obvious in the comment he wrote on January 6, 1839, on page 89 of the same notebook: "The rudiment of a *Tail*, shows man was originally *quadru < manous > «ped.*" (The various sideways open triangles set off words, word fragments, or thoughts Darwin deleted when he reread his notebooks; thus the original word "quadrumanous," meaning four-handed, was later changed to "quadruped," meaning four-footed.)

If we search further through Darwin's notebooks for insight into his thoughts on human origins, we find the following comment, which was written on August 16, 1838, on page 84e of Notebook M: "Origin of man now proved." But, as is obvious from other passages in the note-books, this statement was not a declaration of "man's" relatedness to any particular primate. Rather, it was an expression of Darwin's conviction that "man" was fundamentally similar to a diversity of mammals in aspects of behavior, which, in humans and various primates, might be present in modified form. Thus, even in his notebooks—and it is in Notebooks M and N that Darwin developed ideas used in *The Descent of Man*—we find no anatomical evidence for his published conclusions about either human-ape relatedness or human origins. Among the ideas that Darwin did formulate in his notebooks, and on which he elaborated in the second and longer volume of *The Descent*, were those that introduced sexual selection as a specific kind of natural selection in which mate choice, for instance, might affect the evolution of a sexually reproductive species as a result of members of one sex—often female—selecting features in the opposite sex.

When, in *The Descent*, Darwin did present an argument for the general relatedness of humans to other mammals and, more specifically, to the great apes, it was not based on morphology but rather on such matters as the development of intelligence and emotions, which are more developed in humans. We see these thoughts in shorthand in Notebook C (in which entries were made between early February through the last week of June 1838), on, for example, pages 77–79. (The quote in Latin means "with divine face, turned towards heaven.")

study relation of fossil with recent. the fabric falls! But Man—wonderful Man. 'divino ore versus coelum attentus' is an exception.—He is Mammalian.—his <has> origin has not been indefinite—he is not a deity, his end «under present form» will come, (or how dredfully we are deceived) then he is no exception.—he possesses some of the same general instincts, <as> & <moral> feelings as animals.—they on other hand can reason—but Man has reasoning powers in excess. instead of
(next page)
definite instincts.—this is a replacement in mental machinery—so analogous to what we see in bodily. that <I> it does not stagger me.—What circumstances may have been necessary to have made man! Seclusion want &c & perhaps a train of animals of hundred generations of species to produce continents proper.—Present monkeys might not,—but probably would.—the world
(next page)
now being fit, for such an animal.—man. (rude, uncivilized man) might not have lived when certain other animals were alive, which have perished.—

Let man visit Ourang-outang in domestication, hear expressive whine, see its intelligence when spoken; as if it understood every word said—see its affection.—to those it knew.—see its passion & rage, sulkiness, & very actions of despair; «let him look at savage, roasting his parent, naked, artless, not improving yet improvable» & then let him dare to boast of his proud preeminence.—«not understanding language of Fuegian, puts on par with Monkeys»

If we read the last two paragraphs of *The Descent of Man,* which capture the essence of some of Darwin's thoughts on human evolution, we can see how much of what he had jotted down on these pages in Notebook C was transformed:

But there can hardly be a doubt that we are descended from barbarians. The astonishment which I felt on first seeing a party of Fuegians on a wild and broken shore will never be forgotten by me, for the reflection at once rushed into my mind—such were our ancestors. . . . He who has seen a savage in his native land will not feel much shame, if forced to acknowledge that the blood of some more humble creature flows in his veins. For my own part I would as soon be descended from that heroic little monkey . . . as from a savage who delights to torture his enemies, offers up bloody sacrifices, practices infanticide without remorse, treats his wives like slaves, knows no decency, and is haunted by the grossest superstitions [p. 613].

As we read these and other passages in *The Descent* and in the notebooks, we also become aware of the fact that Darwin's discourse on human origins embodied yet another element: After deriving humans from a common ancestor shared with chimpanzees and gorillas, he extended the continuum through an ascendancy of modern humans that began with the wild and barbaric. Although Darwin did confront the issue of human "races" and did argue that all living humans belong to the same species, he was not exempt from the more widespread notion that, within the species, human races formed a graded hierarchy from "the savage" to "the civilized." Perhaps such a ranking did not seem unreasonable to Darwin because, in order for his version of evolutionary change to occur, it has to proceed through a sequence of gradations.

As Darwin wrote in *On the Origin of Species*, "natural selection can act only by the preservation and accumulation of infinitesimally small inherited modifications" (p. 95).

It would seem, then, that the picture was complete. Humans were closely related to the African apes ("these two species are now man's nearest allies") and, after originating in Africa from their apelike ancestor, had evolved through a series of stages from the "savage" to the "civilized." What was novel about this scheme was that Darwin anchored human evolution in Africa instead of in Asia, where the sentiment of the scientific majority lay. But, in regarding human evolution as the final segment of a sequence along an ascending scale that had its roots in monkeys and apes, he continued a longstanding tradition.

Faces, Races, and Human Origins

The interpretation of modern human races as constituting a graded morphological series was a totally acceptable activity among "scientists"—whether or not they were evolutionists. During the eighteenth and nineteenth centuries, and before thinking in evolutionary terms became widespread, western European anatomists, "phrenologists," and "physiognomists" were endeavoring to deal with and explain modern human diversity—but in the framework of a Great Chain of Being, in which diversity had to be ranked as stages of increasing perfection. The common theme was that one group or race represented this pinnacle of perfection. But how did the other races originate?

One popular theory, which was apparently first proposed in 1744 by the British anatomist John Mitchell, was that humans originated in Asia. Mitchell, who studied skin pigmentation, came to the conclusion that skin color was somehow correlated with the climate in which a group lived as well as with the group's way of life. As he saw it, Noah and his sons (remember, this is a biblical interpretation of the origin of living humans) had the "complexion" of either Mongols or northern Chinese. Writing in the late eighteenth century, the eminent and influential French natural historian Comte Georges Louis Leclerc de Buffon expressed the belief that, given its climate, Asia would have been the perfect place for the origin of humans and for the rise of civilization. The idea was popularized in England during the 1840s by James Cowles Pritchard. In the 1850s the French paleontologist Marcel de Serres narrowed the Asian model of human origins to a "Mongoloid" origin.

But Buffon speculated further on the subject of racial origins than did his contemporaries and successors. His general model was that human races became distinct through a process of degeneration. According to Buffon, after the first humans appeared in Asia, their unaltered descendants migrated west and are now represented by the people living near the Caspian Sea. From this geographic "hub," humankind degenerated into its various races, being affected by such environmental influences as climate, diet, disease, life-style, and interbreeding. Buffon's proposition became known as the "geographical degeneration of man" and was favored from the latter part of the eighteenth century into the beginning of the next by many scientists, including the German anatomist often referred to as the "father of anthropology," Johann Friedrich Blumenbach.

Blumenbach coined the term *Caucasian* to refer to the people of the Caspian Sea, taking the name from one of the region's mountains, Mount Caucasus. He identified Caucasians as representing the "Original Perfection," the Caucasian skull as being the skull of "most beautiful form," and the color "white" the color of the skin of progenitors of modern humans. The "races" graded divergently from Blumenbach's race of "Original Perfection," with one racial gradient proceeding east, to the "Mongolian," and another south, to the "Ethiopian." One of Blumenbach's other claims to fame was that he used his own extensive collection of skulls to devise the technique of orienting or positioning skulls that he felt best showed off the skulls' "racial characters."

Pieter Camper, a Dutch anatomist and craniologist and a contemporary of Blumenbach's, also subscribed to the notion that the environment played a role in creating racial differences. As Camper saw it, however, races arose by a process of differentiation into different "types," not by a process of degeneration from one "perfect type." Camper became very influential among scholars and laypeople alike because of his studies on skulls. His method used different angles and positions of skulls to demonstrate a supposed morphological sequence—

which was also seen as a demonstration of the Great Chain of Being—from, for example, dog, to monkey, to ape, to "Negro," to "Kalmuch" (= Mongolian), to European. A major trend in such a morphological "progression" was the reduction of facial protrusion, which purportedly proceeded from a snouty or "prognathic" condition to a short-faced and straight-jawed, "orthognathic" condition. Unfortunately, the "ape-Negro" comparison within the supposed sequence of facial reduction, in which the Hottentot was the favorite "Negro" example, gained much support among Camper's colleagues and contemporaries and continued to be a favored comparison through the remainder of the nineteenth century and on into the twentieth.

In the essay "On Some Fossil Remains of Man," Thomas Huxley took issue with Blumenbach's, Camper's, and others' attempts to character-ize animals and humans by way of facial angles or similar contrivances. He did so in the context of trying to assess whether two particular fossil skulls represented racial, but now extinct, variants of living *Homo sapiens,* or whether one or both of these fossil crania represented a species different from our own. One specimen—a skull cap—had been discovered in a cave in the Neander Valley, near Düsseldorf, Germany. The bone of this skull cap was thick, the forehead long and slanted, the back or occipital region of the skull compressed from top to bottom, and the frontal region above the orbits distended into prominent brow ridges. The second specimen, which consisted of a skull cap with its occipital region and base still attached, came from the Engis caves, which lie in the valley of the Meuse River, near Liège, Belgium. Com-pared to the Neandertal (this is the preferred spelling nowadays, rather than Neanderthal) skull cap, the Engis skull was more elevated in outline and bore well-developed but relatively smaller brow ridges.

Huxley's primary criticism of the various versions of Camper's facial angles was that the cranial landmarks used in calculating prognathism versus orthognathism were so malleable that they were, at best, only rough approximations of shape. What was needed first, Huxley wrote, was to understand the "organic relation of the parts of the skull" and to establish "a relatively fixed base line, to which the measurements, in all cases, must be referred." Because the base of the skull develops—first as cartilage and then as bone—before the sides and roof of the skull do, Huxley concluded that "the base of the skull may be demonstrated developmentally to be its relatively fixed part, the roof and sides being relatively movable" (p. 193). In studying a series of mammalian, including human, skulls, Huxley found that "the basicranial axis is, in the ascending series of Mammalia, a relatively fixed line, on which the bones of the sides and roof of the cranial cavity, and of the face, may be said to have revolved downwards and forwards or backwards, according to their position. . . . Now comes the important question, can we discern, between the lowest and the highest forms of the human cranium anything answering, in however slight a degree, to this revolution of the side and roof bones of the skull upon the basicranial axis observed upon so great a scale in the mammalian series?" (p. 196). Huxley, as one might expect, answers his own question "in the affirmative."

The human skulls that Huxley chose to compare descriptively and diagrammatically were those of an "Australian," a "Negro," a "Tartar," and "a well developed round skull from a cemetery in Constantinople, of uncertain race." As Huxley knew beforehand, the former two human crania would be prognathic and the latter two orthognathic. He summarized:

> It appears, at once, that the prognathous skulls, so far as their jaws are concerned, do really differ from the orthognathous in much the same way as, though to a far less degree than, the skulls of the lower mammals differ from those of Man. . . . But it is singular to remark that, in another respect, the prognathous skulls are less ape-like than the orthognathous, the cerebral cavity projecting decidedly more beyond the anterior end of the axis in the prognathous, than in the orthognathous, skulls [p. 199].

Huxley was quick to comment that "until human crania have been largely worked out in a manner similar to that here suggested . . . I do not think we shall have any very safe basis for that ethnological craniology which aspires to give the anatomical characters of the crania of the different Races of Mankind" (p. 200). In spite of his own words of admonition, however, he nonetheless proceeded to discuss the geographical distribution of prognathic versus orthognathic "races" and to make various points that were relevant to his assessment of the Neandertal and Engis crania.

One point that Huxley strove to make was how similar humans from Australia and its neighboring islands were to "Negroes" with regard to "the oblong skull, the projecting jaws, and the dark skin." The purpose of this comparison was to draw attention to the Australian Aborigine as another potential model of a cranially "primitive" human. Huxley described the Australian Aborigine skull as being "remarkable for its narrowness and for the thickness of its walls, especially in the region of the supraciliary [brow] ridges" (p. 201). After pointing out various other details, Huxley summarized his observations on the Australian Aborigine skull in general terms: "Many Australian skulls have a considerable height, quite equal to that of the average of any other race, but there are others in which the cranial roof becomes remarkably depressed" (p. 202). And it is the latter feature in particular that would stick in the literature—it is still used to describe Australian Aborigine skulls, in spite of the fact that this is not, as far as I can tell, a constant or prevalent feature of Aborigines.

On the next page of this essay, Huxley published a line drawing of a skull of an Australian Aborigine on which was superimposed the outline of the Neandertal skull cap. The Neandertal's much more massive brow ridges protruded much farther forward than the comparatively benign brow ridges of the Australian Aborigine. The contour of the Neandertal skull cap was not as rounded or as highly vaulted as the Aborigine's. And the occipital, or posterior, portion of the Neandertal skull cap protruded farther back than the Aborigine's skull. Then, with the confidence of a soothsayer, Huxley proclaimed that it would be a simple matter to transform one skull into the shape of the other, as if this were indeed proof that such a transformation had occurred: A "small additional amount of flattening and lengthening, with a corresponding increase of the supraciliary ridge, would convert the Australian brain case into a form identical with that of the aberrant fossil" (p. 203). After bringing the Engis skull into the discussion, Huxley concluded that, with the exception of the brow ridge, its "contours and measurements agree very well with those of some Australian skulls which I have examined" (p. 204). Huxley summarized the situation this way:

In no sense, then, can the Neanderthal bones be regarded as the remains of a human being intermediate between Men and Apes. At most, they demonstrate the existence of a Man whose skull may be said to revert somewhat towards the pithecoid type. . . . And indeed, though truly the most pithecoid of known human skulls, the Neanderthal cranium is by no means so isolated as it appears to be at first, but forms, in reality, the extreme term of a series leading gradually from it to the highest and best developed of human crania. . . . It is closely approached by the flattened Australian skulls . . . from which other Australian forms lead us gradually up to skulls having very much the type of the Engis cranium [p. 206].

Taxonomically, Huxley could see no reason to distinguish either the Engis skull or the Neandertal skull as a species apart from *Homo sapiens*.

The attention Huxley drew to the Australian Aborigine carried with it certain consequences, some more obvious than others. With the Australian Aborigine now "well-established" as a primitive human "type"—at least cranially—and with presumably favorable comparisons having been made between skulls of Australian Aborigines and the Neandertal and Engis skull caps, Asia again became a viable focus for evolution-based theories of human origins because Asia was the obvious place from which human migration into Australia and other islands would have occurred. This is not a trivial point because, as I reviewed earlier, Asia had been cited during the 1700s and was still being cited in Darwin's time as having been the place of origin of modern humans.

When Darwin came to write *The Descent of Man*, he obviously was faced with a history that favored Asia, and then Europe, as the continents of choice for the origin of modern human populations. He also was faced with a choice of who among modern humans represented the most primitive group. Was it an African—a Hottentot, or perhaps a Bushman—or an Australian Aborigine? It is obvious from his notebooks and from passages in *The Descent* that Darwin believed that the natives of Tierra del Fuego also should be considered as being representative of the most savage and barbaric stage in the postulated ascendancy of modern humans. This sentiment reemerges time and time again in his writing. For example, on page 244 of Notebook C, Darwin penned as part of a series of thoughts: "Hensleigh says the love of the deity & thought of him «or eternity», only difference between the mind of man & animals.—yet how faint in a Fuegian or Australian! why not gradation."

But while it seemed clear to Darwin that there was a gradation among modern human populations from the "savage" to the "civilized," he still had to confront a more troublesome problem. Where should he set the origin of the human ancestor? Darwin ruled out Australia for two reasons. One reason, upon which he remarked more than once in *The Descent* and in which he was heavily invested, was that he thought it unlikely that new species of animals could evolve on "oceanic islands"; animals only invaded islands. The other reason was that, had the human ancestor inhabited Australia or other islands, such as New Guinea or Borneo, they "would not have been exposed to any special danger, even if far more helpless and defenseless than any existing savages" (p. 62). And danger—in, for example, the form of potential predators or harsh physical and climatic conditions—represents a primary source of Darwinian natural selection, culling the fitter in each successive generation. Two geographic areas did, however, present themselves to Darwin as being potentially dangerous enough. As he wrote in *The Descent*, "No country in the world abounds in a greater degree with dangerous beasts than Southern Africa; no country presents more fearful physical hardships than the Arctic regions" (p. 61). But it is only broadly in one of these regions that apes as well as "primitive" people are found. The place is Africa. The apes are the chimpanzee and the gorilla. And the "primitive" people are "the negro." Thus the stage is set for Darwin to put the package together:

> In each great region of the world the living mammals are closely related to the extinct species of the same region. It is therefore probable that Africa was formerly inhabited by extinct apes closely allied to the gorilla and chimpanzee; and as these two

species are now man's nearest allies, it is somewhat more probable that our early progenitors lived on the African continent than
elsewhere [p. 151].

From Darwin back to Dart

Again I ask, did Darwin derive the justification for concluding that the
African apes "are now man's nearest allies" from any assumptions
other than his own? The orang-utan is ruled out because Asia is ruled
out. With the orang out of the picture, a great ape group falls apart and
only the chimpanzee and the gorilla remain together. But there is
another reason for seeking human origins via an ancestor shared with
the African apes. Supposedly primitive humans often have been
thought of and caricatured as looking like African apes, particularly the
gorilla. Early systematists sought links in their Great Chains of Being
between Hottentots and apes. Huxley's choice of the gorilla as a source
of favorable comparisons with humans was certainly not without prece-
dent, unconscious or otherwise. And the commonplace references to
various features of, for example, Tasmanians and "negros" as being of
a "very low type" that "indeed retain much of the gorilloid heritage"
were still very much alive in the scientific literature of the early 1900s.
(In fact, these very quotes are from a very widely read and cited
volume, *The Origin and Evolution of the Human Dentition*, published
in 1922 by one of this country's most influential paleontologists, William
King Gregory.)

Apparently favorable comparisons between the gorilla and supposedly primitive humans were not lost on Darwin, as is obvious in *The
Descent* when he sought to thwart criticism that might be levied against
his arguments by virtue of the "great break in the organic chain between man and his nearest allies" (p. 152). This "break," Darwin
argued, should not bother "those who, from general reasons, believe in
the general principle of evolution." In fact, we should probably consider ourselves lucky to have the African apes at all for comparison with
"primitive" people, because, as Darwin argued further, "the civilized
races of man will almost certainly exterminate, and replace, the savage

races throughout the world," and "at the same time, the anthropomorphous apes . . . will no doubt be exterminated." When this happens, Darwin concluded, the "break between man and his nearest allies will then be wider . . . instead of as now between the negro or Australian and the gorilla."

What of the fact that African fossils linking "man and his nearest allies" were as yet then unknown? Darwin tackled this potential objection as well: "No one will lay much stress on this fact who reads Sir C. Lyell's discussion, where he shows that . . . the discovery of fossil remains has been a very slow and fortuitous process. . . . Nor should it be forgotten that those regions which are the most likely to afford remains connecting man with some extinct ape-like creature, have not as yet been searched by geologists" (p. 152).

And this is where Dart comes in. It was he who was presented with the first fossil that could represent the link "connecting man with some extinct ape-like creature." And it was he who could vindicate Darwin's rejection of Asia as the seat or origin of humans. However, in order for Dart to validate Darwin's predictions, he had to subscribe to Darwin's arguments, those on selection as well as those about who among the apes represented "man's nearest allies." And, as I pointed out before, Darwin's theories were not, on the whole, taken seriously in the early twentieth century. Neither was Dart's interpretation of his "discovery."

Although Dart's pronouncements on the Taung child were rejected by the scientific community, physician and amateur paleontologist Robert Broom took up the search for additional specimens of South African "man-like apes." He believed they could serve as vehicles not for demonstrating that human evolution in South Africa was driven by Darwinian natural selection, but for demonstrating that there was a "plan" behind human evolution. And, all the while, other paleoanthropologists continued to search for fossils in Asia that would provide further links between modern humans and apes by connecting with the lowest, but now extinct, end of the great chain of human races, Neandertals.

.   .   .

The study of human evolution is rife with a history of imbedded assumptions, which still fuel current debates on all aspects of human evolution. In the nineteenth century of Darwin and Huxley, speculation focused on human-ape relationships and the relatedness of humans and Neandertals. Although our knowledge of the human fossil record is now beyond anything that could have been imagined even thirty years ago, things haven't changed that much since the nineteenth and early twentieth centuries. Contentiousness surrounds theories of human origins, not just with regard to the recognition and potential evolutionary relationships of a multitude of hominid species, but still with regard to the relatedness of humans and apes as well as of modern human and Neandertals. Before I pursue the touchy arena of humans and apes, I shall first tackle the Neandertals.

■

COPING WITH NEANDERTALS:

THE FIRST TWELVE DECADES

One of the oddities of paleontology, or any discipline that relies heavily on discovery for its grist, is the nature of discovery itself. In human evolutionary studies, the historical sequence of discovery has, oddly enough, divulged new species in reverse order to the sequence in which they are these days typically thought to have evolved.

The First Discoveries

The Engis cranium that Huxley studied was only one of the specimens recovered from excavations of the Engis and Engihoul caves, which lie across the Meuse River from one another. Collectively, and according to written documentation, the Engis and Engihoul skeletal remains constitute the first hominid fossils that were actually discovered, saved, and pondered over in terms of their potential antiquity as well as in terms of their relationship to modern humans or, at least, to the perceived races of modern humans. The year was 1833 and the investigator was Professor Paul Charles Schmerling.

The fragmentary skeletal remains of three humanlike individuals were found in the Engihoul caves. The Engis caves, however, yielded not only humanlike skeletal material but a pointed bone implement, some flint tools, and the bony remains of extinct animals, including mammoth, hyena, and woolly rhinoceros. The human-looking Engis remains consisted of one partial and one relatively complete cranium as well as various fragmentary postcranial remains, primarily from the arms, hands, and feet. Altogether, Schmerling thought he had bones from three individuals. But what Schmerling found most astonishing was that the humanlike bones were stained the same colors as, and in a state of preservation similar to, the bones of the extinct animals from the site.

The Engis cranium was relatively complete, however, only so long as it remained in the ground. When Schmerling tried to remove it from the floor of the cave, it crumbled into unreconstructible fragments. Schmerling was, however, able to tell that the skull had come from a young individual because the permanent molars had not begun to erupt into the jaws. With this skull of little further use, the most potentially important specimen from the Engis skeletal collection was the partial cranium, which, some thirty years later, would figure prominently in Thomas Huxley's essay "On Some Fossil Remains of Man."

Schmerling wanted to evaluate this partial cranium in terms of its racial affinities to modern humans using Blumenbach's popular racial criteria. But, because the specimen's facial skeleton was missing and facial features were critical to the Blumenbach approach, he could not. Schmerling realized that other cranial criteria might be less reliable in determining a skull's racial affinity. Still, he was impressed by the overall length of the Engis cranium as well as by its pronounced occipital region, its minimally elevated, narrow and elongate forehead, and its distinctive orbital region—features that, to his surprise, were supposed to be more characteristic of an Ethiopian's skull than a European's. Because he should have found the skull of a European in Europe, Schmerling interpreted the general features of the Engis skull as indicating that the individual had been of limited intellectual faculties, which, in turn, implied that the individual had been relatively uncivilized.

The most important contribution Schmerling made to the field of paleontology in general was not his discovery of the skeletal remains of primitive humans lying in the *same* deposits with the remains of extinct animals, but his recognition of the fact that the bones of these primitive humans were actually *contemporaneous* with the bones of extinct animals—that humans, at least a primitive type of human, had inhabited the earth at a time when types of animals no longer extant had also existed. But the "scientific" community was unconvinced of this contemporaneity. Humans, even primitive humans, could not be so ancient as to have been contemporaneous with now-extinct animals—not according to the Bible or any other acceptable source of historical information.

It was not until 1863, when Charles Lyell, Britain's most prominent geologist—in fact, the acknowledged "father of modern geology"— confirmed Schmerling's interpretation of the Engis material that the contemporaneity of primitive humans and extinct animals was accepted as fact. In that same year Thomas Huxley corroborated Schmerling's conclusions about the Engis cranium: It represented the fossilized skull of a primitive human. But, according to Huxley, the Engis cranium compared most favorably with various Australian Aborigine skulls, not those of Ethiopians or other black Africans. It was not until the 1930s, when a broader sampling of fossil remains were available for comparison, that the Engis cranium was eventually recognized as having been a Neandertal's.

Enter Neander Thal

The second fossil hominid—to be discovered and not discarded— emerged in 1848, during the mining of Forbes' Quarry, on the Rock of Gibraltar. The specimen was a relatively complete adult's skull. Although it was saved, the skull remained unknown to the scientific community until 1862, when it was "rediscovered" in a cupboard and sent to England. But by then the skull cap from the Neander Valley had been discovered and described in several publications. Thus the Neander Valley skull cap became the second fossil hominid of historical importance after the Engis partial cranium.

The skeletal remains from the Neander Valley ("Thal" means valley in old German), consisting of a reasonably well preserved skull cap and some fragmentary postcranial bones, were unearthed in August 1856 during limestone quarrying of a cave identified as Feldhofer Grotto, which lies approximately seven miles east of Düsseldorf, Germany. Fortunately, the Feldhofer remains, which the quarrymen did not recognize as being humanlike, were collected and turned over to Carl Fuhlrott, a local schoolteacher who had an avid interest in natural history. Fuhlrott also had his own private collection of bones.

Almost immediately after receiving the bones, Fuhlrott realized that he was not looking at the skull and skeletal fragments of a modern human. They were of something else entirely—something that seemed to be well outside of the expected range of human variation. Fuhlrott sent a plaster cast of the skull cap to the eminent professor of anatomy at the University of Bonn, Hermann Schaaffhausen. This cast did more than just pique Schaaffhausen's curiosity. In fact, on February 4, 1857, at a meeting of the Lower Rhine Medical and Natural History Society and on the basis of the plaster cast alone, Schaaffhausen presented a paper in which he emphasized the skull cap's "remarkable conformation." Fuhlrott decided to give his entire cache of bones to Schaaffhausen for study.

On June 2, 1857, Fuhlrott and Schaaffhausen gave a joint paper on the Neandertal remains at the General Meeting of the Natural History Society of Prussian Rhineland and Westphalia, which was held in Bonn. Fuhlrott spoke first. He summarized the nature of the discovery of the remains and argued that the nature of crystallization in the bones indicated that these were ancient bones and thus truly fossils.

When Schaaffhausen took the podium, he began by arguing that, although the Neandertal skull cap looked odd, it had not been artificially or otherwise deformed. Rather, the features of the skull—thick-boned and elongated, with a long and low forehead, enormous brow ridges, and distended occipital region—were normal for that individual. As such, Schaaffhausen concluded, the skull cap represented a form of human now "not known to exist, even in the most barbarous races." He did, however, speculate that the Neandertal skull cap might have come from an individual who was "in all probability derived from one of the wild races of North-western Europe, spoken of by Latin writers" and who had inhabited the region before the invasion of the Celts and Germans. Schaaffhausen believed that the bones were of some antiquity, but, he acknowledged, he could not prove this or even that the bones were truly fossils.

The following year Schaaffhausen published a much more detailed appraisal of the Neandertal remains. His observations are of significance even now. Of particular note is that the bone of the Feldhofer Neandertal skull and postcranial skeleton was remarkably thick and the depressions and elevations onto which muscles attached quite pronounced. Curiously, the ribs were not compressed as in modern humans, but oddly rounded in cross-section; they also had a more abrupt curve to them than is typical of modern humans. Schaaffhausen suggested that the unusual configuration of the ribs was probably correlated with "an unusually powerful development of the thoracic [rib cage] muscles" of the Feldhofer Neandertal.

The skull was unusually large, long, and elliptical. The huge brow ridge, which came together across the midline of the lower forehead, was so large and protrusive that it created a depression along the base of the forehead as well as at the root of the nose. Internally, large frontal air sinuses pervaded this massive brow ridge extensively throughout.

In contrast to the brow ridge of the Feldhofer (or any) Neandertal, a modern human's brow ridge—no matter how large or small—is formed as a pair of discrete, bipartite units. Thus, in a modern human, the superior margin of each eye socket is adorned by a "brow ridge" composed of two distinct components. One component, which is covered by the inner half of the eyebrow, is mound shaped. The other component, which lies beneath the outer half of the eyebrow, angles back and gives more of an edge to that portion of the orbit's margin. The frontal sinuses of a modern human are relatively small and confined to the brow beneath the inner portion of the eyebrow and the region of the frontal bone in between the eyebrows.

After comparing the Feldhofer remains with many modern human skulls, Schaaffhausen had to admit that "the human bones and cranium from the Neanderthal exceed all the rest in those peculiarities of conformation which leads to the conclusion of their belonging to a barbarous and savage race."

Apparently Thomas Huxley had been inspired by Schaaffhausen's study of the Feldhofer Neandertal remains. In his essay of 1863, "On Some Fossil Remains of Man," Huxley set out "to inquire . . . how far the recent discoveries of human remains in a fossil state bear out, or oppose" the view that "the Anthropini, or Man Family, form a very well-defined group of the Primates, between which and the immediately following Family, the Catarhini, there is, in the existing world, the same entire absence of any transitional form or connecting link, as between the Catarhini and Platyrhini." Did the Engis and Feldhofer crania, which Huxley accepted as being ancient fossils, provide significant links with the "Apes"? Or were these crania merely variants of modern "Man"? When Huxley made comparisons with skulls of Australian Aborigines, he thought that "the Neanderthal cranium . . . forms, in reality, the extreme term of a series leading gradually from it to the highest and best developed of human crania." Huxley also felt that the Engis skull could be accommodated easily within that graded series of skulls. Consequently, he concluded that "the fossil remains of Man hitherto discovered do not seem to me to take us appreciably nearer to that lower pithecoid form."

But Huxley's discourses on these fossil crania did not merely demonstrate that they fit nicely into a series of human skulls that could be arranged so as to grade from the most "primitive" to the most "developed." In a follow-up article on the morphology of the Feldhofer Neandertal skull cap, Huxley's more general concerns with taxonomy and classification emerged. Just as his ultimate concern in the essay "On the Relations of Man to the Lower Animals" was with classification—classifying humans within the order Primates—so was his motivation in discussing the relations to humans of the Feldhofer Neandertal cranium. "Inasmuch," Huxley wrote in 1864, "as a complete series of gradations can be found, among recent human skulls, between it [the Feldhofer cranium] and the best developed forms, there is no ground for separating its possessor specifically, still less generically, from *Homo sapiens*." As far as Huxley was concerned, the Feldhofer cranium represented just another type of *Homo sapiens*—not a different species, and certainly not a different genus. And this opinion continues to pervade, and even dominate, the current paleoanthropological literature.

Schaaffhausen and Huxley's interpretations of the Neandertal remains were not, however, the only ones forthcoming. In 1864 William King, a professor of geology at Queen's College, in Galway, Ireland, presented his views on the matter at a meeting of the British Association for the Advancement of Science. There King concluded that the Feldhofer Neandertal cranium did not represent merely a primitive racial variant of *Homo sapiens*. Rather, King felt that the very features of the cranium to which others had pointed as being so primitive actually far exceeded the range of variation known for—and in important ways were so different from—recent and subrecent modern human-looking skulls. Thus the Feldhofer individual should be regarded, at the very least, as representing a different species. As such, King proposed the name *Homo neanderthalensis* to distinguish this type of hominid from anatomically modern-looking humans. Fuhlrott accepted King's proposal and, in 1868, was the first to use the species in a scientific publication.

One of the publications on the Neander Valley skull cap was an annotated translation from the German by George Busk, a well-known British expert on cranial measurements. It was also Busk who, in 1868, introduced the Gibraltar, Forbes' Quarry, skull—which had been found eight years before the Feldhofer skull cap—to the scientific community, at the annual meeting of the British Association for the Advancement of Science.

Busk thought that the Gibraltar skull compared favorably in its proportions to skulls of Tasmanians and various western Australians. Further study of the skull by Busk and a colleague, Hugh Falconer, convinced them that it was not only a real and very ancient fossil but that it belonged to a separate species of the genus *Homo*. In recognition of the old name for Gibraltar—Calpé—Falconer suggested that the species name *calpicus* might be used for the Forbes' Quarry skull. Eventually scholars realized that this skull, although less extreme in some of its features, was otherwise remarkably similar to the skull cap from the Neander Valley.

But these suggestions—that one, if not two, different species of

Homo might have existed in the past—were swamped by claims that the Feldhofer and other Neandertal crania actually could be incorporated into a meaningful group with modern-looking humans. The supporting arguments for these claims were based on the assertions that these fossils either represented the low end of a racial gradient or that, particularly in the case of the Feldhofer skull cap, the cranial oddities were pathological—the result of either physical illness or psychological derangement.

If any doubts remained about the Feldhofer skull representing a distinct type of human, they were dispelled in 1886, with the publication by the anatomist Julien Fraipont and his colleague, Max Lohest, of a report on two humanlike skeletons that had been discovered in a cave in the commune of Spy (pronounced "Spee"), in the province of Namur, Belgium. Significantly, these two skeletons (Spy No. 1 and Spy No. 2) were indisputably associated with Paleolithic stone tools as well as with the bones of extinct animals—which demonstrated, once and forever, that there had been ancient and primitive humans. Although the comparable parts of the skulls and skeletons of the Spy individuals were not exact duplicates of the Feldhofer remains, the two assemblages were sufficiently similar that now a group of humanlike people, whose features became referred to as "Neandertaloid," could be discussed.

The Spy crania were similar to the Feldhofer skull cap, for example, in being long and low and in bearing huge brow ridges. The Spy facial skeletons were massive and heavy. The equally robust lower jaws demonstrated conclusively that Neandertals lacked a chin—the presence of which is one of the hallmarks of anatomically modern-looking humans—and thus the front of a Neandertal's mandible sloped backward from top to bottom. The postcranial skeleton was stout and the thigh bones were oddly curved; these features were interpreted as indicating that Neandertals walked bent at the knees. Although Fraipont and Lohest believed that the Spy individuals "possessed a greater number of pithecoid characters than any other race of mankind," they also thought—as Huxley had earlier opined with regard to the Feldhofer cranium—that "between the man of Spy and an existing anthropoid ape there lies an abyss." The "ancestral type of men and the anthropoid apes," according to Fraipont and Lohest, should be sought in much earlier deposits than those yielding Neandertaloids.

Although discoveries of Neandertal remains continued, the evolutionary interpretation of Neandertals took a twist for the more complex during the very last years of the nineteenth century, due in large part to the efforts of the Dutch physician Eugène Dubois.

Dubois's "Ape-like Man"

In 1887 Eugène Dubois set out for the southeast Asian island of Sumatra. His self-appointed mission was to look specifically for fossils that would fill in the gap between humans and their "pithecoid" ancestors. If the popular theory of Asian human origins was correct, it was in Asia, not Europe, that potential human ancestors should be sought.

Upon his arrival on Sumatra, Dubois worked in a hospital and spent his free hours scouring the caves of the island for human "ancestors." After a fruitless year of fossil hunting, Dubois learned of the discovery on the nearby island of Java of a humanlike, possibly ancient, skull from the site of Wadjak. So, off to Java he went. But, to Dubois's dismay, this skull was not ancient and, for all intents and purposes, looked like a modern Australian Aborigine. Nevertheless, Dubois remained in Java and continued his search for fossils. Eventually he was rewarded with a series of discoveries at the site of Trinil. From 1890 through 1892 Dubois excavated during the dry seasons and unearthed, from the same stratigraphic level, a skull cap, a femur, and two molar teeth of something that not only fulfilled but surpassed his own expectations.

The skull cap was relatively small and the bone was thick. It was the most "pithecoid" of any found so far anywhere. It was definitely more "pithecoid" than any modern human skull cap, including the favorite comparison, an Australian Aborigine's. The skull was very low and elongate, the brow ridges markedly protrusive, shelflike, and laterally flaring, and the occipital region, which was compressed from top to bottom, was quite distended and angular. The teeth were large, larger than most human molars, including, again, an Australian Aborigine's.

According to Dubois, the shapes of the crowns and the disposition of the cusps were decidedly apelike. But the femur was perhaps the most surprising part of this package. Although it was remarkably stout, it also bore the unmistakable features of the femur of an upright biped. If the skull cap, the teeth, and the femur went together, they portrayed an individual that was apelike from the neck up as well as apparently human, at least from the waist down.

But Dubois was convinced—and eventually convinced the majority of his potential critics—that this seemingly incongruous assemblage of bits and pieces did indeed belong to the same individual. The bones had been discovered in the same stratigraphic layer. They were identical in their states of fossilization, color, and preservation. And although bones of other animals were also present in the same deposit, there were no other remains of humans or nonhuman primates with which the skull cap, teeth, or femur could otherwise be associated more convincingly.

Dubois had discovered not just a "man-like ape," but an "ape-like man"—and an erect-walking "ape-like man" at that. To emphasize the upright stance of his human ancestor, Dubois created a new species name, *erectus*, which he presented in 1894, in his first publication on the Javanese material. The genus Dubois chose for his new discovery was *Pithecanthropus*, which had been coined in 1870 by German evolutionist Ernst Haeckel in prediction of the discovery of a link between humans and apes—of, as Haeckel portrayed it, "speechless Primitive Men *(Alali),* who made their appearance in what is usually called the human form . . . but yet being destitute of one of the most important qualities of Man, namely, articulate speech."

"I believe," Dubois wrote, "that it now hardly admits of a doubt that this upright-walking ape-man . . . represents a so-called transition form between men and apes . . . and I do not hesitate now . . . to regard this *Pithecanthropus erectus* as the immediate progenitor of the human race."

Dubois's discovery of a hominid more ancient and primitive than any that had been known previously opened the door for new and different interpretations of Neandertals. The German anatomist Gustav Schwalbe produced a series of papers between 1897 and 1906 in which he argued that Neandertals were so "pithecoid," especially in their cranial morphology, that they should be set apart from modern humans in their own species. Rather than use William King's *Homo neandertha-lensis* for this purpose, Schwalbe promoted the species *Homo primigenius*, which Ernst Haeckel had coined earlier to refer to a hypothetical "Primaeval Man."

More Neandertals

Early twentieth-century discoveries of Neandertal remains in France provided further grist for the species mill. On August 3, 1908, the Reverends J. Bouyssonie, A. Bouyssonie, and L. Bardon discovered a skeleton in a grotto in a valley in the Dordogne, near the commune of La Chapelle-aux-Saints. In their earlier prospecting at this site, the reverends had uncovered finely worked Paleolithic artifacts but no bones. But now they had the bones of something humanlike. Upon unearthing the skeleton, they found that it was oriented with its head pointing west. It lay on its back, with its head resting on a pillow of stones. Its legs were bent. The arms were flexed at the elbow; the right hand was situated closer to the skull than the left hand. A few large pieces of animal bone lay above the head. An articulated lower part of the leg of a cowlike animal also was associated with the skeleton. The reverends gave the humanlike remains to the French paleoanthropologist Marcellin Boule for study. Boule's first paper on these bones was presented on his behalf (as is the custom) to the Academy of Sciences in Paris on December 14, 1908, by Edmond Perrier.

In this paper Boule expressed his belief that the individual had been a male and had been quite old at the time of his death. Measurements of long bones indicated that "he" had stood about five feet tall. The brain case was much larger than that of most modern humans. In fact, Boule was astonished to find that such a short individual had had such a large skull. Boule was also struck by the remarkable fact that, in comparable parts, the man from La Chapelle was very similar to the specimens from Feldhofer and Spy.

The bone of the La Chapelle skull was unusually thick. The skull was long and low, and it lacked a forehead. The enormous brow ridges were continuous across the midline and were delineated above by a marked horizontal depression along the base of the slanted "forehead" and below by a depression above the nose. The occipital region was distended. The entire facial skeleton was situated anteriorly on the cranial vault as an extension of it. And the lower facial skeleton projected so far forward that it made the face look "puffy," with the region below the orbit and above the teeth lacking the depression otherwise found in modern humans. The orbits were large, as was the opening of the nasal region. The nasal bones themselves, however, did not protrude very much from the rest of the face. The lower jaw was also distinct; for instance, the bone was thick and it lacked the chin found in modern humans. Although the teeth were missing, it was obvious that the jaws were somewhat parallel sided, as in various nonhuman primates, and not squatly parabolic, as in modern humans. Boule concluded that the skeletal and especially the cranial remains of the man of La Chapelle were distinguished from those of modern-looking humans and similar to those of other Neandertal skulls, "by the general collection of simian or pithecoid characteristics."

But whereas the Huxleys of the paleoanthropological world interpreted this collection of characteristics as representing the low end of a racial gradient that incorporated living humans, Boule interpreted these characters as being of greater taxonomic significance.

"Can one create a species," Boule speculated, "or even a genus?"

Not a genus.

The skeletal differences did not seem to warrant such a distinction, even though, Boule acknowledged, the Neandertaloid group of fossils "represent[ed] an inferior type closer to the Apes than to any other human group."

A species, though.

This did not seem too outrageous. This species would fit "morphologically . . . exactly between the Pithecanthropus of Java and the more primitive living races," regardless of whether or not this represented a real evolutionary sequence. But as far as Boule was concerned, this apparent but fabricated morphological sequence—as played out by Pithecanthropus → Neandertaloid → primitive living human races—"does not," he warned, "imply . . . the existence of a direct genetic descent." Taxonomically, however, if one were dealing with another, nonhuman animal, such as a monkey or a carnivore, "one would not hesitate," Boule pointed out, "to distinguish, by a specific name, the skull of La Chapelle-aux-Saints from skull of the other human groups, fossil or living." William King's *Homo neanderthalensis* was available and Boule used it.

The Early Twentieth Century Tries to Deal with Neandertal

By the early twentieth century, the debate over "who, or what, was Neandertal?" was well established. Neandertals could have been another, now extinct, variant of *Homo sapiens*—at least this was the interpretation of one camp. For other paleoanthropologists, Neandertal morphology was just too odd, too distinctive, too unique in its own right, to be squeezed into a morphological and racial gradient within modern human populations. If uniqueness were to be translated into taxonomic terms, *Homo neanderthalensis* certainly deserved distinction from *Homo sapiens*.

In his broadly influential monograph of 1915, *The Antiquity of Man*, Sir Arthur Keith (who, ten years later, would oppose Dart's *Australopithecus*), argued for the distinctiveness of *Homo neanderthalensis*. In historical faithfulness, however, I should point out that his thoughts on human evolution and antiquity were bound up in many legacies, not the least of which was a kind of paleoanthropological nationalism. Basically, the cruel facts were that, while fossils of all sorts of import morphologically and chronologically were being exhumed from the soils of other European and even Asian countries, England's fossil contribution to the picture of human origins was essentially nonexistent. By 1915 the only claims Great Britain had to any potential human fossils consisted of one modern-looking skull, which had been found at Galley Hill, Kent, and one odd conglomeration of bony bits and pieces from Piltdown Common, in Fletching, Sussex. Given the inaccuracies in dating geological deposits and the tendency among various paleoanthropologists to stress the potential ancientness of modern humans, the Galley Hill specimen was believed to be older than 200,000 years and the Piltdown "hominid" older than 400,000 years.

The Piltdown "specimen" consisted of a partial cranium of something modern looking, a large piece of a lower jaw in which two molars were still preserved, and an isolated lower canine tooth. The lower jaw looked surprisingly apelike, but the two molar teeth, although large, were more human than ape in appearance. An isolated lower canine was found—a year later—in the same gravels that had yielded the skull and lower jaw. Although the lower jaw did not preserve the portion where this canine would have resided, this tooth was quickly accepted as having come from that jaw, which had already been accepted as belonging to the skull.

According to Keith's view of human evolution, the races of modern humans began to differentiate about 400,000 years ago. The Galley Hill specimen represented an early member of the European race. The Piltdown "hominid" was seen as one of the near-terminal representatives of a lineage that had split off about 300,000 years earlier from the "line" leading to modern humans. Although the hypothesized Neandertal lineage also was thought to have diverged at about the same time as the Piltdown lineage, Keith interpreted the latter as being closer to the modern human lineage. He believed that Neandertal-bearing deposits were younger, perhaps even considerably younger, than that which yielded the Galley Hill specimen.

In 1915 the most ancient non-British European humanlike fossil known came in the form of a complete lower jaw, with most of its teeth in place, which had been found at a site near Heidelberg, Germany. Keith and others interpreted this stocky and chinless mandible, which was thought to be slightly younger in age than the Piltdown remains, as representing a member of the Neandertal lineage. Dubois's *Pithecanthropus*, although a potential contemporary of the Piltdown "hominid," was seen as a near-terminal representative of a lineage that had diverged hundreds of thousands of years prior to the origins of the Neandertal, Piltdown, and modern human lineages. Keith speculated that the common ancestor of these three lineages "was a form of man in which the brain had attained a human size, but in which the mandi-

ble, the teeth, and the skull still remained anthropoid in conformation."
Accordingly, the Piltdown lineage had retained the more primitive
lower jaw and teeth, whereas the Neandertal lineage "preserved the
ancestral simian features of the skull." Neither type of hominid represented a modern human ancestor. In fact, as far as Keith was concerned, Neandertal "was so different from modern man in every point
of structure that, in order to account for his structural peculiarities, we
have to represent his phylum as separating from that of the modern
human type at an early date."

Keith translated this structural dissimilarity taxonomically and distinguished *Homo neanderthalensis* from *Homo sapiens*. An equally eminent colleague of Keith's and a describer of the Piltdown remains, Sir
Arthur Smith Woodward, had glorified the Piltdown "hominid" by
creating for it the genus and species *Eoanthropus dawsoni*. But, Keith
argued, if Neandertals were separated from modern humans only at the
species level, then this should also be the case with Piltdown. If Piltdown was to be delineated taxonomically at all, Keith conceded, *Homo
dawsoni* would be the appropriate genus and species.

One of the most influential of American vertebrate paleontologists at
the time, William King Gregory, a curator at the American Museum of
Natural History in New York City, also leapt into the fray of human
evolutionary studies. As early as 1916 Gregory had come to reject
Eoanthropus dawsoni—on all counts. Following a trail forged the year
before by Gerrit Smith Miller, a curator of mammals at the National
Museum of Natural History of the Smithsonian Institution in Washington, D.C., Gregory argued that Piltdown's lower jaw was that of a fossil
chimpanzee—at least that's what the morphology of the preserved
molar teeth made him think of. He interpreted the modern human-
looking brain case, on the other hand, as having come from a modern
human. Miller and then Gregory also disagreed with Woodward's identification of the isolated Piltdown tooth as a lower right canine. Rather,
they thought that it was a chimpanzee's upper left canine; the manner
and degree to which the tooth was worn down at its tip appeared
similar to the way in which upper canines of old female chimpanzees
are worn down. (It turns out that the lower jaw with two molars as well
as the isolated canine had come from an orang-utan; the teeth had been

filed down, in part to obscure the wrinkled enamel characteristic of orang molars.)

Gregory was not too enthusiastic about Dubois's *Pithecanthropus* either. As he wrote in 1920: "The association of gibbon-like skull-top, modernized human femur and subhuman upper molars . . . , if correctly assigned to one animal, may perhaps define *Pithecanthropus* as an early side branch of the Hominidae, which had already been driven southward away from the primitive center of dispersal in Central Asia, by the pressure of higher races." Even though he embraced Asia, rather than Africa, as the center of human origin, Gregory nonetheless did not envision a central position for *Pithecanthropus* in human evolutionary events.

With *Eoanthropus* and *Pithecanthropus* out of the way, Gregory could comfortably emphasize the humanlike dentition of the Heidelberg mandible. Because of the antiquity attributed to this specimen, and the nonapishness of its teeth, Gregory felt the Heidelberg mandible was a "good ancestor" for both humans and Neandertals. He also accepted the taxonomic allocation that the describer of the Heidelberg mandible, Otto Schoetensack, had in 1908 bestowed upon it: *Homo heidelbergensis*.

Compared to a Neandertal's mandible, the Heidelberg mandible was even more massive. From this observation alone, Gregory concluded that, "as the jaw of the Heidelberg man is lower in type than that of the Neanderthals, it seems likely that his intelligence was also of a lower order, the face extremely heavy, and the forehead retreating." As farfetched as Gregory's reconstruction of "Heidelberg man" may seem to us, it arose as a logical consequence of his approach to reconstructing the evolutionary history of organisms, which was to try to line up fossil and living species in a sequence that supposedly demonstrated change within a lineage. Having done this for the human fossil record, Gregory could manufacture the missing elements of *Homo heidelbergensis* on the basis of the skeletal and nonskeletal attributes of the species he had placed on either side of it in this transformation sequence leading to modern humans.

And what of the Neandertals? Gregory duly noted what he and others considered to be the "very low" characters of these hominids.

• The front part of a Neandertal's brain, as judged by endocasts, was not expanded, as ours is.

• The Neandertal cranium was relatively long compared to ours, and its face was stuck onto the front of the brain case instead of being tucked underneath it. This difference is reflected in the fact that the base of the Neandertal cranium was flatter than ours, which is more noticeably flexed.

• The bony nasal opening (from which the fleshy nose protrudes) of a Neandertal's facial skeleton was enormous and remarkably wide. Ours is absolutely smaller.

• The areas of the skull with which the right and left ends of the mandible articulate were relatively flat in Neandertals. When our jaw is closed, each articular end of the mandible slides into a depression that is bordered in front by a downward swelling of bone. When we open our mouths, not only does the front of the mandible drop down as the mandible rotates around its articular ends, but the entire mandible drops down as its articular ends move along the contour of this swollen hump of bone. The mandible would not have worked the same way in a Neandertal.

• The Neandertal mandible lacked a chin. We have one.

• The pulp cavities within the molar teeth of a Neandertal were taurodont, that is, huge and vacuous and extending well down into the roots. Our molar pulp cavities are much smaller and confined to the center of the crown of the tooth.

• The spines of a Neandertal's neck or cervical vertebrae were elongate and not bifurcate at their tips, as in apes. Most of our cervical vertebral spines are short and bifurcate at the end.

And the list goes on.

Boule and Keith's reconstruction of Neandertal portrayed it as being brutish and stooped, with its massive head jutting forward. Gregory accepted this picture of Neandertal, adding that the massive head would have been supported "by a short, heavy, forwardly-sloping neck." However, in the decades that followed, and with the discovery of more completely preserved skeletons, the picture of a stooped, brutish—and thus obviously apish and primitive—Neandertal would change. For instance, it turned out that degenerative changes of the bone—due to age and even, in some cases, disease—had caused some of the distortion that led to the "brutish" reconstructions of Neandertals. The skeletal differences in bone thickness and specific detail noted between Neandertals and you and me are real, but Neandertals otherwise would have carried themselves as we do, upright and bipedally. Until the earlier errors of reconstruction were recognized, the stooped image of Neandertal helped to reinforce—and was perhaps even in part inspired by—the notion that this was a primitive, archaic hominid.

Gregory entertained the possibility that the development of large molar pulp cavities was a specialization that, therefore, "exclude[d] Neanderthaloids from direct ancestry to any of the later human races." However, he preferred to interpret the overall Neandertal skeletal morphological pattern as being primitive. Thus Gregory "regard[ed] the neanderthaloids, or some of them, as structural ancestors—primitive or perhaps archaic types surviving into a later epoch—of higher races." As Gregory saw it, *Homo heidelbergensis* gave rise to *Homo neanderthalensis* from which, in turn, *Homo sapiens* arose.

Hrdlička's Neandertal Phase

By the early twentieth century, many paleoanthropologists had come to believe that Neandertals in Europe had been replaced—almost suddenly, catastrophically—by anatomically modern, technologically more sophisticated humans. Neandertal skeletal morphology and the rough-hewn Neandertal stone tool kit, which archeologists classify as the Mousterian tool culture (named after the French Neandertal site, Le Moustier), seemed to end without issue. From somewhere else—farther east it seemed—Cro-Magnon-like, anatomically modern humans invaded Europe, bringing with them a more refined type of stone tool kit, which became known as the Aurignacian (named after the type site of Aurignac, which is in the Haute Garonne of France). The Aurignacian tool kit was based largely on the production of finely worked blades and the modification of bone and antler. The Mousterian tool kit was dominated by various kinds of flakes that were used as they were struck from a prepared block of, for example, flint or quartzite.

William King Gregory, who was committed to the discovery of morphological transformation, did not go along with the notion that Neandertals just died out. Ales Hrdlička, of the National Museum of Natural History in Washington, D.C., and the dominant U.S. physical anthropologist of the early twentieth century, also rejected that idea. He attempted to discredit every part of this popular reconstruction of human evolutionary events. In 1927, as the honored Huxley Memorial Lecturer, Hrdlička gave one of his most detailed arguments against Neandertal replacement. He presented his case not in the United States but in England, at the Royal Anthropological Institute, on the turf of Sir Arthur Keith, one of the proponents of the theory of Neandertal replacement.

In the course of his presentation, Hrdlička argued first that "on the whole the Mousterian industry, though characteristic, does not provide evidence of something entirely new and strange, intercalated between the Acheulean [an earlier, primarily hand-axe industry] and the Aurignacian, beginning abruptly by displacing the former or ending suddenly through displacement by the latter." In fact, Hrdlička suggested, "there is much . . . at either end that may prove to be, more or less, of a transitional nature." In support of this contention, Hrdlička made reference to the difficulties others had had at various sites in distinguishing between the late Acheulean and the early Mousterian, or between the late Mousterian and the early Aurignacian. As Hrdlička saw it, "the more the initial and the terminal stages of the Mousterian industry are becoming known, together with the late Acheulean and the earliest Aurignacian, the less abrupt and striking appear their differences and the greater grows the feeling that they are not absolutely separated."

Obviously, Hrdlička's interpretation of the archeological record was incompatible with the model of Neandertal replacement. "The coming of a distinct and superior species of people," he argued, "ought to have left a very tangible record on the sequence and nature of the cultural levels of the two stocks." But Hrdlička had just begun to attack the notion, as he paraphrased it, of "Aurignacian man . . . who came from somewhere outside the Neanderthal area, overwhelmed completely the established less capable species, and annihilated or at least wholly replaced it, over all the great domain over which it once extended."

First off, Hrdlička pointed out, this purported invasion and subsequent conquest would have coincided with the last of the four glaciations that had assaulted Europe. In the face of such unpleasant conditions, it seemed unthinkable that anyone in his or her right mind would want to invade Europe at all. Rather, if people were going to migrate, movement to sunnier climes would be expected. Second, Hrdlička argued, an invasion from the east would have required a large, coordinated army, which probably would have been beyond the capabilities of the obviously "imperfect social organization" of such people. And, in any case, Hrdlička asked, where is the archeological evidence of the preinvasion bastions of these hordes of invaders? If, on the other hand, these Aurignacian people had migrated peacefully into Mousterian Europe—and especially if this migration had taken place in small or gradual increments—it would be reasonable to think, so Hrdlička argued, that this "would lead to an amalgamation with, rather than the extinction of, the native stock."

Even though Hrdlička had obviously satisfied himself with his arguments against an Aurignacian replacement of a Mousterian people and culture, he still had to deal with Neandertal morphology:

> The crucial part of the whole question of Neanderthal man is . . . the skeletal material, for it is essentially upon this that the separateness and discontinuance of the Neanderthal type of man has been based. It would probably be easy to harmonize all the rest of the differences between Neanderthal and later man with the idea of a simple evolution and transmission, were it not for the obstacle of the Neanderthal man's skulls and bones. These impress one by such marked differences from those of any later man, that bridging over of the gap has, to many, seemed impossible.

As we can anticipate, Hrdlička did his best not only to bridge but to eliminate that "gap" between "Neanderthal and later man."

Although he admitted that "the Neanderthal remains . . . constitute a very respectable array of precious material," Hrdlička informed his audience that, were we to see them all together, "we should be struck by the prevailing aspects of inferiority." Such "inferiority," we are told, takes the form of the "whole differing widely in colour, weight, state of petrifaction, and in principal morphological characters." In addition, were we to attempt to arrange this material "by their antiquity, from the oldest to the latest," we would find that "a satisfactory chronological grading of them becomes very difficult and uncertain."

Now that he had begun to sow the seeds of distrust of previous ideas about the relation of Neandertals to present-day humans—at least ideas that were contrary to his—Hrdlička went on to discuss the "somatological characteristics of the skulls and bones themselves" by referring to previous analyses of Neandertal morphology by such "eminent anatomists and anthropologists" as Boule, Keith, and Schwalbe. As a result of these scholars' work, Hrdlička acknowledged, "the main features of the average Neanderthaler are therefore fairly well known." He then proceeded to list them:

> They include a moderate stature, heavy build, and a good-sized, thick, oblong skull, with pronounced supraorbital torus [brow ridge], low forehead, low [cranial] vault, protruding occiput, large, full upper maxilla [upper jaw], large nose, large teeth, and a large, heavy lower jaw with receding chin. To which may be added stout bones of the skeleton, particularly the ribs and the bones of the lower part of the body, femora and tibiae with heavy articular extremities, the tibia relatively short and with head more than not inclined backward, a peculiar astragalus [the ankle bone just under the end of the tibia], and various secondary primitive features.

But, of course, as far as Hrdlička was concerned, if the Boules, Keiths, and Schwalbes *really* looked, they would see that "from this generalization there are many aberrations," because, in reality, it is not

possible to arrange the "material for satisfactory grading." The reason
for this difficulty is that "in one and the same skeleton are found parts
and features that are very primitive and far away from man's later
types, with parts and features that are almost like modern."

I do not, however, see this as inconsistent at all. It makes perfect
sense that some bones, or parts of bones, of one species may be primitive relative to the same skeletal elements in another species, while the
same two species also can share certain similarities. This is what we
expect to find in two species that are closely related to one another.
Related species share certain similarities because they inherited these
features from one or more distant common ancestors. Related species
also may differ from one another in features that may reflect the fact
that at least one species became different from the other by developing
even more unique features.

But if a systematist's particular view of evolution is that species grade
one into another—so that the fossil record should reveal a continual and
gradual transformation series leading from the older and, by assumption, more primitive species into the more recent and, again by assumption, more modern species—then this combination of presumably
primitive and modern features in the same skeleton will seem inconsistent. And indeed, this is precisely how Hrdlička interpreted the
Neandertal situation: It was inconsistent with a presumption of continual and gradual evolutionary transformation from the old, and thus
primitive, to the modern, and thus advanced.

"Here is facing us," Hrdlička wrote, "a very noteworthy example of
morphological instability, an instability, evidently, of evolutionary nature, leading from old forms to more modern."

As Hrdlička saw it, the skull of a Neandertal was its most primitive
part. The thigh and lower leg bones were somewhat less primitive. And
the bones of the upper arm were the least primitive. Hrdlička thought
that the teeth preserved in one of the Spy Neandertals looked fairly
modern. But there was some variability among the known Neandertal
remains, particularly in aspects of the skull. Some specimens had higher
cranial vaults and foreheads than others. Some had less protrusive
occipital regions than others. Higher cranial vaults, higher foreheads,

less protrusive occipital regions—these, so it seemed, were obviously more modern features.

Hrdlička compared Spy No. 2, which had the "higher" and "less protrusive" variety of skull, with Spy No. 1, which had the "lower" and "more protrusive" variety of skull, and proclaimed "that the morphological distance between the two is greater than that between [Spy] No. 2 and some of the Aurignacian crania." Mind you, the comparison between Spy No. 2 and these Aurignacian crania is not exact. However, *if* someone was disposed to finding graded series, then the nature of "higher" and "less protrusive" in Spy No. 2 would seem to be *on the way to becoming* even higher and less protrusive, and would thus compare well with human crania, which are highly vaulted, have high foreheads, and are not remarkably protrusive in the occipital region.

Hrdlička went even farther in trying to break down the morphological barrier between Neandertals and modern humans by focusing on the lowness of the cranial vault and forehead. Because he was the most knowledgeable human craniologist in the United States, and perhaps the world—having measured and cataloged thousands upon thousands of skulls in the collections of the Smithsonian—Hrdlička could throw his weight around with unmatched authority. "There exists to-day," he declared, "a whole great stream of humanity, extending from Mongolia deep into America, which is characterized by a low vault of the skull . . . [and] low foreheads are frequent in prehistoric America." As far as the protrusive occipital region went, Hrdlička could not make the same assertion and was forced to admit that this feature "would be difficult to fully match in later man." However, in order to diminish the weight of such a character, Hrdlička felt that it was sufficient to point out that not all Neandertals had the same degree of occipital extension.

With regard to the large supraorbital torus, or brow ridge, Hrdlička admitted that it "is common to Neanderthal skulls, [and] is not found in later man." But, then, as with the other characters, he proceeded to downplay this difference. For example, "not all the Neanderthalers," Hrdlička pointed out, "had the torus equally developed (*e.g.* Gibraltar)." Furthermore, "there are later male skulls in which there is a marked approach to the torus. . . . Moreover," he declared, "it is well known that, first, the torus is essentially a sexual (male) and adult feature; second, that a reduction of such characters is easier than that of those which are more deeply rooted; and third, that in the civilized man of to-day a continuance of such reduction is still perceptible." (What the first comment has to do with the price of beans, or anything of significance in the interpretation of Neandertals versus modern humans, is beyond me. And you'd have to be a soothsayer to know the points Hrdlička claims to know in the third and especially the second comments.) Nevertheless clearly Hrdlička felt that he had beaten down the significance of large brow ridges in Neandertals as a feature distinguishing these hominids from modern humans.

What about Neandertals having massive, chinless lower jaws and modern humans having less massive, chinned jaws? As he had done with the other characters, Hrdlička began the discussion of these features by admitting that they "are among the most striking characters of Neanderthal man." And, it is true, "jaws such as these are not known in later skulls." But, Hrdlička immediately pointed out, some Neandertal jaws are a bit less massive than others, and there are some modern humans with large, "nearly chinless, and even receding jaws." It obviously did not make any difference to Hrdlička that even his nearly chinless modern human examples still had a chin. But, once again, for him, a *real* comparison of Neandertal with modern human morphology revealed that *real* distinctions *really* do not exist. The "gap" between Neandertals and modern humans is thus made to appear as small as that between the fingertips of God and Adam, with Neandertal morphology extending up toward the lower end of modern human morphology.

By this time in the lecture, Hrdlička must have felt that he had made his point about Neandertals and modern humans actually forming a graded series, because he just breezed over the postcranial skeleton and the brain. As for the rest of "the bones of the skeleton," Hrdlička stated matter-of-factly that "there are scales of gradation from forms that stand considerably apart from those of later man . . . to forms that approach to, or merge with, the modern." With regard to the brain, Hrdlička focused on a partial skull from Mugharet-el-Zuttiyeh, a cave site in Israel. At the time, this skull was referred to as the Galilee skull;

it is now referred to as the Zuttiyeh skull. Although only the frontal or forehead region and the face below were preserved, the Zuttiyeh skull served Hrdlicka's needs. "In its mass and its markings," he stated in reaffirmation of Keith's initial assessment of the skull, it had "reached at least to the level attained by individuals in living races—such as that represented to-day by the aborigines of Australia."

Having decided that Neandertal morphology had indeed been transformed into that of modern humans, Hrdlička had to come up with an explanation, a scenario, of how this could have been accomplished. Fortunately, the earliest Neandertal remains then known were thought to have come from deposits that had accumulated right before the beginning of the last glaciation—just as things were going from warm and balmy to cold and miserable. If the climate changes, so must the hominid. But let's let Hrdlička tell it:

> During this period man is brought face to face with great changes of environment. He is gradually confronted with hard winters, which demand more shelter, more clothing, more food, more fire, and storage of provisions; there are . . . new adaptations and developments in hunting; and there are growing discomforts . . . that call for new efforts. . . .
>
> Such a major change in the principal environmental factors must inevitably have brought about . . . greater mental as well as physical exertion and . . . an intensification of natural selection, with the survival of only the more, and perishing of the less, fit. But greater sustained mental and physical exertion . . . leads inevitably towards greater efficiency attended by further bodily and mental development, which, with the simultaneous elimination of the weak and less fit, are the very essentials of progressive evolution.
>
> Strong evidence that a relatively rapid, progressive change, both mental and physical, was actually taking place during the Neanderthal period, is furnished by the great variability of the skeletal remains from this time.

Hrdlička collapsed the apparent differences between Neandertals and "later man" into two categories of morphological change—changes he thought could easily transform "Neandertal" morphology into "modern" morphology. To begin with, there was supposed to have been a "reduction in musculature" associated with the jaws as well as with the postcranial skeleton. In conjunction with the reduction in jaw musculature were supposed to have come "changes in the teeth, jaws, face, and vault of the skull," which, according to Hrdlička, are "now going on in more highly civilized man, of whatever racial derivation." The second area of change from Neandertal to "later man" involved a reduction in size of the brow ridge, or supraorbital torus. Evolutionary diminution of the supraorbital torus was perceived of as the counterpart of brow ridge development. Children lack a brow ridge, but this feature may develop in some individuals as they mature into adults. However, various groups of modern humans characteristically lack brow ridges as adults because they retain the juvenile condition, in which this feature is absent. This sometime phenomenon—whereby juvenile features are retained in the adult—was formalized in terms of evolutionary process and referred to as progressive infantilism. Progressive infantilism became quite popular and, as Hrdlička acknowledged, was "commonly accepted as the explanation of the differences of the negrillo from negro, and for the greater average reduction of the supraorbital ridges in the negro than in the whites."

In this context, Hrdlička felt justified in concluding that, as far as "later man" was concerned, "it is impossible . . . to conceive of his origin without a Neanderthal-like stage of development."

Now, it is one thing to demonstrate morphological variation within a species, or even a group of individuals. Species, to whatever extent they are indeed real units in nature, are agglomerations of individuals. Almost by definition, some morphological noise will be present, some variation from one individual to another. It is another thing altogether, however, to demonstrate variability over a continuum such that a group of organisms represents an intermediate stage or phase relative to two other groups. Species as real units in nature—in time and space—cannot exist if continual transformation is the rule. If continual transformation is the rule, then species can be recognized only by arbitrarily cutting up the continuum into artificial segments. But Hrdlička envisioned evolutionary history, especially human evolutionary history, in this way. Indeed, as Hrdlička concluded, "there appears to be less justification in the conception of a Neanderthal *species* than there would be in that of a Neanderthal *phase* of Man."

Along with the text of his lecture, Hrdlička published an evolutionary tree representing "the Phylogenetic Relation of Neanderthal and Later Man" as he saw it. On one side of a diagram that looks like a balding squirrel's tail is the genus name *Homo*. On the other side, lower and obviously earlier in time, is the abbreviation *"neanderth."* (for *neanderthalensis*). Midway up the "tail" is *"Aurign."* (for Aurignacian). And farther up again is *"praes."* (for *praesapiens*).

1927: A Recapitulation

By 1927, the year in which Hrdlička gave this lecture, seventeen separate hominid discoveries—sometimes of remains of more than one individual—had been made in Europe from sites that were interpreted as being Mousterian, both culturally and chronologically. In addition to the Heidelberg mandible, only two other hominid localities had yielded skeletal remains that were thought to predate the Mousterian. In general, these hominid remains were perceived of collectively as being more or less Neandertal, or "Neandertaloid." Ten Aurignacian sites and almost twenty post-Aurignacian sites had yielded human remains that were definitely and inescapably the remains of modern humans. Southeast Asia had divulged *Pithecanthropus erectus*, which, for some reason, Hrdlička did not even mention in his presentation. In an alternative evolutionary diagram he did, however, depict *Pithecanthropus* as being directly ancestral to *"neanderthalensis,"* which was, in turn, depicted as being directly ancestral to *Homo sapiens*. But he rejected this evolutionary scheme in favor of the balding squirrel's tail.

Henry Fairfield Osborn, director of the American Museum of Natural History and one of this country's most influential scientists, also published an article on human origins and antiquity in 1927. But Osborn at least dealt, albeit briefly, with *Pithecanthropus*. Although the *Pithecanthropus* brain was small, Osborn thought that it also showed "a fairly well-developed forebrain or intelligence area." As such, he proclaimed, "we may now regard *Pithecanthropus erectus* as a case of arrested development, of a very primitive type, possibly related to the Neanderthal stock, surviving in the southern subtropical forests of Asia." Because Osborn held tenaciously onto the theory of Neandertal replacement, no fossil of any antiquity then known could qualify as being an ancestor of modern humans.

The year 1927 was also the time when the first hominid remains— actually, only one tooth—from Chou Kou Tien (now Zhoukoudien), a site near Beijing (formerly Peking), China, were excavated. Referred by its discoverer, Davidson Black, a professor of anatomy, to a new genus and species, *Sinanthropus pekinensis*, this tooth and subsequent finds of skulls and jaws came to be known collectively as "Peking Man." If Hrdlička had known about *Sinanthropus*—the tooth anyway—he did not let on.

This was two years after Dart's report in *Nature* on the new genus and species *Australopithecus africanus* and its importance as an ancient link between proper hominids and the apes. But none of the publications by the paleoanthropological big shots even mentioned it. It's as if the Taung child and Dart's report had never existed.

As mentioned, Robert Broom did not entirely embrace Dart's interpretation of *Australopithecus* as being somewhere between ape and human, a "man-ape," either. While in 1937 Broom allowed as to how the preserved premolars and molars of an adult *Australopithecus*-like skull he had found did indeed "resemble much more closely those of primitive man—especially those of Mousterian man," he also thought that the teeth of this specimen resembled those of various apelike fossils that were being unearthed from much more ancient deposits in the Siwalik Hills of India. As for *Australopithecus* in general, Broom considered it a fossil ape, not a fossil man-ape. However, in contrast to the fossil apes from India, "there seems no doubt," he wrote, "that it [*Australopithecus*] is the fossil ape nearest to man's ancestor at present known."

But the paleoanthropological world was little moved by the noises and discoveries coming from so far away in South Africa. As far as the majority of paleoanthropologists was concerned, the only relevant discoveries were those from Europe and Asia. And the only relevant debates on human evolution—*real* human evolution—had to do with how these fossils related to modern humans.

Neandertals in the Near East

Discoveries made in two cave sites in northern Israel seemed to provide a link in both time and place between Neandertals and modern humans as well as between Europe and lands farther east. These neighboring caves, identified as Tabūn and Skhūl, are located in the Mount Carmel range, which flanks the Mediterranean coast, just north of Tel Aviv. From April 1929 to August 1934, these caves were excavated under the direction of British archeologist Dorothy Garrod. All of the stone tools, animal bones, and hominid material were meticulously (for that time, at least) recorded and saved.

The cave of Tabūn yielded the remains of two hominids. The first individual, Tabūn I, an apparent female, was represented by a complete skeleton. Tabūn II, which was identified as a male, was represented by the mandible alone.

Bits and pieces of five very fragmentary individuals were found at Skhūl. These remains consisted of the partially damaged and incomplete skeletons of an apparent male and female as well as the complete skeletons of a child and two adults, both presumably male. These latter individuals may even have been interred intentionally by their comrades. As Theodore McCown, who had excavated Skhūl, commented in 1937 in the first volume on the excavations: "We have to do with a deliberate, if carelessly made burial." Sir Arthur Keith joined Theodore McCown in the analysis of the hominid skeletal material, and, in 1939, they put the Mount Carmel specimens into a broader scenario of human evolution.

McCown and Keith appear to have been overwhelmed by what they thought they saw represented among the teeth, jaws, skulls, and postcranial skeletons from both sites. The Tabūn hominids, although smaller, were essentially identical in details of skull and mandible to the Neandertals of western Europe. The Skhūl hominids, on the other hand, were strikingly similar to the modern human–looking European fossils, such as Cro-Magnon. In fact, in the context of the prevailing tendency to try to line up fossils in a progression from primitive to modern, McCown and Keith had to admit that "on strictly anatomical grounds one would presume that the Skhūl was the later type." However, despite these and other differences that seemed to distinguish one group from the other, the two men were "move[d] to regard all the specimens from both sites as members of the same species or race."

McCown and Keith gave three reasons for having decided that the skeletal material from these two caves represented "the same species or race." The first was that there did not seem to be a distinction between the Tabūn and the Skhūl individuals in tooth morphology. The second reason was that, in terms of the stone tools that were excavated, the people of Tabūn and Skhūl seemed to have been fairly similar culturally. And the third reason was that the caves in which these people lived, or which they at least used, were in the same place and were presumably contemporaneous. McCown and Keith also thought that the Mount Carmel hominids were more ancient than the western European Neandertals.

But if the Tabūn and Skhūl individuals were in many ways so distinct from one another morphologically, how could this be reconciled with the interpretation that they were nonetheless members of the same species? Because McCown and Keith thought that "all members of the groups possess certain characters in common," they felt justified in constructing a transformation series of what they perceived to be "intermediates" that could be fit in between the extremes. From the Tabūn, or Neandertal-looking, type of Mount Carmel hominid, McCown and Keith thought they could trace a sequence of increasing Neandertal-ness from the Near East to contemporaneous specimens from Krapina, a site near Zagreb, Yugoslavia. From Krapina, the trail seemed to lead to Germany, near the city of Weimar, to a contemporaneous skull and two contemporaneous mandibles from the site of Ehringsdorf as well as to a somewhat younger, very Tabūn-like skull from the site of Steinheim. From Germany, the morphological trail continued to those specimens from southwestern and central Europe that were clearly Neandertal. As far as McCown and Keith were concerned, "western Europe . . . had become an evolutionary backwater." For them, "the centres of active evolutionary progress lay much farther to the east, probably in western Asia."

Because the Tabūn and Skhūl individuals, when taken together, seemed to share features with both Neandertals and modern-looking, Cro-Magnon-type humans, McCown and Keith concluded "that the Mount Carmel people represent a series which can be arranged between a Neanderthal form at one end and a Cromagnon form at the other." From this they could argue that because Skhūl was located in the Near East, the modern human–looking features of the Skhūl individuals must have evolved in the absence of the glaciation-induced selection pressures Ales Hrdlička had invoked as being responsible for the development of anatomically modern humans from Neandertals. But did the peoples of Tabūn and Skhūl demonstrate this transformation? McCown and Keith believed they did not.

The people of Skhūl were sufficiently similar morphologically to the Cro-Magnons that McCown and Keith were convinced that the former represented "a very particular form of modern man, one of the white or European type, for concerning the racial status of Cromagnon man there should be no doubt." As such, their "belief [was] that at Mount Carmel we have reached a transitional zone which leads from one ancient area of racial differentiation (the Neanderthal or Palaeoanthropic) to another ancient area lying farther to the east, a Neanthropic area where the proto-Caucasian (or proto-Cromagnon) type of man was being evolved."

But because the Mount Carmel people were interpreted collectively and not as the distinct type of hominid they represented morphologically, McCown and Keith believed they could not be the ancestors of the Cro-Magnon people—some were just too Neandertaloid. There had to be some other explanation. And McCown and Keith came up with one—one that had been used previously. The ancestors of the Cro-Magnon people, they argued, must be sought farther to the east, where "a progressive and conquering type of humanity was being evolved in western Asia in the remote times at which the Mount Carmel people lived." With their numbers and strength increasing, McCown and Keith continued, these people kept pushing west, eventually "replacing and extinguishing the native Neanderthalians."

By way of analogy, McCown and Keith summarized their conceptions of Neandertals and the people that had replaced them. "In brief," they proposed, "our theory assumes that Europe became the 'Australia' of the ancient world . . . and that the people who colonized it and extinguished its Neanderthal inhabitants, as the whites are now ousting the 'blacks' of Australia, were Caucasians evolved in western Asia." Although McCown and Keith used the term *race* to refer to what they saw as the core group of Neandertals as well as to the Neandertals of Krapina, Ehringsdorf, and Mount Carmel, the scheme of classification they offered to accommodate these supposedly different types belies the deeper concept that equates "race" with species.

First of all, McCown and Keith segregated all of the "primitive" Near Eastern–European types into a genus other than *Homo*. They chose the genus *Palaeoanthropus*, meaning "ancient man," which had been used previously for the Heidelberg mandible. Then each regional variant, or "race," was segregated into its own species. *Palaeoanthropus heidelbergensis* was the species of "Heidelberg Man." *Palaeoanthropus ehringsdorfensis* subsumed the fossils from the site of Ehringsdorf, in Germany. *Palaeoanthropus neanderthalensis* incorporated the Feldhofer and La Chapelle type of Neandertal. *Palaeoanthropus krapinensis* represented the Krapina Neandertals of Yugoslavia. And *Palaeoanthropus palestinensis* subsumed both the Tabūn and Skhūl types as well as the Galilee (Zuttiyeh) skull.

Perhaps because these were fossils, allocating them to different species seemed inoffensive enough, even though, until they put them into a classificatory context, McCown and Keith had argued that these fossils formed a graded morphological series from the Near East, through Yugoslavia and Germany, and into the heart of Neandertal country. And, indeed, the two continually referred to these regional variants as "races." Clearly, the act of segregating fossil humanlike "races" taxonomically into different species is not at all dissimilar to the actions of eighteenth-century polygenist taxonomists who defined modern human "races" in subjective ways and then put species boundaries around them.

Franz Weidenreich's Stages of Human Evolution

The fine art of interpreting humanlike fossils in a racial context persisted well into the 1940s—even if the segregation of regional variants of Neandertals into different species did not. By the mid-1940s the world's leading paleoanthropologists had come to the conclusion that *Pithecanthropus* and *Sinanthropus* were quite similar to one another morphologically. The slightly smaller *Pithecanthropus* was taken as the more primitive of the two. But this was acceptable because *Pithecanthropus* was supposed to have been a bit more ancient than its Chinese relative. With the end of World War II, an additional set of skulls, which had been found in Javanese deposits during the early 1930s, was finally accessible for study. These skulls were noticeably larger than the *Pithecanthropus* skulls, were presumably from somewhat younger deposits, and were considered to represent a more developed type of hominid. Taking all of these factors into consideration, this Javanese hominid was placed into the genus *Homo*, but in the species *soloensis*. The species name reflected the fact that the site which yielded these specimens, Ngandong, is located near the Solo River.

The world's expert of the 1940s on the Asian hominids was Franz Weidenreich, who had been at and had studied the hominid material discovered in the late 1920s and 1930s at the Zhoukoudien cave site near Beijing. While there Weidenreich took copious, detailed notes of the series of skulls that had emerged from the cave's deposits. He also made a complete set of molds of the skulls. It is fortunate that he did, because this wonderful series of skulls disappeared without a trace as they were being transported to safety during the Sino-Japanese war. To this day, no one knows what happened to them—they're just gone. But we at least have Weidenreich's scrupulously careful descriptions and illustrations. And we also have casts of the original *Sinanthropus* skulls and jaws, so that we can study the external morphology of the specimens, at least to the degree of accuracy that was recorded in the molds Weidenreich made.

As the world's expert on the Asian hominid material and thoroughly versed in the European Neandertal material, Weidenreich could claim a virtually unrivaled authority in paleoanthropology. In the mid to late 1940s, and with all of his clout behind him, Weidenreich began to formulate his own view of human evolution. Because his concept of "who among the fossils qualified as being a hominid" did not include *Australopithecus,* Weidenreich's view began with the Asian hominids. In his eyes, all hominids should be regarded as constituting a single species, regardless of where they resided in time and place. Weidenreich based this claim on his, and others', belief that "if all hominid types and their variations . . . are taken into consideration, their arrangement in a continuous evolutionary line, leading from the most primitive state to the most advanced, does not meet with any difficulty." In certain geographic areas, where the predicted intermediate or transitional forms were lacking from the fossil record, Weidenreich used as temporary substitutes fossils from other parts of the Old World that were from the appropriate time period. Thus, for example, the "gap" between *Sinanthropus* and the younger, morphologically Chinese, skulls from Zhoukoudien was filled by the European and especially the Near Eastern Neandertals.

But this was just the tip of Weidenreich's evolutionary iceberg. He may have begun with the seemingly simple belief "that *any* modern type must have had a more primitive forerunner," but his conclusion was biased. Weidenreich perceived of human evolution as a series of phases analogous to the developmental stages of an individual. First there was the embryonic phase, which was represented, for example, by *Pithecanthropus* and *Sinanthropus.* This was followed by the infantile or Neandertal phase. And the adult phase was represented by brainy and socialized modern "man."

Given the analogy of human evolution with human development, the logical conclusion, according to Weidenreich, was that there should have been early fossil representatives in the same geographic regions where today groups of humans are found. This picture was seemingly borne out in the near-recent fossil record of living humans. Fossil specimens eminently relatable to the groups now living in various geographic regions had been found in Java (remember the Wadjak skull Dubois had gone to see), Australia, Asia (the younger specimens from the upper cave deposits of Zhoukoudien), Africa, and eastern and western Europe (such as Cro-Magnon). The Neandertal phase had fossil representatives in Europe and the Near East as well as supposedly in Africa (with a skull from Broken Hill, a site in what was then called Rhodesia and is now Zambia). The Near East was sufficiently close to Asia for Weidenreich to feel that Asia was represented in the sequence. The earliest phase, although known only from Asian specimens, also would have had its representatives in the other major areas of the Old World, Africa, and Europe. It was therefore only a matter of time before these fossils would be found.

The apparent discrepancy in the Old World-wide distribution of hominids through time and space was not, however, a problem for Weidenreich. "That these voids in the distribution of the fossil hominids are chiefly due to incomplete exploration is proved," he declared, "by the recent discoveries which brought missing types to light from regions where they were not known before or were even not expected to be found." And, in any case, Weidenreich could find features between living human groups and fossils from the same continents that seemed to demonstrate beyond reproach that, for each human group, a line of evolutionary continuity had to have been in existence from the fossil equivalent of the embryonic phase.

From what, by any present-day standards, seems like the flimsiest of bases, Weidenreich nonetheless was convinced that the fossil record really was good enough to make detailed claims about human evolution. "All this points," he concluded, "to an already world-wide distribution of early phases which transmuted into more advanced types by vertical differentiation, while they split into geographical groups by horizontal differentiation." Furthermore, it seemed perfectly clear to him that "the human stem produced more advanced types under favorable circumstances at a certain period and in one place on earth, while it remained stationary in another." According to Weidenreich, examples of this were readily available; for instance, it could be seen in the fact that "the Vedda [the original inhabitants of Sri Lanka] and the Australian bushman are less advanced human forms than the white man; that is, they have preserved more of their simian stigmata."

But what kind of human evolution is this? Weidenreich's work is not just a treatise on the origin of modern *Homo sapiens*—all of them, all of us. It is an argument that bestows an antiquity to the development of modern human races by grounding it in the fossil record. As such, the earliest fossil hominids—whether known or only hypothesized—were the geographic ancestors of the modern "races" of humans. As Weidenreich put it, because "human forms preceding those of modern man were distributed over the entire Old World and differed typically from each other, just as is true of any present geographical variation . . . it seems that there must have been, not one, but several centers where man has developed." In support of this theory, Weidenreich offered a few comparative examples. One such example, and one that continues to be cited today in certain paleoanthropological quarters, is a link between *Pithecanthropus* and *Homo soloensis* and Australian Aborigines. The two fossil forms have elongate, low, and posteriorly sloping foreheads. They also have large brow ridges. And the occasional male Aborigine can be found with an elongate, low, and posteriorly sloping brow ridge and larger-than-usual brow ridges. Ergo, there is a continuum.

The problem Weidenreich had to face in discussing the origin of modern "races" was "the tendency of man to interbreed without any regard to existing racial differences." Thus, he was compelled to admit, "the chance to meet 'pure' races—provided they should be recognizable—diminishes correspondingly." Because he could see for himself that geography did not isolate human populations from one another, Weidenreich was not convinced by the popular notion that geographical isolation had been the basis of "racial" differentiation among modern human populations in the first place. But he was not willing, as were some of his anthropological colleagues, to deny the existence of human "races" even if "the number of individuals who conform to established racial schemes in all proclaimed characteristics is minimal." Confronted by this dilemma, Weidenreich, a confirmed paleontologist, felt that "by tracing back the really characteristic features to fossil forms where they first become recognizable, we will finally gather more knowledge of the history of, and relationship between, the races of today than can ever be inferred from vague descriptions handed down in folk tales and sagas."

Carlton Coon and the Origin of Races

By the late 1940s and on into the 1950s, the paleoanthropological picture began to change in a number of ways. For example, as Great Britain's foremost comparative primate anatomist and paleoanthropologist, Sir Wilfrid Le Gros Clark's pronouncement on *Australopithecus* in 1947 validated the recognition of these South African specimens as hominids. The 1940s also had witnessed ground-breaking symposia during which, for the first time, geneticists, paleontologists, and neontologists (scientists who study recent organisms) met to try to learn each other's evolutionary language. These meetings gave rise to what was called the "synthetic theory of evolution." The "synthesis" was really an attempt to break down barriers between different disciplines in the hope of advancing our understanding of the processes of evolution and the ways in which we might go about trying to unravel its mysteries. One consequence of the synthesis was an expansion away from the narrow-minded and historically limited notions of "neo-Darwinism." As is clear from the writings of those involved, there was not, or not necessarily, a single theory of process. And the "synthesis" is still ongoing.

New ways of looking at the fossil record spilled over into paleoanthropology in various profound ways. As one consequence, the multiplicity of genus and species names were lumped into just two genera—*Australopithecus* and *Homo*—and only a handful of species. Harvard evolutionary biologist Ernst Mayr performed this taxonomic surgery in 1950. Mayr also speculated that there had been only one hominid species in existence at any given point in time. For Mayr and others, human evolutionary history was perceived of as a straight-line event and not as being similar to the evolutionary histories of other animals—replete with bursts of diversification, contemporaneity of multiple species, and episodes of extinction.

Within the genus *Homo*, Mayr recognized only two species, *erectus* and *sapiens*. Neandertals and an assortment of other fossils were placed in *Homo sapiens*. *Pithecanthropus*, *Sinanthropus*, the Heidelberg mandible, and various other fossils were subsumed in *erectus*. *Homo erectus* gave rise to *Homo sapiens*. When, during the 1950s, "Piltdown Man" was exposed as a fraud, the presumed continuum of evolution within the genus *Homo* seemed even more probable. Although the Victorian racism that had been kept alive in the early twentieth century was eliminated from the paleoanthropological literature of the 1950s, the evolutionary scheme stayed essentially the same. Races of people could now be discussed with the same dispassionate objectivity that would be used to refer to regional variants of lizards or squirrels.

Out of this period of revelation and intellectual discovery emerged a new way of thinking about human diversity. If there were only two species of *Homo*, how could the huge amount of variation created by the diversity of morphologies that were now lumped into *Homo sapiens* be explained? The explanation offered in the 1950s, and often even today, was couched in terms of adaptation and natural selection. Neandertals were variants of *Homo sapiens* who came to look the way they did—for instance, in having thick bone, large nasal openings, huge molar pulp cavities—because they had become adapted to the cold climate of the glaciation. Of course, if we accept the premise that such a morphologically distinct hominid as Neandertal is nothing but a variant of another group of morphologically distinct hominids—that is, of anatomically modern humans—then we have to try to come up with some explanation for the striking differences between the two.

Notions of adaptation and natural selection also were applied to the question of the origin of modern human races. The prominent figure in this endeavor was the American physical anthropologist Carlton S. Coon, who presented his ideas on human evolution and the evolution of human racial diversity to scientific as well as to popular audiences. In the early 1960s Coon dusted off Weidenreich's theory of multiregional origins of modern human "races" and reformatted it. "The separation of man into races," Coon proclaimed, "is the work of geography, acting in the guise of natural selection shaping genetically plastic living material."

Coon's scenario posited that racial differentiation actually began when an early, primitive, *Australopithecus*-like hominid spread throughout Africa and Eurasia. By half a million years ago at the very latest, *Homo erectus* was not only on the scene, but the species already had become differentiated into five geographical races. *Homo erectus* in Java gave rise to the group of modern humans Coon identified as the Australoids (actually, Javanese *Homo erectus* was supposed to have been the first Australoid). Modern Australoids were the Australian Aborigines, the Papuans of New Guinea, the Melanesians, the Negrito dwarfs from the Philippines to the Andaman Islands, and some groups living in India. According to Coon, *Homo erectus* in China was already Mongoloid and was eventually transformed into the modern Mongoloids of eastern Asia, the Polynesians, the Inuits and Aleuts, and the American Indians. Caucasoids originated in western Asia and, by about 250,000 years ago, had evolved into *Homo sapiens*. Caucasoid descendants include Europeans, whites of the Middle East, the majority of India's people, and perhaps the Ainu of northern Japan. The Capoids originated in North Africa but were forced south, giving rise to Bushmen and Hottentots. Coon coined the term *Congoid* to refer to "the modern Negroes and Pygmies." According to Coon, "*Homo erectus* . . . evolved into *Homo sapiens* . . . not once but five times, as each subspecies or race living in its own territory passed a critical threshold from a more brutal to a more sapient state."

Coon readily admitted that his "thesis [was] at variance with the dogmas of 1962, which insist on a single, relatively recent emergence of man." The dominant theory for the origin of human races was that modern *Homo sapiens* had originated only once—that all modern humans share a common ancestor that was itself anatomically modern. From this ancestor, modern humans spread throughout the world, differentiating some 30,000 years ago into modern races. But, Coon countered, if in other animals, "races of a single species can evolve in concert," then why not in *Homo sapiens*?

Coon just could not accept a single-origin explanation for the diversity of modern human populations. "If this were true," he asked, "how does it happen that some peoples, like the Tasmanians and many of the Australian aborigines, were still living during the nineteenth century in a manner comparable to that of the Europeans of over 100,000 years ago?" Surely, he continued, "this would have entailed some major cultural backsliding which the archaeological record does not show. . . . To me there was something pat, dogmatic, and wrong about the anti-Weidenreich point of view."

But if modern races can trace their origins well back in time, to *Homo erectus*, how is it that they did not become increasingly different from one another as time went on? What kept these races together as the same species?

Coon suggested that the races had never really been genetically separate from one another. He had to make this point, because systematists believed genetic separation to be the major criterion by which different species could be delineated from one another. One of the ways in which gene flow could be maintained between racial groups, Coon speculated, was by men engaging in wife-trading or by their capturing wives from other groups. As he proffered, whereas men in general "remain faithful to their own races, at least if their own women are with them . . . men traveling alone have no such compunctions."

Transforming Homo erectus *into* Homo sapiens

Although the racial component of Coon's multiregional theory of modern human origins set him apart from his peers, he was only one of many who subscribed to the overall picture of human evolution that *Homo sapiens* had evolved from *Homo erectus*. He also was not alone in trying to explain the contradictions that this evolutionary formulation generated.

Justification of this supposed unilineal transformation, from *Homo erectus* to *Homo sapiens*, was sought in two different arenas. The differential displacement of natural selection by culture was one increasingly popular form of speculation. Just as natural selection was supposed to act on other organisms in order to fine-tune each species for a specific ecological niche, so culture was to have become the hominid ecological niche. Thus, by dint of making "culture" synonymous with "ecological niche," it was impossible to allow for the existence at any point in time of more than one hominid species. The evolutionary—the morphological—transformations that must have occurred during later human evolution resulted solely and directly from the development of culture. Hominids had developed their own adaptive mechanism for survival, one that removed them from the grasp of nature and the whims of the evolutionary processes that uncompromisingly took their toll on all other forms of life.

The second arena in which the unilineal transformation from *Homo erectus* to *Homo sapiens* gained supposed validation was more traditionally based on the chronological sequence of fossil remains and stone tools. Morphological transitions from *Homo erectus* to and within *Homo sapiens*, and then within *sapiens*, were seemingly discovered not often, but frequently enough that the belief in the transformation could be maintained. Different approaches to dating paleontological and archeological sites helped. For example, the Mount Carmel cave site, Tabūn, which McCown and Keith thought was contemporaneous with the nearby cave of Skhūl, was subsequently thought to be the older of the two caves, by almost 20,000 years. The Neandertal-like hominid of Tabūn, therefore, preceded the quite modern-looking hominid of Skhūl. Surely this was evidence of transition.

Farther west, in Europe, various sites—such as Steinheim in Germany, Fontéchevade in France, and Swanscombe in England— came, through chronological manipulation, to fill the "gap" between *erectus* and later *sapiens*. These specimens made "good" intermediates, not just because they seemed to fit into the sequence chronologically but because they did not represent a uniform morphological assemblage. Taken together, as if they constituted a real sample, a mixture of those morphologies that would be expected in a transitional stage could be found.

The Steinheim skull was small, and its sloping forehead, long and low brain case, large brow ridges, huge nasal opening, and massive (for its size) upper jaw definitely fit the image of a primitive and archaic transitional form, from which Neandertal could have evolved. The larger, incomplete brain cases from Fontéchevade and Swanscombe appeared to be more modern *sapiens*-like, at least in having larger, less demonstrably squat crania. The Fontéchevade cranium also seemed to lack the large, Neandertal type of brow ridges. Thus it appeared that *Homo sapiens,* in its various guises and versions, really had been around for a long time.

But the apparent fact that modern *sapiens*-like specimens predated the earliest known appearance of definitive Neandertal was bothersome to some paleoanthropologists, who continued to believe that the classic type of Neandertal, such as was found at La Chapelle, had not become transformed into modern-looking *Homo sapiens.* Of course, each side of the argument was prey to the disparaging barbs of the other. Each side thought that the missing parts of the partial crania from Fontéchevade and Swanscombe would prove its case.

Would the Swanscombe forehead be vertical or sloping? Because the occipital bone and the left parietal bone, which forms one-half of the middle upper portion of the skull cap, had been found at different times, and a few yards away from one another, perhaps more bones could be found. Perhaps the frontal bone, which constitutes the forehead and the brow ridge region, would be found. Or the face. Had the lower face of the Swanscombe hominid been "puffy," as in Neandertals, or indented at the root of the cheekbone, as in modern-looking humans? Perhaps the lower jaw would be discovered. Was it chinless or chinned? What about the limb bones? Were they thick-walled and thickened at their ends or thin-boned and lightly built?

Serious attempts to find more, especially of the Swanscombe skull, were made—even as recently as 1970. I know. I was there.

∎

STILL COPING WITH NEANDERTALS:

ARE THEY ONE OF US, OR NOT?

Enter Swanscombe

The quiet town of Swanscombe lies near the Thames River, not quite two hours by train east of London. Its claim to paleoanthropological fame came in the 1930s, when dentist and amateur fossil hunter and archeologist Alvan T. Marston made a series of discoveries that included some stone tools, the bones of various extinct animals, and two cranial bones from something that was definitely humanlike. These two bones—the occipital and the left parietal bones—represented, respectively, the back and most of the top and upper part of the left side of an individual's brain case. Although they were found on different occasions and separated from one another by a few yards, these two bones had to have been from the same individual because they fit together so perfectly. Marston compared his specimen to the Piltdown skull and concluded that, because it was apparently the more ancient and primitive of the two, his "Swanscombe skull is to be regarded definitely as a precursor of the Piltdown type." Although this partial cranium was thought to have been a woman's, the specimen was nonetheless often referred to as Swanscombe "man."

A few years later Sir Wilfrid Le Gros Clark was enlisted to head a committee—the Swanscombe Committee—whose mission was to study the Swanscombe occipital and left parietal in the context of a broader comparison with European fossil material. The Swanscombe cranial bones were thick, almost as thick as some of the Neandertal remains from mainland Europe. But the Swanscombe cranium had more height to it; it was more elevated, more highly vaulted than was typical of European Neandertals, whose crania were typically lower. In reconstructed outline, the Swanscombe skull looked more like a slightly peaked roof, whereas the classic Neandertal skull was more bologna shaped. The Swanscombe occipital bone was not markedly distended as it is in many European Neandertals, but only modestly swollen. And, given how the Swanscombe skull had been reconstructed, its greatest width, from side to side, was measured relatively high up—not quite as high up along the side of the skull as in modern humans, but not as far down on the skull as in European Neandertals.

Although the comparisons more consistently seemed to show Swanscombe as being somewhat *sapiens-* rather than Neandertal-like, the committee was most impressed by the moderate position of its greatest cranial width in conjunction with the thickness of the cranial bone. As a result, the general consensus among the committee members was that the Swanscombe skull compared well with the Steinheim skull—well enough, as a matter of fact, that their frontal bones and facial skeletons also must have been similar and somewhat Neandertal-like. Later, in the 1950s, Henri Victor Vallois, Marcellin Boule's student and successor at the Museum of Natural History in Paris, would argue that the *sapiens*-like features of Swanscombe should be weighed more heavily in any assessment of the specimen's evolutionary relationship to other hominids.

Historically, the Swanscombe skull was important for various reasons, not the least of which was that it had been found in British soil. One of the most crucial "features" of this specimen, however, had nothing directly to do with its morphology or its potential evolutionary relationships (as I, at least, would go about trying to resolve them). The

Swanscombe individual's importance also was determined by the particular evolutionary scheme that was brought to bear on the interpretation of its apparent mixture of morphologies. Could Neandertals have interbred with modern-looking humans?

Based on stratigraphy, geology, and associated animal remains, the Swanscombe skull was supposed to be quite old—older, at least, than the last glacial period, which was when most Neandertals were thought to have existed. The Swanscombe individual had apparently lived during the interglacial period that preceded the glacial appearance of European Neandertals. (Modern dating techniques indicate that Swanscombe is about 225,000 years old.) Given such antiquity, finding out if the Swanscombe individual was more Neandertal-like than it was modern human–like, or vice versa, was of paramount importance.

The Swanscombe individual also was set apart by its stone tools. Swanscombers manufactured flakes struck from prepared blocks—as did the manufacturers of the Mousterian tool kit—but the tool kits were not quite the same. The Swanscombe flakes and technique were a bit odder and just did not fit into the more typical European design. This kind of stone tool kit had been found earlier at another site, not too far away, called Clacton-on-Sea. Clacton-on-Sea was thus the type site, and this unusual stone tool assemblage was identified as the Clactonian. (Today this type of tool industry is categorized as a variant of what in Europe is called the Acheulean, a hand-axe–dominated tool industry that preceded and, in some areas, was also contemporaneous with the Mousterian.)

Because in all ways the Swanscombe individual seemed to represent such a distinct and important element in human evolutionary formulations, finding more of this kind of hominid was imperative. It was of particular importance to those who thought that the known parts of the skull were not Neandertal-like. Until more pieces were discovered, these paleoanthropologists could only speculate that the Swanscombe skull had had a modern human-looking face and forehead.

One of these speculators was Montagu F. Ashley Montagu, an anatomist and physical anthropologist who had left England for professorial work in the United States. After stints at New York University in Manhattan, Hahnemann Medical College in Philadelphia, and Rutgers

University in New Jersey, Montagu retired to Princeton. He was a great organizer and editor of books of collected essays on aspects of human cultural and biological evolution and popularized physical anthropology and paleoanthropology as a frequent guest on television talk shows.

A little-known fact about Montagu is that he had actually done some fieldwork at Swanscombe. But his search went unrewarded. No frontal bone. No lower facial skeleton. Nothing. Similar efforts in 1955 by the British archeologist John Wymer were not rewarded with the discovery of the coveted frontal bone or lower facial skeleton, either. However, Wymer did find a right parietal bone—which articulated perfectly with the left parietal and occipital bones that Marston had found twenty years earlier. The back and top of the Swanscombe skull were now complete. But this did not seem to clarify things much. Nevertheless, Montagu adamantly maintained in 1962 that "as for Swanscombe, the morphology of the three known bones is very much more compatible with a *sapiens* face than with a non-*sapiens*." Because of the supposed *sapiens*-ness of the Swanscombe individual, and also because of its presumed antiquity, Montagu concluded that "were it not for the presence of such 'fragments' as Swanscombe . . . I should have thought there could be no doubt of the Neanderthaloid ancestry of *Homo sapiens*."

The last archeological and paleontological stab at Swanscombe was spearheaded by the professor of prehistoric archaeology at the prestigious Institute of Archaeology of the University of London, John D'Arthur Waechter. During the summer months of 1968 through 1971, Waechter led a series of ragtag, motley crews in the search for those all-important pieces of the Swanscombe skull. But, again, in the end, he found nothing.

The 1970 Excavation Season at Swanscombe

While I was still a graduate student, Ralph Solecki, of Shanidar fame, wrote to his longtime friend Waechter to inquire if I could join the excavations of Swanscombe. Because I was going to be working as the osteologist on the excavations at Tell Hesi, Israel, during the summer of 1970, I wrote to Waechter and asked if I could go to Swanscombe for the month of August, after the operations at Tell Hesi shut down. Waechter generously agreed. I had never been out of the United States before, and now I was committed to working on excavations in Israel and England.

Being a novice, I sought the advice of seasoned archeologists. Getting outfitted was complicated, because I was going to work in two different regions, where the climate and working conditions in general were very different. Nevertheless, I was told, I would have to wear the same garb and gear in each place. So, off I went to the army-navy stores to buy all sorts of work shirts and pants, and a clunky, hard-toed, thick-soled, laced-up-the-calf pair of thick leather paratrooper boots that would protect me from lacerating my feet on potentially life-threatening objects and, at the same time, form a protective barrier against all poisonous desert snakes that could not raise themselves more than a foot off the ground. By the time I was outfitted, I could have survived any assault, as long as I didn't have to move to get away from it.

After two months in the heat of the northern fringe of the Negev Desert, I left to work at Swanscombe. I arrived at Gatwick Airport, took the train into central London and then the underground to Holland Park, where I was going to stay for a few days with friends, Jonathan and Jill White. I was supposed to go to Swanscombe that weekend to meet Waechter and to make final arrangements for joining the crew; Jonathan volunteered to drive me out to the site. When we got to the town of Swanscombe, we were given directions that took us through a deserted area that was one big, smoldering garbage dump. On top of one pile of discards we spied a set of chairs. They had been painted too often and in ugly colors but were otherwise in perfect condition.

We finally reached the edge of a small, wooded and thickly overgrown area that separated the dump site from the excavation site. A small camp—made up of small tents, two camper-trailers, a modest shack, and one dripping spiggot sticking out of the ground in the middle of the encampment—had been set up near the edge of the actual excavations. The overgrown thicket extended to the base of a steep palisade, on the top of which Jonathan and I could see a row of houses.

We were down on a terrace, one of the terrace levels cut by the Thames River during its long life. Half of the town of Swanscombe was down on our level. The other half was on the top of the palisade.

Everyone was gone for the weekend. I left a note that I'd be returning on Monday, and Jonathan and I returned to London, picking up the discarded chairs along the way. (When I visited the Whites the following year, they had moved into a larger house, and the refinished Swanscombe chairs were the centerpiece of their dining room.)

I returned by train to Swanscombe on Monday and finally met Waechter. He was tall and imposing, even with his slight paunch. He was balding but sported a mustache that complemented his thick, wiry eyebrows. His brow was deeply wrinkled. His chapped hands were large and always slightly red, except for the adjacent patches of skin on his right index and middle fingers, which were stained brownish yellow from a long history of cigarette smoking. The middle area of his mustache was stained the same brownish yellow, which didn't quite go with the ruddy color of the hair. Waechter comported himself with the authority of the born aristocrat—he was easily serious, stern, professorial, and jocular.

The way I was treated by Waechter's crew, I might have been the rescuer of a shipwrecked group that had been stranded on a desert island for months. I quickly learned that this was a typical welcome to any new person who would share the physical labor.

At Tell Hesi, my tools consisted of a trowel, a tablespoon, a teaspoon, some dental picks, and various brushes, and the earth I dug through was soft and sandy. We also used these tools at Swanscombe, but, more often than not, there was shovel duty. The earth was thick and moist, composed of compacted silts and clays. The weather was gray and damp almost every day, and the soil never dried out. There also were layers of gravel. Heavy gravel, which had been pushed ahead of the advancing glacial ice sheet and left behind when it retreated. We all had to take shifts moving tons of gravel out of the way of the excavation. To do so, two of us at a time had to heave shovelfuls of coal-size gravels *up,* some ten or twelve feet, to a higher level on which an out-of-date but functional conveyor belt was anchored.

My first day at Swanscombe consisted largely of shoveling gravel. By

dusk I was covered with mud and dirt, every muscle, tendon, and joint
was sore, and I was very cold and hungry. Whatever we had for dinner,
which was prepared by one of the crew over a burner in the shack, was
barely distinguishable from the layer of unremovable stuff that formed
a thick lining on the inside of the camp's pot.

The crew working at Swanscombe was made up of students. Some
were studying at the Institute of Archaeology. The woman who was the
conservator—she would use preservatives or special wrappings to protect the items that were found—was from Denmark. Her nickname was
Mus, which, although pronounced "Moose," is actually the genus name
of the mouse and had been bestowed upon her in reference to her
diminutive size. There was a Malaysian student, Pisit (rhymes with
cheese-it). About fifteen years ago I saw a *Time* magazine article about
an important Bronze Age site Pisit had found in the jungles of his
homeland. There were also a few not-so-serious types. But one crew
member, Chris Stringer, has become one of the world's experts on
Neandertals and is right in the thick of all the current debate. Chris has
been at the Natural History Museum in London now for years and is
head of the newly formed Human Origins Group.

Although we continued Waechter's streak of not finding more of the
Swanscombe skull, we did do some interesting archeology. We found
various skeletal parts of now-extinct mammals, such as the antler of a
large deer, something like the red deer that now inhabits parts of
Europe. We also found evidence of mammals that would no longer be
able to survive in England, much less northern Europe. One particularly spectacular specimen was the complete skull of an extinct species
of rhinoceros. In order to get it out of the ground in one piece, we left
it in place while we excavated a small moat down and around it. When
we got down far enough that there was a good layer of earth supporting
the skull, we dug in a bit under the whole thing. Our moat now went
down and partially under the skull and its earthen pedestal. We didn't
go too far in, though, for fear of having the heavy and awkward mass
topple to one side or having the earthen support crumble underneath.

Mus then arrived with her materials and canisters of chemicals. She
started soaking plaster-of-Paris–laden gauze bandages in water, and we
began wrapping the skull and its earthen base. A few layers later we

had solidified the whole mass in a plaster jacket. Then Mus took two different cans of stinky, viscous liquid and dumped them into a large bucket. Immediately the concoction began to bubble and foam and expand uncontrollably. We had been forewarned of the speed with which this chemical reaction would take place and were prepared to start pouring this expanding foam down the moat around our specimen. We filled the moat almost to the top with that batch. A second batch completely filled the moat, with enough left over to cover the top of the plaster cast. Almost as quickly as the concoction had begun to expand, it set up and hardened into a Styrofoam cocoon. We now had to dig another moat around the pedestaled specimen so that we could try to wrest it from the ground in which it had lain for over 200,000 years. With wooden planks as levers and all the muscle power we had, we eventually hauled the rhino skull out of the ground and onto a low cart. We last saw this huge Styrofoam pod sitting in a pile of soft material in a crate in the van that came to take it to the Natural History Museum in London.

Presumably, at least some of the animals' bones we were finding represented the spoils of hunting. And, presumably, there had been more than one Swanscombe individual living and hunting, and dying, around the site. In fact, the area we were digging seemed to be an ancient campsite. Careful excavation revealed a natural slope to the terrain, a slope that went down to what had been the shallow banks of the Thames River, before the river assumed its current position. Spread out along the slope were various chunks of flintlike material. Some of these pieces were bladelike, others were smaller chips. Some of these chips may have been waste products of the process of stone toolmaking. Other chips, however, may have been blanks for small scraping, gouging, or boring implements. We also found what remained of the original block—the core—from which all these flakes of different thicknesses and sizes had been struck. After we isolated and pedestaled all the pieces, and recorded their positions along the slope of the old bank of the Thames, we collected them and tried to put them back in their original positions, as they were before they were struck from the core. It was like doing a strange jigsaw puzzle. Eventually we got it. All of the pieces we had found were back in their original positions. By undoing the jigsaw puzzle, we could then reconstruct the order in which the flakes had been struck off and the techniques used to do it. It was obvious, however, that we had not recovered the entire core. The useless outer layer that covers these stone nodules—the cortex—was not found, nor was a whole set of flakes, taken off after the core was removed, that must have been used and discarded elsewhere.

Whatever we might think about the level of sophistication of our modern technology, it was overwhelming and awe-inspiring to hold that reconstructed core and peel off the flakes, one by one, in the order in which they had been struck off more than 200,000 years ago by some master flintknapper. And it was no less amazing to imagine how this Swanscombe individual had to have envisioned the whole process, thinking steps ahead of the flake that was being struck at any given moment—because, in this particular process of flintknapping, the outer side of a flake and its shape is modeled by the flakes that have been removed previously.

But we didn't find any more of the Swanscombe skull. And neither did Waechter the following year, which was the last season he dug at Swanscombe.

"Archaic" Homo sapiens *and the Reemergence of the Multiregional Model*

By the mid-1970s various specimens had been discovered that were similar in age to the Steinheim and Swanscombe specimens. This morphological grab bag of specimens—including Steinheim and Swanscombe—was referred to collectively as "archaic" Homo sapiens. Included in this temporal assemblage were a mandible and the front part of a skull from a site in France called Arago. The facial skeleton, brow ridges, and jaws of the Arago hominid were remarkably large. A second specimen, from the site of Petralona in northeastern Greece, was a mineral-encrusted skull. The Petralona skull in general and the face and upper jaw in particular were huge. This skull and the Arago specimen resemble one another much more than either does the smaller Steinheim skull or any classic Neandertal.

Even more striking than the massiveness and breadth of their facial skeletons was the fact that the brow ridges of the Arago and Petralona specimens, although reminiscent of *Homo erectus* and Neandertal because of their massiveness, were distinctly different in their configuration from either of the latter hominids. To be sure, the brow ridges of the Arago and Petralona specimens followed the contour of the upper margin of the orbits and were continuous across the midline—as in Neandertals, not *Homo erectus*. But the brow ridge of a Neandertal is distinct in its own right in that it is fairly uniform in height and thickness from one side of the face to the other. In the Arago and Petralona crania, on the other hand, the brow ridge is thickest near the midpoint of the upper margin of the orbit and thins most noticeably toward the orbit's outer edge. A Neandertal's brow ridge is smoothly rounded throughout its length; it flows into the base of the forehead without a discernible break. In the Arago and Petralona crania, the front surface of the brow ridge is essentially flat; as such, it bears a distinctly angular upper border. In facial and brow ridge morphology, and also in general massiveness of features, the Arago specimen, and especially the Petralona skull, are more similar to two crania from African deposits than either is to a Neandertal.

One of these skulls had been found in the early 1920s in Zambia (then Rhodesia), at a site called Broken Hill. This specimen, which is now referred to as the Kabwe skull, had given paleoanthropologists problems. Some who studied it were impressed by its apparent *Homo erectus*–like features. Others saw more Neandertal-like features in it. And yet other paleoanthropologists were overwhelmed by the skull's seemingly modern human attributes. Another apparent problem—a major obstacle to many, in fact—was that the specimen had been found during mining operations and could not be associated firmly with a date that would confirm its antiquity. Yet the Kabwe and Petralona skulls in particular do share real uniquenesses in various cranial features, such as the morphology of the brow ridge.

Equally real is the presence of the same kinds of uniquenesses in a partial skull dating back 200,000 or so years that was discovered in the late 1970s by a team led by John Kalb, Glenn Conroy, and Cliff Jolly. The specimen was found in the general vicinity of where Don Johanson and his colleagues had earlier found the specimen nicknamed Lucy. This area of Ethiopia, called the Afar Triangle or Depression, encompasses paleontological and geological exposures of various ages. The fossil hominid–bearing deposits span the period from approximately 4.5 million to about 200,000 years before the present (B.P.). The skull, perhaps of a male, that Kalb and crew found was from the uppermost of a series of geological deposits referred to as the Bodo Beds. While often touted as an archaic *Homo sapiens*, or something close to it, the resemblances—from the general massiveness of facial features to the details of the brow ridges—would associate the Bodo skull with the specimens from Kabwe and Petralona, as well as perhaps Arago. (As I discussed in chapter 1, it was on the Bodo skull that Tim White found scratch marks that could have resulted from the intentional defleshing of this individual by his companions in their preparation of the body for burial.)

But in spite of the morphological inconsistencies that were created by so doing, the Steinheim, Swanscombe, Arago, Petralona, Bodo, and Kabwe specimens were lumped together as a group of "archaic" *Homo sapiens* that, by virtue of the variation they reflected, could be seen as representing an intermediate stage between *Homo erectus* and later *Homo sapiens*.

By the mid-1970s any residual racial connotations had been expunged from Weidenreich and Coon's multiregional model of human evolution, and the theory came to claim if not a large following, at least a vocal one. According to Sherwood Washburn, professor of physical anthropology at the University of California, Berkeley, and subsequently C. Loring Brace, professor of physical anthropology at the University of Michigan, the driving force in the postulated evolutionary transition from *Homo erectus* into *Homo sapiens* was culture. The cultural-force torchbearer of the 1970s was, and still is, Milford Wolpoff, a professor of physical anthropology at the University of Michigan.

Wolpoff, Thorne, and the Multiregional Model of Modern Human Origins

The general idea of culture as driving human evolution, as Wolpoff summarized it in 1980, is that "once hominids embarked upon the evolutionary path of dependence on culture for survival, there is a certain inevitability to the course of human evolution." Basically, there was "continued feedback between culture and technology on the one hand and human morphology on the other." The difference between cultural change and morphological change, according to Wolpoff, is that the former "is additive and cumulative," whereas the latter "depends on the forces of evolution acting on existing gene pools."

Culture, especially in the form of developing technology, is supposed to be one of the forces, presumably one of the *evolutionary* forces, that changed the face—literally—of *Homo sapiens*. As Brace and Wolpoff have maintained, advances in tool technology led to a reduction of the size of the teeth (particularly of the anterior teeth) because tools supposedly took over the function of teeth. In turn, reduction in tooth size led to the reduction of the face and even the cranium. For Wolpoff, the impetus for all of these changes occurred during the Middle Paleolithic with the development of such tool technologies as the Mousterian. This new technology was based on flakes being struck from a prepared block or core. Wolpoff offers functional reasons for how such a sequence of morphological changes could have been initiated and maintained.

With Middle Paleolithic tools doing all sorts of tasks supposedly more efficiently than ever before, so the argument goes, the jaws and teeth would not have to work as hard, especially as a vise to hold on to and pull items that were being worked on. With the jaws and teeth ceasing their roles as stress-bearing structures, they were therefore free to reduce in size. Bulk was no longer necessary to absorb the stresses of rigorous activities. A further consequence of the reduction in stress upon the masticatory system was the reduction in size of the brow ridge. An unbuttressed, vertical forehead alone was sufficient to absorb the normal stresses of chewing generated by the anterior teeth. The more forward displacement of the facial skeleton itself was no longer necessary to help in taking up the stress loads. Thus the face receded, losing its puffiness with the shrinking of the maxilla, maxillary sinuses, and cheekbones. With the reduction in facial protrusion and in the size of the upper jaw, the lower jaw had to reduce in size accordingly. As a result, the gap between the back of the last molar and the vertical part of the mandible, which is seen in *Homo erectus* and Neandertal, closed. Changes in the mandible also resulted in the development of a defined chin.

Another consequence of reduction of the face and jaws was a lightening of the overall weight of the skull. With a less heavy head to hold and move around, the neck muscles could become smaller. In turn, smaller neck muscles caused changes in the occipital bone, both in size and of the areas onto which these muscles attached.

The beauty of this model, according to Wolpoff, is that it "is based on the hypothesis that selection would change existing archaic *sapiens* gene pools in the direction necessary to account for the appearance of populations with more modern features" without requiring "new genetic material . . . to account for these changes." The differences between regional populations of modern humans are due in each case to different rates of change from *Homo erectus* to *Homo sapiens*. It's all a matter of frequency. In some populations, such as Australian Aborigines, more *Homo erectus*–type features are supposedly preserved. In certain European groups, more Neandertal features are thought to be retained. Thus regional continuity can be traced back hundreds of thousands of years, back to the variants of *Homo erectus* that had inhabited those general geographic regions.

In the 1980s Wolpoff was joined by Australian paleoanthropologist Alan Thorne in expanding this argument, which has become identified as the "multiregional continuity model of modern human origins." Thorne had already gotten his paleontological feet wet in the late 1960s with the discovery of some of the most important fossil hominids from a site called Kow Swamp, which is located in the northern part of Victoria, Australia. The dating of Kow Swamp is not, however, very precise; some analyses yield a date of at least 13,000 years, while others suggest that the site may be up to 4,000 years younger. Thorne discovered the first Kow Swamp specimen under a layer of dust in the National Museum of Victoria. Eventually the remains of forty additional individuals were excavated from the site. Although there were many interesting aspects to the archeology of these specimens—these were real burials, some with stone tools, animal teeth, and red ocher included, and some individuals had been cremated—it was the morphology of the skulls that seemed to lend credence to the regional continuity model.

The bone of the Kow Swamp skulls was thick and the forehead was very sloping and flat. Five of these skulls also bore brow ridges, but not of the specific kind seen in Neandertals of Europe. The configuration of these brow ridges was apparently more reminiscent of *Homo erectus*, particularly as seen in the Sangiran 17 cranium, which had been discovered in the late 1960s and is the only Javanese specimen of *Homo erectus* in which the face and skull cap are still together. Also in apparent similarity to *Homo erectus*, the occipital region of some of the Kow Swamp skulls was distended and bore a bony strut. Other cranial features, however, such as a deep cavity in which the articulating end of the mandible sits and an enlarged bony process just behind this cavity, where a major muscle of the neck attaches, were morphologically modern human in appearance. Thorne, and also Wolpoff, believe the apparent mixture or, to use a popular term, "mosaic" of features seen among the Kow Swamp specimens is indicative of evolutionary continuity in Australia between *Homo erectus* and modern humans—the sequence was *Homo erectus* → Kow Swamp → modern Aborigine. The occasional male Australian Aborigine who can be found with large brow ridges and sloping forehead seemed to fortify one of the key elements of the model of regional continuity—that traces of primitive or archaic features still can be found among living groups.

But not everyone is convinced of this supposed demonstration of regional continuity in southeast Asia and Oceania. Soon after Alan Thorne's initial publications on the Kow Swamp specimens, alternative explanations, especially of the sloping and flattened forehead, were forthcoming. Perhaps, it was suggested, this cranial configuration was due not to the retention of *Homo erectus* characteristics but to purposeful cranial deformation—the deliberate alteration of head (and thus skull) shape. Culturally motivated, purposeful, artificial cranial deformation is well documented among humans. While on a fellowship a few years ago at the American Museum of Natural History, I came across hundreds of examples of cranial deformation as I rummaged through thousands of skull-size boxes in search of specimens to use in the project I was pursuing.

The Incas and Mayas of the New World preferred long, tapering heads; this shape was probably created for beauty's sake. Indians of the American Southwest often had flattened occipital regions, which resulted from infants' being bound to the swaddling boards on which they were carried. Cranial deformation was also common among the early civilizations of the Mediterranean and Middle East. Archeologists have long known that the Pharaonic Egyptians favored long, tapering heads. Larry Angel, with whom I was involved in "fetusgate," had in one study found that occipital flattening was prevalent about 5,000 years ago among Neolithic (New Stone Age) people from Cyprus. When I was doing osteological research on Cyprus in the early 1970s, I identified additional examples of Neolithic occipital flattening and also found that different cranial shapes were being "manufactured" a couple of thousand years later among Late Bronze Age Cypriote people.

Having now studied different varieties of cranial deformation, I have learned that a few constants seem to go along with each kind of shape. For example, in skulls that have been elongated, the forehead becomes sloped and the frontal bone itself becomes elongated. With the forehead low and sloping, instead of being more vertical, the brow ridge region is emphasized, even in the most gracile of skulls. This might have been the case with the Kow Swamp specimens as well.

Various analyses have indicated that at least some of the Kow Swamp skulls had been deformed. Detailed comparative studies by, for example, Don Brothwell of the Institute of Archaeology and one of England's top human osteologists indicate that this deformation was induced by compressing the head with boards. Various Melanesian groups still practice this form of cranial deformation. This insight, in combination with more recent analyses of the Kow Swamp specimens that demonstrate that they are truly modern morphologically, point to the fact that evolutionary continuity has not been demonstrated—that there is not a succession from *Homo erectus* to the Kow Swamp people to modern Australian Aborigines.

But the search for such a link continued. And, to this end, Alan Thorne discovered another skull that seemed to bear out the regional continuity model of modern human origins.

This specimen, cataloged as WLH (Willandra Lakes Hominid) 50, was found near Lake Mungo, which is in the Willandra Lakes region in western New South Wales. Up to 15,000 years ago, these lakes were filled with fresh water. Now they are dry. The fossil specimen, which is radiant because it became opalized, consists of a faceless skull cap. It may be older than 30,000 years. But Alan has suggested in conversation that the skull may in fact be much older than that.

The robustness of the specimen's bone, brow ridge, and distended occipital region, as well as the degree to which the forehead slopes backward, are unmistakable. In fact, and especially in profile, WLH 50 seems to be a perfect match for some of the skulls from Java that had been found at the site of Ngandong, near the Solo River. These Javanese skulls, now referred to the species *Homo erectus* instead of *Homo soloensis*, may be as old as 200,000 years. Thus, Alan suggests, if there is regional continuity from the past to modern aborigines via WLH 50, it extends back perhaps another 160,000 or 170,000 years, to the Ngandong *Homo erectus*.

Alan brought a set of lifelike casts of some of the Australian hominid fossils to New York City for a new exhibition hall on human evolution that Ian Tattersall is putting together for the American Museum of Natural History. I must admit, the features of these Australian fossil specimens are quite overwhelming. But WLH 50 is remarkable. And it certainly looks convincingly like the museum's casts of the Ngandong skulls to which Ian and I compared it.

But Alan pointed out one peculiarity of the WLH 50 cranium that had been bothering him. The thick bone of this skull cap was not uniformly dense from the outer to the inner surface. Instead, a thick layer of spongy bone was sandwiched between thin layers of dense outer and dense inner bone. Now, this was odd. Typically among mammals, including apes, the bone of the skull cap is composed primarily of dense bone, with little development of a middle spongy layer. Even in modern human crania, in which a middle layer of spongy bone does develop with some consistency, this spongy layer is not thicker than the dense bone of the outer and inner layers—even in the thicker-boned specimens of Australian Aborigines I found in the American Museum's collections. In fact, in those modern human skulls with somewhat thick-boned skull caps, it is the outer and inner layers of dense bone that are relatively thick. The same is true of thick-boned fossil hominids: The thickness is dominated not by spongy bone but by dense, compact, cranial bone.

Could the features—all of them, some of them, or at least the degree to which they are expressed—of the WLH 50 skull cap be due to its unique development of such an expanded middle layer of spongy cranial bone? It doesn't actually matter, I think, because the main point is that WLH 50 is set apart from modern humans and known fossil hominids by the degree to which its spongy layer of cranial bone is expanded. WLH 50 is obviously unique in this regard—which raises an interesting problem of interpretation. WLH 50 could be a descendant of Ngandong *Homo erectus*, which, in the course of its own evolutionary history, became distinctive in developing an expanded spongy layer of cranial bone. However, precisely because WLH 50 is unique at least in this regard, it could *not* have been ancestral to any modern human.

Howells and the Distinctiveness of Neandertal

Even if we don't have a clue about anything else that goes on in evolution, we would still have to agree that an ancestor cannot be more unique or specialized than its descendant. A descendant can develop uniquenesses or specializations not seen in its ancestor—surely that makes sense. But not the other way around. If, however, you choose to use time—chronology—as your guide for determining ancestor-descendant sequences, then whatever configurations you would find in modern humans would have to be interpreted as being more unique or "evolved" than features in an older specimen, such as the 300,000 plus-year-old WLH 50. I, however, subscribe to an increasingly popular philosophy that does not accept at face value that fossil chronologies reflect ancestor-descendant sequences. I believe that the relative relationships of species first must be worked out on the basis of their shared uniquenesses. If it turns out that a particular species is no more unique in any feature than is its closest relative, then, perhaps, that species has retained the ancestral condition. If this species also happens to be a fossil, or is the more ancient of the two species, then perhaps there is a case for an ancestor-descendant sequence. As I see it, a systematist has to go through a lot of comparative analysis before she or he can make a claim for demonstrating ancestry and descent.

Thus I and various colleagues come into conflict with Milford Wolpoff, Alan Thorne, and others who support the model of regional continuity in modern human origins on the very fundamental grounds of how we approach reconstructing evolutionary relationships. How can we debate the matter? We can't. We don't even speak the same language, even though we are all interested in modern human origins and we all study the same specimens. Odd, isn't it? You'd think that the historical whims of fossil discovery, as well as the problems of dating fossils—some will never be datable, others keep having their antiquity revised—would cause some hesitation about relying on fossil sequences as real and representative of things as they really happened. But not everyone bases evolutionary reconstructions on a succession of fossils through time.

The beginnings of an alternative way of thinking about the relationships of Neandertals to modern humans—an alternative to the most recent formulation of a multiregional model of human origins—started to emerge around the early to mid-1970s. One of those spearheading this reinterpretation was William Howells, now professor emeritus at Harvard University. Howells had begun to try to cope with the differences in skull shape between Neandertals, specimens thought of as Neandertal-like or Neandertaloid, and anatomically modern-looking humans by comparing skulls not only morphologically but by way of statistical analyses of cranial measurements, called morphometrics.

Howells's motivations may actually have been in reaction to C.

Loring Brace's 1964 diatribe in the journal *Current Anthropology*, which was, as Howells described it, "a vigorous attack on the whole paleoanthropological establishment, which he [Brace] alleged to be ignorant of evolution and to be blindly opposed to direct descent." Howells, who had been one of those invited to comment on Brace's article, had been among those whom Brace accused of such evolutionary ignorance. To Howells's surprise, Brace's updating of Hrdlička's suggestion of a "Neandertal phase" in human evolution actually gained quite a following. What bothered Howells was that, although Brace may have been "right about weaknesses in the views of many writers, . . . at the same time, his cannonading was so wide-ranging that it concealed his own failure to provide evidence for an opposite view, legitimate as it may be."

Brace believed that a greater reliance on increasingly sophisticated tool technologies had been responsible for a decrease in the size of jaws and teeth from Neandertals to modern-looking humans. As such, Brace had modified Hrdlička's definition of Neandertal ("the man of the Mousterian culture") to read "the man of the Mousterian culture prior to the reduction in form and dimension of the Middle Pleistocene face." (The Pleistocene, which is the geological epoch that preceded the one in which we are living [the Holocene], is now dated from almost 2 million to about 10 thousand years ago. In 1964, however, the Pleistocene was thought to have lasted for only about half a million years; thus the term *Middle Pleistocene* meant something different then and will alter every time the dating is changed.)

For Howells, Brace's definition of Neandertal was unacceptable. "This epitomizes a view," Howells wrote, "which ignores any real examination of the structure of the Neanderthal face (except to refer to it as the supporting architecture for the teeth)." Howells didn't find Wolpoff's development of Brace's ideas any more acceptable, especially when it came to swallowing up even earlier, non–*Homo erectus* specimens into the realm of Neandertal. "The result," Howells wrote concerning this re-redefining of Neandertal, "is a monster, whose morphological character is merely large cranial size and large brows and whose range of variation is simply illegitimate."

From both his morphometric and straightforward morphological comparisons of Neandertals with *Homo erectus* and modern-looking humans, Howells was convinced that there was something special about the Neandertal skull and, in particular, about the Neandertal face and jaws. While recognizing the existence of individual variation in certain features among Neandertals—just as there is variation among modern humans, or any other animal—Howells concluded that there was nonetheless a "characteristic morphology."

The Neandertal skull is certainly big. It is also, as described by Howells, "long, low, and bulging at the sides; and in the so-called 'classic' form of western Europe it protrudes rather pointedly in the rear, although the occipital torus, with the limit of the neck muscles, is placed fairly well down." The low forehead "carries projecting brow ridges of a characteristic kind: fairly even in size all across, arching over each eye, and bending back somewhat at the sides." These brow ridges are invaded by large frontal sinuses that, contrary to the frontal sinuses of modern humans, traverse the midline and do not extend up into the bone of the forehead.

"But," for Howells, "the striking feature of the Neanderthals is the face, which is both high and prominent." The height of the face contributes to the roundness of the bony eye sockets. The prominence of the Neandertal face is due, uniquely, to the jaws and teeth being quite forwardly placed—which is correlated, in part, with the receding Neandertal chin. The Neandertal nose is not only broad but forwardly projecting. The forward position of the face and jaws is manifested in several distinct ways. It makes the distance from between the ear hole to the margin of the front teeth relatively much longer than in other hominids. It is reflected further in the last molars (the third molars, or wisdom teeth) of the lower jaw being typically well in front of, instead of being partially hidden behind, the vertical part of the mandible. And it is emphasized by the gentle backward slope of the cheekbones, which, in other hominids, are otherwise more forward-facing and angular at their sides. "Thus, in Neanderthals," Howells summarized, "the sides of the face, including the outer rims of the eye sockets, give an impression of being pulled back, [which is] actually due to the extraordinary prominence of the middle of the face from top to bottom."

Howells also cited observations others had made previously on Neandertal peculiarities. In particular, he emphasized features of the ear region. If you poke around your skull with your fingers, you will feel a substantial, downwardly tapering, bony projection that is partially hidden by your fleshy ear. You also can feel this projection if you place your fingers at the back edge of the vertical part of your lower jaw. If you still can't find it, turn your head to one side—make it to the left—and follow the thick, cordlike muscle bulging along your neck that goes from the top of the breastbone to just below your right ear. The large bump below your ear, to which this muscle attaches, is the bony projection I'm talking about. In anatomists' terminology it is called the mastoid process. The mastoid process is longer (from front to back) than it is thick (from the skin side of your head to the side that faces the middle of the cranial base). In modern humans, the mastoid process is characteristically well developed and is one of the most downwardly projecting elements of the cranial base. The human mastoid process often extends even lower than the occipital condyles (the bumps on either side of the foramen magnum that articulate with the first vertebra).

Modern humans are the only hominids in which a mastoid process of any significance develops. Apes and monkeys don't have projecting mastoid processes at all. Most Neandertal skulls don't have a prominent mastoid process, which is odd considering how large and bulky their long skulls are.

In modern humans, between each mastoid process and the occipital condyle closest to it lies a crest of bone, called the occipitomastoid crest, which is oriented front to back. In Neandertals, this crest is particularly well developed and delineated on its outer and inner sides by a deep depression. When present in other hominids, this crest is typically less pronounced than in Neandertals and is delineated only on its outer side by a groove. The Neandertal occipitomastoid crest is characteristically so prominent that not only does it project farther down than the neighboring occipital condyle, but it may even project downward as far as, if not farther than, the mastoid process. Furthermore, the Neandertal occipitomastoid crest lies along the suture between the occipital bone and the temporal bone from which the mastoid projects. In modern humans, and hominids in general, this crest typically lies only on the temporal bone.

What does, or did, the peculiarly large Neandertal occipitomastoid crest do? Who knows? A specific muscle does not attach to the structure in modern humans. Rather, in modern humans, a muscle—the posterior belly of the digastric muscle—attaches in the groove or depression that intervenes between the occipitomastoid crest and the mastoid process; the anterior belly of the digastric, which is connected to the posterior belly by a tendon, attaches to the inside of the lower jaw, just behind the chin. The double-bellied digastric muscle, by way of a complex association with other muscles, elevates the hyoid bone (which produces the "Adam's apple") and pharynx and is involved in swallowing. Among nonhuman primates, however—gorillas, for example—one of the neck muscles attaches to the groove. But, regardless of the function of a large occipitomastoid crest, it is certainly a unique feature among primates, one that adds to the distinctiveness of being Neandertal.

In reviewing the rest of the Neandertal skeleton, Howells fleshed out the picture of its uniquenesses. For instance, the Neandertal hand bones are quite unusual. The last segment of a Neandertal's thumb and fingers (the segment on which the nail grows) is relatively much longer than in modern humans; these bones are also longer, broader, and flatter at their ends than in modern humans. The opposite is true of the first segment of a Neandertal's thumb and fingers (the segment closest to the body of the hand): These bones are relatively shorter than they are in modern humans. In Neandertals, the ends of the bones in the palm that articulate with the first segments of thumb and fingers are distinctly broad, broader than in modern humans. Scars on the hand bones where muscles would have attached indicate that Neandertals had quite a powerful grasp. Neandertals would not have been as good at pinching things between the tips of their thumb and index finger as we are, but they would have been proficient at grasping an object between the thumb and the side of the index finger, as you and I would hold a key.

In contrast to modern humans, and other hominids for which the parts are known, the Neandertal pelvis is also uniquely distinctive. Of particular note is that the distance from the hip joint to the pubic symphysis is absolutely and relatively longer in Neandertals than in modern humans. Neandertal pubic bones are also distinctively thin and become platelike toward the pubic symphysis.

Howells added to this list of Neandertal skeletal peculiarities the long-noted breadth and size of the articular ends of long bones and of the talus (the ankle bone that articulates with the lower leg bones). He also made mention of a distinct muscle-related groove pattern on the shoulder blade, or scapula, that is found in only about 20 percent of modern humans but is present in more than 60 percent of Neandertal specimens. This groove occurs along the border of the scapula that angles down and away from the shoulder joint. In modern humans this groove usually lies on the side that faces the rib cage, whereas in many Neandertals it lies on the outer surface, away from the rib cage. Attaching to this groove in modern humans is an arm muscle, the teres minor muscle, whose other end attaches to the back side of the humerus, or upper arm bone. Regardless of where on the anterior border of the scapula the teres minor muscle attaches, it acts to pull the arm into the shoulder joint. When this muscle attaches to the outer surface of the scapula, as it did more frequently in Neandertals, it also acts to turn the arm so that the palm faces outward. Because the major shoulder muscles turn the arm palmside-in when they pull the arm down, a teres minor muscle that attaches to the outer surface of the anterior border of the scapula will tend to counteract the inward rotation of the arm and hand.

How did Howells interpret these odd and unique features of Neandertal—features that others interpreted as being primitive in their scenarios of Neandertals being transformed into modern-looking humans? With regard to the face, for example, Howells argued that, rather than being primitive, "the Neandertal form is in fact a specialization . . . and is not a generalized, all-purpose leftover from the Middle Pleistocene." The same can be said about the postcranial skeleton. "In other words," Howells concluded, "although there obviously were steps in many places between *Homo erectus* and modern man . . . the Neandertals do not represent one of them."

Stringer, Howells, and the Single Origin Model of Modern Humans

By the mid-1970s Chris Stringer had emerged as another voice in the debate over the reality of a "Neandertal phase" in the evolution of modern humans. In his early publications Chris relied more heavily on morphometric analysis than he does now.

When applied to adult crania, Chris's morphometric analysis demonstrated in numbers what our eyes tell us: Neandertal and Neandertal-like specimens are distinct from modern-looking humans. Chris also included data on the skulls of Neandertal children and found that juvenile Neandertals "are closer to modern populations than the fully adult specimens in several of the analyses." As a Neandertal youth matured physically, she or he changed from being cranially similar to us into being cranially Neandertal. This developmental deviation struck Chris as indicating not that Neandertal morphology was primitive or "ancestral" to modern human morphology, but that it was the other way around. Rather, some aspects of modern human cranial morphology are primitive relative to their counterparts in Neandertal cranial morphology.

"Thus it is possible," Chris argued at the International Primatological Society meetings of 1976, "that Neandertals are rather 'advanced' or 'specialised' in a number of respects compared to their precursors, but not necessarily 'advanced' in a direction leading to modern man. . . . In other words, the late Neandertals show derived characteristics, some of which are not shared with anatomically modern populations."

Chris then focused his attention on the modern-looking human skulls that had been discovered at the site of Qafzeh, in Israel. These skulls had emerged in Chris's morphometric analysis as being very similar to one skull in particular from the cave of Skhūl, in northern Israel. And while the Skhūl material was still believed to be younger than the unquestionably Neandertal Tabūn fossils, the Qafzeh crania were apparently older than the Tabūn fossils. If Neandertals were sandwiched chronologically between modern human–looking specimens, then there would seem to be some question of morphological continuity. The nice picture of continuity between Neandertals and modern-looking humans was complicated even further, as Chris pointed out, because the "Qafzeh specimens have a modern vault shape and facial form yet are associated with artefacts which are apparently not of the more advanced Mousterian varieties "known from the near-east."

Chris felt that both his morphometric analysis of crania and the case of the Qafzeh skulls contradicted the "scheme of human evolution leading from Neandertal to modern man advocated by Brace . . . Wolpoff and others." As an alternative scheme, Chris proposed that the ancestral condition from which Neandertals and modern humans had diverged in their independent courses of evolution was represented by a small cranial vault with a large face. Neandertal evolution primarily involved an increase in cranial vault size as well as changes in facial shape. In modern humans, cranial vault shape changed (for instance, in height) and facial size decreased.

But while Chris Stringer and William W. Howells concluded from their analyses that Neandertals were too distinctive in their own right to be just a primitive phase in the evolution of modern-looking humans, they held on to the taxonomic notion that these different hominids represented different versions of *Homo sapiens,* not different species of the genus *Homo.* Thus, although Stringer and Howells posited an origin for modern humans that did not include the Neandertals, their model still sought the origin of *Homo sapiens* in *Homo erectus,* as did the broad multiregional continuity and the more restricted "Neandertal phase" models of modern human origins.

The continuity model postulated that regional variants of modern humans evolved from regional variants of *Homo erectus* more or less in situ, as they currently are found distributed throughout the Old World. At every stage of this continuum, genetic continuity—gene flow—among its diversifying populations held intact the disparate and diverse species *Homo sapiens.*

The Stringer-Howells model sought the origin of modern humans once, from one local ancestor. From this local (but of unspecified location) ancestor, modern humans spread out and diversified. Independently within *Homo sapiens,* Neandertals diverged, becoming more specialized in some bony ways than modern-looking humans, and then they died out.

Neandertals Meet the Young Turks

Given the number of comparisons that have been made over the years between Neandertals and *Homo erectus,* it is odd that no one thought to suggest that, maybe, Neandertals and *Homo erectus* were more closely related to one another than either was to modern-looking humans. But, in 1975, Niles Eldredge and Ian Tattersall, of the American Museum of Natural History in New York City, did. Their article was primarily a theoretical discussion of determining potential evolutionary relationships not on the basis of overall similarity or on the chronological ordering of fossils but on the basis of uniquely shared features.

At the end of the theoretical discussion, Niles and Ian applied this approach to reconstructing the evolutionary relationships of hominids. As such, thick cranial bone, large brow ridges, a sloping forehead, a long, low cranium, and the development of a moderately distended occiput emerged not only as features that are present in Neandertals and *Homo erectus* but as features that are present *only* in Neandertals and *Homo erectus* among the species of *Homo.* In other words, these features are shared uniquely by Neandertals and *Homo erectus.* As they put it:

> those features of the Neandertal skull which have generally been viewed as "primitive" . . . are in fact specializations which align their possessors with *Homo erectus* rather than with modern *Homo sapiens*: the *Gestalt* of the typical Neandertal (or Neandertaloid) skull is that of a *Homo erectus* with an inflated brain. . . . In this view, a worthwhile question to ask of the Neandertals . . . is not so much whether they gave rise to modern man, but whether *Homo erectus* and the Neandertals form a true sister group, or represent iterative offshoots.

The linking of Neandertals with modern humans would always require an explanation of why these two hominids are so different, cranially and postcranially.

In Niles and Ian's diagram of potential evolutionary relationships among hominids, they offered two alternative hypotheses for the relationship of Neandertals. Either Neandertal is the closest known relative of *Homo erectus*, or it is the closest fossil relative of modern humans. In spite of the points they argued about Neandertals being derived relative to modern humans in many skeletal features—some unique to themselves and others uniquely shared with *Homo erectus*—Niles and Ian nevertheless identified Neandertals in their diagram as a subspecies of *Homo sapiens, Homo sapiens neanderthalensis,* and modern humans as *Homo sapiens sapiens.* However, two years later, in a reworking of their article for a more general audience, Ian and Niles (co-authoring in this order now) no longer lumped Neandertals taxonomically with modern humans. Although they did represent modern humans in their diagram as *Homo sapiens sapiens,* with Neandertals identified just as "Neandertaloids," they clearly referred in their text to Neandertals and *Homo sapiens* as distinct entities.

Niles and Ian's articles were not met with much enthusiasm from the establishment, which had come to embrace supporters of the multiregional as well as the single origin model. The bold suggestion that Neandertals were indeed derived or uniquely specialized in various features compared to modern humans was not, by itself, so threatening. William Howells, and then Chris Stringer, had pursued that argument. But the possibility that Neandertals might not be closely related to modern humans at all? Now that was too much. And that Neandertals should not be subsumed in *Homo sapiens?* Unthinkable.

But before we can deal adequately and rigorously with the reconstruction of Neandertal relationships among hominids, we have to go back to square one and try to define on the basis of discrete, unique features just exactly what "Neandertal" means or constitutes. With Neandertals being *Homo sapiens,* and *Homo sapiens* supposedly having evolved from *Homo erectus,* the species *sapiens* had grown to include an overwhelming diversity of morphologies. Because more and more specimens were being shunted into *Homo sapiens*, the amount of variation within the species increased accordingly. This fact made it increasingly difficult to differentiate among Neandertals, Neandertal-like individuals, and modern humans.

The first and, for the longest time, the only attempt to deal with this "problem" came in 1978, in a study by Albert Santa Luca, who was a graduate student at Yale University. As Santa Luca saw it, previous definitions of Neandertal were based on gross morphologies (such as large brow ridge or sloping forehead) that were too general and impressionistic and not diagnostic of, or specific to, being Neandertal. In order to begin to clarify the issue, Santa Luca realized that he first had to try to define characters that would specifically delineate a group we could call "Neandertal." Then and only then could those specimens that had come to be thought of as Neandertal-like be assessed—those specimens that had been swallowed up into *Homo sapiens* because they were from deposits that were supposed to be too young to yield *Homo erectus*, but that morphologically did not seem to be either truly Neandertal or truly modern human.

Santa Luca began his analysis by trying to isolate any character or characters that would be uniquely present in, and therefore distinctive only of, a group he called the "core group of Neandertals." This core group consisted of specimens that all paleoanthropologists accepted as being Neandertal—they all had those telling features of being Neandertal. Among the core group were the skulls from La Chapelle-aux-Saints, Forbes' Quarry (Gibraltar), Tabūn, and Spy. These skulls are blatantly similar to one another.

What, if anything, is truly distinctive about them? Santa Luca was in a good position to undertake a broad comparative analysis because he had already done his dissertation research on *Homo erectus*.

One of the features he isolated as being uniquely Neandertal had been cited previously, by William Howells and others, as being something that was not only peculiar about but was seen only in Neandertals. This feature was the large occipitomastoid crest at the base of the skull. In addition, Santa Luca found two features that hadn't been pointed out before and one that had cropped up in descriptions of some specimens, but which had not been considered significant in previous attempts to define Neandertal.

The first distinctive Neandertal feature Santa Luca discovered was the development of a round protuberance, or bump, on the outer surface of the mastoid process (the downward bony projection behind your ear). We and other hominids have a variably developed crest that runs across the upper extent of the mastoid process. But the mastoid bump was entirely different.

The second Neandertal feature he isolated had to do with the specific configuration of the distended occipital region. In *Homo erectus*, the occipital bone is uniquely extended backward to a blunt edge and can be described as V shaped, with the V lying on its side. Modern humans, if they have anything developed back there, have a more discrete midline projection of the occipital bone, called the external occipital protuberance. On either side of this projection lies a scallop-shape region where muscles attach. Neandertals, however, have a uniformly thick, horizontally oriented strut of bone that runs across and is confined to the occipital bone; this strut of bone is called the occipital torus. In addition, Neandertals develop an elliptical depression, sometimes rimmed by an elevation of bone, that lies above this uniquely configured occipital torus. This depression had been noted in earlier descriptions but had not been considered of any consequence.

Although these isolated, apparently uniquely derived, Neandertal features were few in number, Santa Luca felt that he was on somewhat safe ground because they occurred uniformly within the core group of Neandertals. And, besides, he had to start somewhere.

Santa Luca then turned his attention to an array of specimens that, at one time or another, had been thought of as being either regional variants of Neandertal or in some way Neandertal-like. Did any of these specimens share any of the specifically Neandertal features with the core group? The Kabwe (Broken Hill) skull from Zambia (Rhodesia) didn't. And neither did the Ngandong (Solo) skulls from Java. In fact, as Santa Luca concluded in his dissertation, which focused on the Ngandong skulls, these particular skulls shared with undisputed *Homo erectus* a suite of unique *Homo erectus* features and were, therefore,

Homo erectus. (This is not a trivial point because it was popular in the 1960s and 1970s to refer to the Ngandong specimens as Asian Neandertals [that is, *Homo sapiens*], in part because they had larger cranial capacities [and presumably larger brains] than other Asian *Homo erectus*, and because they were then thought to have been contemporaneous with European Neandertals.) In addition to the Kabwe and Ngandong skulls, the Skhūl and Qafzeh skulls from Israel and other modern-looking skulls from Africa (Omo 2 from Ethiopia and Jebel Irhoud from Morocco) also lacked the diagnostic features of the core group of Neandertals. Thus, Santa Luca concluded, there seemed no evidence of an Old World–wide Neandertal phase in the origin of modern humans.

As for the "archaic *Homo sapiens*" in his sample—the Steinheim and Swanscombe skulls—Santa Luca reaffirmed other paleoanthropologists' observations: These specimens did indeed possess features otherwise diagnostic of the core group of Neandertals. T. Dale Stewart, the Smithsonian physical anthropologist who had studied the Shanidar Neandertals, had, for instance, suggested that the portion of the occipitomastoid crest present on the Swanscombe occipital indicated that its intact crest probably had been as large as those seen in Neandertals. And Franz Weidenreich thought that both the Swanscombe and Steinheim skulls had a horizontally oriented but weak occipital torus; the Swanscombe occipital bone even bore a depression above the occipital torus. More specifically, Santa Luca found that the depression in the Swanscombe occipital was surrounded by a rim of bone and that, although somewhat damaged, the Steinheim occipital region may also have borne a slight depression above the occipital torus. Thus, of those specimens grouped as "archaic" *Homo sapiens*, Santa Luca felt that only the Steinheim and Swanscombe skulls could be described as Neandertal-like.

Santa Luca concluded from this study that, of the various specimens that had been grouped with Neandertals or had been perceived of as being Neandertaloid or "archaic *Homo sapiens*," only Steinheim and Swanscombe bore relevant morphologies—which would lead, at least tentatively, to the suggestion that Steinheim and Swanscombe were either true Neandertals or closely related thereto. Although others before him had reached these conclusions, Santa Luca felt that his results were all the more viable because "the results of a significantly different kind of morphological analysis also support them. . . . Most importantly," he concluded—and I agree—"this study demonstrates that the concept of Neandertal-like fossils must be revised." That statement was published in 1978. I am writing in the 1990s. What's happened in the intervening years?

The Inescapable Distinctiveness of Neandertal

In 1978 French paleoanthropologists began to reemerge in the forefront of the debates on modern human origins. For instance, for his doctoral dissertation, Jean-Jacques Hublin studied the finer details of the Neandertal occipital torus and of the odd depression that lay just above it. From his broad comparative analysis, Jean-Jacques, who is now a faculty member at the Université de Paris, found, for example, that the Neandertal occipital torus is unique not only in being a uniformly thick horizontal strut of bone but in being subdivided longitudinally, so that it looks like a pair of lips.

In 1978 Bernard Vandermeersch, who is on the faculty of the Université de Bordeaux, described what was considered to be the oldest unquestionably Neandertal specimen. Consisting of the back half of the skull, the specimen came from the site of Biache, in northwestern France, and dates to at least 125,000 years ago. A few years after the Biache publication, Vandermeersch came out with a monographic study of the Qafzeh fossil hominid material. There he solidified the reasons why this population as well as that from Skhūl should be considered modern human and not Neandertal. With experience on both sides of the Neandertal–modern human battle line, Vandermeersch was well qualified to address the issue of which morphologies were truly distinctive of each hominid. He found that an area of the Neandertal skull replete with unique morphologies was the general region of the mastoid process (the downward bony projection behind your fleshy ear). Of particular note were features of and near the bony ear region itself.

If you were to stick a pencil into your ear canal, you would eventually crunch into your eardrum. The canal along which your pencil traveled before reaching the eardrum is a flesh-lined bony tube that grows out of the petrosal bone and thus lies along the cranial base. As you might be able to feel with your fingertips, the opening of this bony tube is sandwiched between the mastoid process (behind) and the region where the mandible articulates with your skull (in front). (If you stick your index finger into your ear canal, your thumb will rest on the mastoid process and your middle finger will be over the area of mandibular articulation.) Because the bony tube is part of the ear region, it is referred to in technical jargon as the auditory tube.

In modern humans, the lower edge of the auditory tube is compressed into a crest. This crest extends along the length of the tube, from its outer opening, all the way to the body of the petrosal bone. Because the outer opening of the auditory tube lies extremely close to the front of the mastoid process, this crest abuts and often fuses with the mastoid process. While a fellow at the American Museum of Natural History a few years ago, I discovered that in some human populations—especially among Inuits—this crest can become distended downward into a prominent sheet of bone. But it still merges with the front surface of the mastoid process. In functional terms, the auditory tube forms a wall against which the articular end of the mandible can move. The more the depth of this wall is increased by expansion of the crest, the more the mandible can drop down along this bony wall.

Vandermeersch found that Neandertals also develop a crest in the vicinity of the auditory tube. However, in contrast to modern humans, a Neandertal's crest is not confluent with but remains distinctly separate from the mastoid process.

In modern humans, approximately one-quarter to one-third of an inch in from the outer edge of the auditory tube, a tapering spikelike projection of bone juts down. The length and robustness of this bony spike varies from individual to individual and is characteristically different among human populations. This thin bony process—called the styloid process—is a different structure altogether from the mastoid process; different muscles, which do different things, attach to it. In some of the skulls I studied, the downward extension of the auditory tube was so massive and sheetlike that it even draped itself down the entire length of a very long styloid process. In modern humans the styloid process lies behind the articular end of the mandible. In Neandertals, however, Vandermeersch found that the styloid process is located at the very inner end of the auditory tube, near the petrosal bone. The Neandertal styloid lies, therefore, to the inner side of rather than behind the articular end of the mandible.

In modern humans, three muscles originate from the styloid process: one to the tongue, another to the hyoid bone (the "Adam's apple"), and the third to the pharynx (the muscular tube that connects the back of the mouth with the rest of the digestive system). These styloid muscles, when contracted, participate in the action of swallowing—the hyoid bone and the pharynx are elevated and the tongue is elevated and pulled back. Because the styloid process is located in a different position on the base of the skull in Neandertals, they might have swallowed somewhat differently than we do.

Vandermeersch argued that a few more features in and around the mastoid region were specific to being Neandertal, but I think I've made my point. There is an abundance of distinctly unique Neandertal morphologies.

The Distinctiveness of Modern Humans

Although there has been an increase in the number of studies focusing on the delineation of Neandertal uniquenesses, similar analyses of modern human morphology have been few and far between. This makes some sense—it is a relatively simple matter to delineate apparent Neandertal uniquenesses because Neandertals are so blatantly different from modern humans and are easily distinguished from *Homo erectus* and other hominids as well.

This is not to say that modern humans are not also obviously different from Neandertals in their own right—we *know* that we are unique. But, aside from pointing to the development of a chin, thinner bones, and a smaller face and smaller jaws, it wasn't until the early 1980s that an attempt was made to define uniquenesses of modern humans without couching the discussion in terms of deriving modern human features from Neandertal or other "archaic" hominid features.

This attempt arose from a collaboration between Chris Stringer and Michael Day, a professor of anatomy at the University of London and for years a collaborator with Louis Leakey. Michael and Chris argued that modern humans could be distinguished in their own right from *Homo erectus,* so-called archaic *Homo sapiens,* and Neandertal not just by the development of a chin and thin cranial and postcranial bone but by a variety of cranial features. Among these modern human uniquenesses, Michael and Chris delineated the following.

The modern human skull is short and high-rising. In this differently shaped skull, the forehead is typically vertical. Also, the parietal bones that make up the top and sides of the skull are, for instance, tall and broad along their uppermost portions and narrow along their bottom edges. According to Michael and Chris, a modern human's occipital bone is noticeably curved, not distended.

A couple of years later Chris, in collaboration with Jean-Jacques Hublin and Bernard Vandermeersch, rethought the issue of what indeed is unique about the modern human occipital bone. They concluded that it is unique in being long, narrow, and not markedly projecting, although a pointed elevation of bone could develop in its midline. Most of you can feel this "bump," or external occipital protuberance, in the middle of and somewhat low down on your occipital bone. The external occipital protuberance in modern humans, when present, is essentially "freestanding." It is not the midline peak of a prominent ridgelike occipital crest, as it is so distinctively in *Homo erectus.*

In modern humans, as I discussed earlier, the supraorbital (or brow ridge) region, regardless of its size, is subdivided over each eye socket into inner and outer portions. The inner portion, when observable, comes up from the bridge of the nose and courses under the hair of the eyebrow. If you drag your finger along your eyebrow, you will feel a break or discontinuity in the contour of the underlying bone, from the swollen and moundlike inner portion, to the flatter and more platelike outer portion of the brow ridge.

But even though Chris Stringer and others could distinguish "anatomically modern humans" by a set of apparent uniquenesses, they still lumped "anatomically modern humans" with Neandertals in the same species, *Homo sapiens*. Curiously, the very publications that sought to delineate the respective uniquenesses of *Homo erectus*, "archaic" *Homo sapiens*, Neandertal, and "anatomically modern" *Homo sapiens* continued to operate under the constraints of Ernst Mayr's 1950 taxonomic revisions. There was *Australopithecus* and *Homo*, and that was that above the species level. Within *Homo*, there was *erectus* and *sapiens*, and that was that as well. When *Homo habilis* was proposed in 1964 by Louis Leakey and two colleagues, Phillip Tobias and John Napier, this new species was inserted into the sequence before *Homo erectus*. *Homo erectus* still gave rise to *Homo sapiens*, regardless of whether a multiregional continuity model or a single origin model of modern human populational diversity was subscribed to.

But what about the increasing success of—and the increasing acceptance of—demonstrations of real, tangible differences between different "kinds" of *Homo sapiens*? Chris Stringer came close, in 1984 and again in 1985, to what might appear to be the obvious conclusion—the recognition of different species to correspond to the morphologically distinct "kinds" of *Homo sapiens*. But he did not do it, even though he did suggest that perhaps only anatomically modern humans should be called *Homo sapiens*.

How Many Species of Homo?

The first taxonomic noises suggesting the recognition of more species than just *erectus* and *sapiens* came in 1984, at the same conference on human ancestors at the American Museum of Natural History at which Chris Stringer more tentatively proposed restricting the use of *Homo sapiens* to anatomically modern humans. The word *noises* is probably inappropriate because the suggestion came from one of the most subdued, and probably the quietest, of paleoanthropologists, G. Phillip Rightmire, of the State University of New York at Binghamton. Rightmire, like many others—but not the Neandertal-phase or multiregional continuity supporters—envisioned later hominid evolution as a branching phenomenon. If there were different branches—the splitting of lineages to give rise to new and different forms—then, Rightmire argued, these new and different forms could receive their own species names. His interpretation of the branching pattern of later species *Homo* reflected the presence "of at least four species of *Homo*, existing after about 1.5 million years (m.y.) BP," or before present.

Rightmire's particular group of interest is *Homo erectus*. From this background, he has a different slant on analyzing the diversity of specimens that had been subsumed under the umbrella of *Homo sapiens*. His scrutinizing of the fossil record of later hominids led Rightmire to conclude that two distinct species, *Homo erectus* and *Homo heidelbergensis*, had been the products of lineage splitting. The former species is represented by specimens from Africa and the Far East and the latter from specimens found in Europe. From *Homo heidelbergensis*, Rightmire suggested, *Homo neanderthalensis* and *Homo sapiens* arose. He also seemed to hint that Middle Pleistocene African hominid material— such as the Kabwe skull—or various out-of-place crania from similarly aged deposits in China may represent distinct species as well. Surprisingly, however, after taking the first step toward correlating discrete morphologies with species differences—which he had pursued within the realm of the *Homo erectus* debate—Rightmire backed off, and for the rest of his presentation referred to the whole non-*erectus* lot as *Homo sapiens*.

But Ian Tattersall couldn't keep a lid on it. In 1986, in the *Journal of Human Evolution*, Ian forced the species question harder and further, in what is now a widely cited article. Ian stated the obvious when he pointed out that "rarely, indeed . . . have paleontologists ever found it necessary to distinguish between 'archaic' and 'anatomically modern' types of the same species, and there seems scant justification for squeezing these distinct hominid morphs [= distinct groups or kinds] into a single species. . . . In any group other than Hominidae," he continued, the presence of several clearly recognizable morphs in the record of the middle to upper Pleistocene would suggest (indeed, demonstrate) the involvement of several species. Any mammalian paleontologist seeing morphological differences on the order of those separating modern humans from their various precursors, and the latter from each other, would have no difficulty in recognizing a number of separate species. And in this decision there is no obvious place for special pleading, even where it is our own closest relatives that are involved.

So, according to Ian Tattersall, when morphology is translated into species, it leads to the recognition of *Homo sapiens* ("anatomically modern humans"), *Homo neanderthalensis* (Neandertals), *Homo heidelbergensis* ("archaic" *Homo sapiens*, as represented by the specimens from Kabwe, Bodo, Petralona, and Arago), and possibly *Homo steinheimensis* (at least Steinheim and Swanscombe). "Recognizing a multiplicity of hominid species in the mid-to-late Pleistocene," Ian admitted, "will go against the grain for many paleoanthropologists. . . . After all, there is a beauty in linear simplicity that the aesthetes among us, in particular, would be reluctant to see vanish." And that, I think, is all too true.

Whatever the motivations, unconscious or otherwise, many paleoanthropologists exhibit an almost insatiable drive to swallow up into one big evolving lineage an odd lot of specimens that would be recognized as separate species if they represented any animal other than *Homo*. However, rather than being so simple, the picture of human evolution may be even more complicated and species-laden than any of us has imagined. For instance, Bernard Wood, a professor of anatomy and paleoanthropology at the University of Liverpool, England, has recently published the results of some very interesting analyses that indicate that not all things dumped into *Homo erectus* may indeed be *Homo erectus*. It seems that some of the East African material that Richard Leakey, who recently gave up fossil hunting for elephant conservation in Kenya, and Alan Walker, a Johns Hopkins anatomist who remains paleontologically active, have found may not be *Homo erectus*, after all. These specimens may be *Homo erectus*–like, but they are not distinguished by the totality of uniquenesses that characterize *Homo erectus* from Asia as well as other, demonstrably *Homo erectus* material from East Africa. And more things may be about to change.

Just as I was in the throes of formulating these chapters on human evolution, Chris Stringer published a general article in *Scientific American* on the single origin versus the multiregional continuity model in which he finally recognized *Homo neanderthalensis* as something different from us. Although this is only taxonomy, it is important because the recognition of uniquenesses as delineating different (in this case) species is the first step toward looking at morphology objectively enough to consider alternative theories of relatedness. As, for instance, Niles Eldredge and Ian Tattersall suggested years ago, Neandertals and *Homo erectus* do seem to share a suite of uniquenesses not shared with other hominids, which, in turn, might be reflective of their being more closely related to one another than either is to any other hominid, *Homo sapiens* included. And more recently Peter Andrews took some time off from his studies on the evolutionary relatedness of fossil and living apes and, from the perspective of one who had not been involved in the debate, undertook an analysis of relationships within the genus *Homo*. Peter's conclusions: *Homo habilis*, as represented by specimens from Louis and Mary Leakey's Tanzanian site, Olduvai Gorge, could be more closely related to *Homo sapiens* than is *Homo erectus*.

If the potential reality of the species *Homo heidelbergensis* and even *Homo steinheimensis* is also acknowledged, the whole picture of evolution within the genus *Homo* acquires an entirely new, and exciting, set of possibilities.

Homo habilis aside, it looks as if there is a *Homo erectus* group, with a full-blown *Homo erectus* species (as seen in specimens from Java, Beijing, and even Olduvai Gorge) and a primitively *Homo erectus*–like species (represented by various specimens from Richard Leakey's sites in Kenya) as well as a group that includes *Homo neanderthalensis* (represented by classic Neandertals) and a primitively Neandertal-like species, *Homo steinheimensis* (Steinheim and possibly Swanscombe). Perhaps related to the *neanderthalensis-steinheimensis* group, by virtue of features of the facial skeleton in particular, is *Homo heidelbergensis* (represented by Arago, Petralona, Kabwe, and Bodo).

Now, is the *neanderthalensis-steinheimensis-heidelbergensis* group more closely related to a *Homo erectus* group (based, for example, on thickened cranial and postcranial bone; long, low cranium; sloping forehead; distended occipital bone; and enlarged, protruding brow ridges) than it is to *Homo sapiens* (based on what)? And what about *Homo habilis*?

It's wild. But why not? Just because Ernst Mayr said there is only *Homo erectus* and *Homo sapiens* doesn't make it so.

But the search for continuity continues. In a talk he gave in 1990 in New York City, Alan Thorne criticized Chris Stringer's attempts to delineate uniquenesses of *Homo sapiens* (that is, anatomically modern humans). Alan suggested that some of the characters Chris cited as being uniquely *Homo sapiens*—such as the vaulted skull with tall fore-head and rounded occipital bone—were relevant only to European specimens. If Chris had looked at some Australian Aborigines, for in-stance, he would have come to a different conclusion—such as seeing the continuity. In the same vein, C. Loring Brace (who had transformed Hrdlička's "Neandertal Phase" into a version of the multiregional con-tinuity model) made the bold assertion at the 1990 annual meeting of the American Association of Physical Anthropologists that any one of us could pick up just about any European skull and find traces of Neander-tal features preserved in it.

Well, it just so happened that my fellowship research at the Ameri-can Museum of Natural History had expanded into a test of the single origin versus multiregional continuity models. By the end of my term there, I had analyzed 500 modern human specimens, sampling different global populations, and had recorded data on more than 100 features of the skull, teeth, and mandible for each specimen. I also had collected data on 300 nonhuman primates, including the great apes, gibbons, and various New and Old World monkeys. After months of trial and error in testing, discarding, and rethinking features that would be develop-mentally sound, reflective of shapes regardless of the individual's sex, and that varied little in their expression from individual to individual, I finally delineated a reliable suite of cranial, dental, and mandibular features. In order to test the single origin model, I had to put together a sample of features that was broad enough to distinguish a potential group we might call *Homo sapiens* as well as subgroups of this *Homo sapiens*. In order to test the multiregional continuity model, I had to include Neandertal and *Homo erectus* features and see how frequently they appeared in modern humans.

As you can well imagine, by the time I was done with the fellowship, I had amassed a huge amount of data. Although I haven't yet worked out the details of the differentiation of subgroups of modern humans, one thing is clear: Modern humans should be recognized as constituting a species apart not only from Neandertal but from other specimens previously attributed to *Homo sapiens*. True, some Australian Aborigines do have more sloping foreheads than other humans. And, true, some Australian Aborigines do have more prominent brow ridges than other humans. But they are anatomically modern, no matter how you slice it. Their brow ridges, regardless of size, are not continuous or smoothly rounded, for example, but instead develop as two components over each orbit. They do not develop *Homo erectus* brow ridges. Their cranial bone is "usual" in thinness, and their occipital bones are not distended into a *Homo erectus* sideways V. Among humans, Inuits consistently develop the thickest cranial bone. However, Inuits typically do not, for example, develop marked brow ridges.

Some of the most prominent brow ridges I found in any humans were among sub-Saharan Africans—which is interesting considering that early twentieth-century notions of "progressive infantilism" were based on sub-Saharan Africans being the least "brow-ridged" of humans. However, these few heavily brow-ridged skulls had *anatomically modern human* brow ridges, which jutted out from *anatomically modern human* skulls. In turn, these human skulls were highly vaulted and thin-boned, with tall foreheads and smoothly arced occipital bones. Apropos of Brace's comment, I could not find anything Neandertal in any European skull I studied. To be sure, various European skulls did display thickenings along the occipital bone. But the details were not those of Neandertals (or *Homo erectus*), but of *anatomically modern humans*—as are the large brow ridges one finds on occasion among humans.

Curiously, and in contradiction to the multiregional model's predic-

tion, the closest I came to finding anything that might at least superficially be thought of as a "Neandertal" character in a human skull
occurred when I was collecting data on sub-Saharan African, not
European, skulls. In fact, there were two such African skulls. One had
a strut of bone along its occipital bone that some might think came
close to the Neandertal type of occipital torus—except that it was
short, located farther down on the occipital bone, bore an external
occipital protuberance, and everything else about the skull was otherwise blatantly modern human. The other skull had a short toruslike
strut and above it a slight depression—but the strut also was located
low on the occipital bone, bore an external occipital protuberance,
and the depression was small and circular, not triangular and subtended by a raised border of bone.

Where Are We Now?

Rather than being close to solving the picture of later hominid evolution, I think we are just beginning to sort things out. The multiregional
continuity group is still battling it out with the single origin group—
which is good, in that it might lead to the continued testing of all
hypotheses that come along.

Besides being the focus of paleoanthropologists, the single origin
model has in recent years received the support of those who analyze
proteins and DNA. Study of a particular kind of DNA, called mitochondrial DNA, has led to the conclusion that modern humans originated in
Africa about 100,000 or 200,000 years ago. Because this type of DNA is
believed to be passed on only through the maternal line, the hypothesized African "mother" of us all has been nicknamed "Eve." Eventually, according to the theory, modern humans migrated out of Africa
and differentiated into populations that came to inhabit Europe and
Asia. The Eurasian groups are, therefore, supposed to be more closely
related to one another than either group is to an African group. Chris
Stringer and colleagues believe that the fossils support the "Africa as
Garden of Eden" theory.

If we look at the distribution of fossils that are "anatomically modern human," they include the Skhūl and Qafzeh material from the Near East as well as one skull from East African and possibly two skulls from South African sites. The ages of these skulls have recently been recalibrated, with the result that they appear to be about 100,000 years old. The implication drawn from these skulls, their geographic location, and their age is that modern humans originated in Africa even earlier than 100,000 years ago and then spread out through the rest of the Old World.

The relatively recent discovery of an undeniably Neandertal skull from the French site of Saint-Césaire, which dates to about 36,000 years ago, documents without question the fact that morphologically distinct Neandertals and modern humans coexisted for a long time. The evidence also documents that Neandertals were contemporaneous with tool types that were thought to have existed only when modern humans came into being. And, conversely, the antiquity of modern human fossils makes them contemporaneous with tool types thought to be associated exclusively with Neandertals or "archaic" Homo sapiens.

As with any situation in which there are competing, alternative interpretations of presumably the same data, voices of dissent have arisen. Some anthropologists suggest that the mitochondrial DNA and other molecular data actually support a multiregional continuity model. And still other analyses of different samples of mitochondrial DNA have been interpreted as indicating a longer period of separation of Asian groups and therefore perhaps an Asian origin for modern humans. My own morphological data, while not necessarily contradicting an African origin for modern humans, indicates at least tentatively that recent Africans may be more closely related to Asians than are Europeans. Because mine is the first morphological study to attempt a global analysis of modern human populations in terms of shared uniquenesses and not simply shared overall similarity, I intend to keep plowing ahead, increasing my samples in size and geographic distribution. Doing so is especially important because it is not fashionable to come to conclusions that are in conflict with those based on DNA or other molecular analyses, which are often taken as providing the final word.

But before we get caught up in the often inappropriate debates over who's right and who's wrong, we should not forget that, when analyzing molecular sequence data or features of a skull, scientists are the ones who ultimately decide on how to interpret the data evolutionarily. And although there is a real—and only one—evolutionary history of life, none of us will know for certain what really happened.

■

FINAL REFLECTIONS

What If?

One of the most obvious ways in which humans differ from virtually all other mammals is that females do not have an estrous cycle, or go into "heat." Dogs, cats, chimpanzees, and gorillas, for instance, do go into estrus. An estrous cycle restricts the period during which a female can and will mate to that part of the ovulatory cycle when the probability of conception will be at its highest. Various signals herald the onset of estrus during each cycle. All animals that go into estus seem to transmit chemical cues in addition to displaying various species specific behaviors. In some animals, including many primates, size and color of the sexual region change. In female chimps, for example, the sexual region can swell up enormously. According to laboratory observations of gorillas, the female's sexual region also changes during estrus, but the changes are much more subtle.

Humans, as we know, are different. Females have the potential to mate any time during the ovulatory cycle they wish. Aside from the possibility that human females transmit chemical cues signaling the peak of the ovulatory cycle and the suggestion in the literature that their frequency of mating may intensify around this peak, human females undergo no visible changes similar to those that characterize animals that do have estrous cycles.

But when did humans, or some distant human relative, lose—in evolutionary terms—the estrous cycle and become different from chimps and gorillas? And why? Was it because some form of natural selection acting on our ancestors made it more advantageous for females to have the potential for being continually sexually receptive? Perhaps to keep one or more males in her company? For protection? For the male's or males' input and assistance in the rearing of offspring?

If a male had a reason to stay with the same female beyond the act of mating, he would be assured of his parentage. Then he would have some biological motivation for contributing to the care of the offspring. Although chimps, for example, travel in bands of females and males and their offspring, they have estrous cycles and, because more than one adult male mates with a female during this period, no male knows with any certainty that any particular child is his. Thus it would seem that early human bands of females and males and their offspring would have to be different in some special way or ways—in large part because of the loss of estrus and all that this would entail.

Perhaps this important event in human evolution occurred with the emergence of one of the earliest species of our group. Perhaps it was one of the species of *Australopithecus* that existed in savanna-covered expanses of Africa a few million years ago. Perhaps the loss of estrus was correlated with the abandonment of a predominantly arboreal existence for one on the ground, a shift that itself was accompanied by the development of bipedalism. And with the development of bipedalism and the loss of estrus, somewhere along the way large, pendulous breasts developed—a feature that distinguishes human females from other mammals.

But when did this occur? And why? Did breasts come to act as some sort of signal for males—perhaps to replace the estrous cycle that had been or was being lost? Or, as some anthropologists have suggested, are human breasts an evolutionary mimic of the buttocks—which are also large in humans?

How do we even "know" that some human ancestor "lost" the estrous cycle?

We only "know" this as a consequence of our having first accepted a specific theory of evolutionary relationships among primates. In this case, we have accepted the hypothesis that chimps and gorillas, or at least one of them, is our closest living relative. And because we actually do know that chimps and gorillas are similar to most mammals in having an estrous cycle, it makes sense in the context of this particular theory of relatedness to infer that the postulated last common ancestor of humans and chimps and/or gorillas also had an estrous cycle. (This hypothesis at least is more parsimonious than one that postulates that this common ancestor did not have an estrous cycle and that the African apes somehow regained it.) Thus, by accepting this particular hypothesis of evolutionary relatedness, we are led naturally to the conclusion that, somewhere during human evolution, the estrous cycle was lost.

What if, however, chimps and gorillas are not our closest living relatives? What if, for the sake of argument, it turns out that the orang-utan is? Would we still be compelled to create an elaborate explanation of how, why, when, or where the loss of estrus occurred during human evolution?

No. Because, as we know from observations in the field and in the lab, orang-utans, in contrast to chimps and gorillas, do *not* have an estrous cycle. The anogenital region of female orangs does not swell at any time during, much less coincident with the peak of, the ovulatory cycle, and female orangs potentially can mate with males throughout the ovulatory cycle. Oddly enough, the sexual region of orang females becomes distended only during pregnancy—which, obviously, is something entirely unique to the orang and does not impact the hypothesized evolutionary relationships of the orang to other hominoids.

If the orang, and not the chimp or gorilla, is our closest living relative, we would not have to hypothesize that the estrous cycle was lost during human evolution. This "event" would already have occurred with or by the time of appearance of the last common ancestor of humans and orangs. Then there would be no need to create evolutionary explanations based on our assumptions—about, for instance, natural and sexual selection, the events of coming down from the trees and evolving bipedalism, and so on—of how, why, when, or where the loss of estrus occurred during human evolution. This event would not have happened in any human species, living or extinct. Thus, whatever formulations we might be inclined to develop to explain certain features of human reproductive and social behavior would have to be constructed within a totally different framework—one that did not include, for instance, the "loss" of estrus.

An Explanation of How Something Might Have Happened Evolutionarily Is Not a Hypothesis of Relatedness

Okay. So you don't like this scheme. But the point is that a lot of what we read in popular as well as scholarly literature is essentially an explanation of how, why, when, or where some evolutionary change occurred. But evolutionary explanations—for example, of how selection could have caused this or that feature to change from this to that—are always based on a previously accepted theory of who is related to whom precisely because we have to know beforehand the points between which this purported change would have occurred. How else could we have any basis for formulating a scheme about how something changed from this to that? All too often, however, an explanation of how something could have happened given a certain scheme of relationships is accepted as representing the rigorous analysis of the evolutionary relationships that have already been assumed.

But this is the wrong way around. Rather than try to defend a particular scheme of relatedness—by arguing how it could have happened—we should first question the assumed evolutionary relationships. Tear the scheme apart. See what makes it tick, what features actually support the theory of relationships.

But this is not usually what happens. It seems to be a common belief—among scientists as well as laypeople—that developing a theory of closeness of relatedness is so simple that anyone can do it. And that, once a majority of interested parties has agreed upon a particular scheme of relationships among a group of species, the matter has been settled, once and for all.

We are in deep trouble, though, if that is true.

Reconstructing the potential evolutionary relationships among species is not a simple matter. There is no simple key to unraveling the mystery of who is related to whom. The anatomies or molecules that may provide insight into the potential evolutionary relationships of one group of organisms are not necessarily the same ones that will arise as being potentially significant in investigating the possible evolutionary relationships of another group of organisms. To make matters even more uncertain, there is no assurance that we will even be able to delineate one, much less many, potentially evolutionarily significant features that could reflect the relatedness of one species to another. However, when we convince ourselves that the species under study are related to one another in a particular way, it will not be because this was the only scheme of relatedness that could be derived from the data; rather we accept it (at least for the time being) because it is the most highly corroborated of the competing, alternative schemes of relatedness that can be derived from the data.

Although there is truly one evolutionary history of organisms out there, we still have to try to find it—even though we never will piece it all together. The evolutionary past presents us with only a fractured sampling of life that existed—those organisms that could be fossilized and those that are not yet extinct. To some systematists only fossils, no matter how chancy their discovery is, provide clues to the past. To others, only living species hold these clues.

Fitting Fossils to the Great Ape Group

When I was a student from the late 1960s to the early 1970s, this is what we learned: Humans were related to a great ape group. Within this great ape group, the two African apes—the chimp and gorilla—were thought to be the most closely related because they are the only primates in which a certain suite of peculiarities of muscle and bone anatomy, particularly of the arm, develop. And, besides, they look like small and large versions of the same animal. There had been suggestions that humans were related only to the African ape group or that they were related to only one of the African apes. But the human–great ape group was the theory that won out.

Fossils from sites in East Africa and the Siwalik Hills of Indo-Pakistan that are 14 million years old or more could be fitted neatly within this human–great ape scheme of relatedness. The generally accepted notion was that there was a group of Miocene fossils (the Miocene was the geological epoch that lasted from about 25 million to 5 million years ago) in which the ancestors of humans and of each ape could be found. This group of Miocene fossils was also referred to as the Miocene hominoids, because "hominoid" is the broad taxonomic group name that refers collectively to living humans and apes as well as to their potential fossil relatives. The group of Miocene hominoids in question was the dryopithecines, which means "wood-apes." Although the first jaw of a dryopithecine was discovered in the mid-1800s in France, the dryopithecines that came to be thought of as being directly ancestral to various living hominoids were discovered in Africa and Indo-Pakistan. In the scenario that became popular in the late 1960s and early 1970s, all of these potential ancestors had evolved from an earlier, more generalized and unspecified dryopithecine ancestor.

The ancestor ultimately leading to humans was supposed to be a form from Indo-Pakistan that had been given the genus name *Ramapithecus*; Rama is one of the major Hindu gods. *Ramapithecus* was first identified in the 1930s as a potential human ancestor by a Yale graduate student, G. E. Lewis, who was studying the larger collection of Siwalik fossil hominoids. The specimen upon which Lewis based his novel conclusion consisted of most of the right side of an upper jaw. Lewis reconstructed the complete shape of this hominoid's upper jaw as being "parabolic, rather than U-shaped as in recent Simiidae [the taxonomic name then used for the apes], and hence the palate broadens posteriorly." Lewis also believed that the face of this fossil hominoid would not have protruded as much as an ape's; humans are contrasted with modern apes in having a shorter face. The preserved teeth and root sockets in this fossil jaw also seemed more human- than apelike, especially in that the upper canine would have been small, as in humans, and would not have overlapped and interlocked with the lower canine as the larger canines do in apes.

Through a series of unfortunate events, however, Lewis's suggestion did not gain acceptance. The fossils lay in a drawer of the Yale Peabody Museum until they were rediscovered in the late 1950s by a young professor of paleontology named Elwyn Simons. But Simons's arguments about the hominidness of *Ramapithecus*, beginning with his first publication on the specimen in 1961, were enormously successful in convincing the scientific community that this Miocene fossil did indeed represent the earliest-known potential human ancestor. Simons was also an expert on the other fossil hominoid material, and in the mid-1960s he published a major revision of the dryopthecines with a graduate student of his, David Pilbeam. Pilbeam went on to popularize the roles of various Miocene hominoids in the evolution of modern apes.

Pilbeam, who subsequently became a professor at Yale and then at Harvard, pointed specifically to two East African Miocene hominoids as being ancestral, respectively, to each of the African apes. The original genus name that subsumed these particular species of African Miocene hominoid was *Proconsul*. In their joint article, Simons and Pilbeam reduced the number of genus names that had been around for decades in the literature for the various Miocene hominoids, and *Proconsul* was one of the victims of this taxonomic lumping. In recent years, however, the genus *Proconsul* has been revived and its distinctiveness accepted by most primate systematists.

Pilbeam recognized three species of *Proconsul*. One came from slightly older deposits than the other two, which led him to suggest that the former was ancestral to the two younger species. Of these two supposed descendants, one, *Proconsul africanus*, was smaller than the other, *Proconsul major*. Of the two living African apes, the chimp is smaller than the gorilla. *Proconsul africanus* was also similar to the chimp in having larger, spatulate upper incisors. *Proconsul major* seemed to be similar to the gorilla in having relatively smaller upper incisors, with the second upper incisor being more conical than spatulate. There were various other features of apparent similarity between the respective pairs of Miocene and living African hominoids, but I think you get the picture. The bottom line, according to Pilbeam, was that *Proconsul africanus* was ancestral to the chimp and *Proconsul major* was ancestral to the gorilla.

The third living great ape, the orang-utan, is now found in the southeast Asian islands Borneo and Sumatra. Evidence primarily from fossil teeth—some as old as 1 million years—indicate that orang-utans used to inhabit the island of Java as well as what is now the mainland of southeast Asia. It might seem impossible to imagine an orang-utan making its way across major stretches of water to get to these islands from the mainland, but these islands did not begin to come into existence until around half a million years ago. Before then—before the Sunda shelf began to sink and was inundated by the sea—the present-day islands were still part of the mainland.

Pilbeam's most likely candidate for the ancestor of the orang-utan was one of the Miocene hominoids then known only from the Siwalik Hills of Indo-Pakistan. This fossil hominoid was represented by species of the genus *Sivapithecus*, so-named after the Hindu god Siva. Between 1910 and 1915 the British paleontologist Guy Pilgrim had collected and named a number of fossil hominoids, and *Sivapithecus* was one of them. Based on the morphology of *Sivapithecus*'s lower jaw and teeth, Pilgrim thought it might be an ancestor of the human lineage. The American paleontologist William K. Gregory, however, thought that Pilgrim had erred in his reconstruction of the shape of that jaw. Gregory's reconstruction confirmed his assessment of the morphology of the canine and first premolar of *Sivapithecus*: This fossil hominoid was more orang-utan–like than anything else.

Molecules and the Demise of the Great Ape Group

During the 1960s another source of information emerged as a means of inferring evolutionary relationships—the study of proteins that are found in the serum component of blood. The impetus for these studies actually dates back to pioneering work published in 1904 by George Nuttall, a lecturer in bacteriology and preventive medicine at Cambridge University.

The idea is simple. Blood is taken from one animal and injected into another animal, which, in turn, produces antibodies to the foreign substance. Blood is taken from the second animal and the antibodies isolated. If these antibodies are mixed with the blood proteins of other animals, there will be an immunological reaction, somewhat like an allergic reaction. If these antibodies are mixed with the blood proteins that were used to get the antibodies in the first place, there would be a large-scale reaction because there would be a specific antibody for every protein—each antibody would be a "perfect match," if you will, for each protein.

Now let's take our original sample of antibodies and use it with the blood of other animals. It turns out that the less similar the blood serum proteins to be tested are to the original sample of those used to produce the antibodies, the less reactivity there will be between the sample of blood serum proteins and the test batch of antibodies. Nuttall referred to this kind of immunological test as demonstrating the "blood relatedness" of organisms. Accordingly, the more similar two organisms were in their blood serum proteins—because their blood serum proteins would have similarly profound reactions with the same sample of antibodies—the more closely related these two organisms were supposed to be to one another.

Although Nuttall's studies were known among some quarters of the scientific community, it was not until the 1960s that this immunological method of testing similarity of blood serum proteins gained much attention in paleoanthropological circles, largely through the work of Morris Goodman, of Wayne State University in Detroit, and Allan Wilson and Vince Sarich, both of the University of California at Berkeley. In 1962 Goodman published a paper in which he concluded that, even though various protein analyses lent themselves to a variety of schemes of relatedness among humans and apes, "as judged by the overall impression of the patterns, man shows more similarity to the gorilla and chimpanzee than to the gibbon or orangutan." Basically, as Goodman saw it, his analyses "show[ed] that the Asiatic apes are more distant from man than are the African apes." The upshot of this was that, if similarity in proteins does indeed reflect closeness of relatedness, the great apes do not represent a real, evolutionarily coherent, group to which humans are related. Humans, so it seemed, were related most closely to the African great apes.

Paleontologists, primate systematists, and physical anthropologists, in general, more or less went along quietly with the breakup of the great ape group. It really did not seem like a big revision, anyway. After all, the African apes were still kept together—which was compatible with their being the only primates to knuckle-walk, that is, to carry the weight of the front part of the body on the surface of the second segment of the fingers. And it happens that chimps and gorillas have to knuckle-walk, instead of walking on their palms, because the short flexor tendons of their arms force an involuntary bending in of their fingers when they straighten their wrists. This uniqueness, along with other specializations of soft tissue and bone of their arms and hands, has led primate comparative anatomists of the past century to conclude that chimps and gorillas are an evolutionary sister pair. Some systematists have even suggested that the chimp and the gorilla are morphologically so similar to one another that they are actually just small and large species of the same genus.

It was a relatively simple matter to go along with a minor breakup of a great ape evolutionary group because the notion of a human–great ape group was replaced by a scheme—human–African ape—that had already been proposed as an alternative theory of hominoid related-ness. One of the more adamant supporters of a human–African ape relationship—but, curiously, in an on-again, off-again fashion—had been William K. Gregory. In addition, the clout of Charles Darwin and Thomas Huxley was, and continues to be, sought in garnering support for a human–African ape scheme of relatedness. For example, as Roger Lewin, a science writer and sometime coauthor with Richard Leakey, has most recently put it in his book *Bones of Contention*, "Darwin and Huxley . . . suggested that in spite of superficial appearances, detailed anatomical comparisons revealed the gorilla and chimpanzee to be closely allied to humans, with the third of the great apes, the Asian orang-utan, more distantly related to humans." But as we saw in an earlier chapter, while people may *think* this was what Darwin and Huxley had been up to, this was not the way in which Darwin came to this conclusion, and this was not at all what Huxley concluded. Nevertheless, Darwin did suggest that humans are possibly most closely related to the African apes—even though his reasons would now be rejected—and it has become increasingly popular in the twentieth century to be seen as a vindicator, rather than a potential detractor, of Darwin.

In 1966 and 1967 Sarich and Wilson published three papers that further impacted the study of primate, and especially human-ape, relationships. Focusing solely on one blood serum protein, albumin, which is a large molecule, they developed a cross-check for using immunological reactivity in the construction of schemes of closeness of relatedness among species. If, for example, one series of reactivity tests was done with one sample of antibodies, another series of reactivity tests was done with antibodies produced against another species to see if degrees of similarity and dissimilarity remained relatively constant. Thus, if there was reciprocity in degrees of reactivity between pairs of species tested, a scheme of relationships could be constructed. Although Sarich and Wilson's results were in some disagreement with Goodman's—for example, Goodman's analyses showed the gibbon as being more similar to humans than the orang-utan, whereas Sarich and Wilson's analysis had it the other way around—the general arrangement of the species studies was compatible with accepted, morphologically based schemes. Chimps, rhesus monkeys, and capuchin (organ-grinder's) monkeys, in that order, were decreasingly similar to humans.

But Sarich and Wilson pushed their albumin studies another step further. They argued from their demonstrations of reciprocity of reactivity that molecules, at least the albumin molecule, changed over time at a constant rate. How else, you might think, could you get reciprocity? And if molecules did change at a constant rate, this could be converted into a molecular clock. But schemes of evolutionary relatedness based on analyses of molecules are abstract formulations when it comes to time. Fossils, however, are timekeepers of a sort. And because the general consensus among paleontologists was that the human-ape group split from a common ancestor shared with an Old World monkey group about 30 million years ago, this was where Sarich and Wilson could begin calibrating the molecular clock. They concluded that the gibbon became distinct about 10 million years ago, the orang about 8 million years ago, and, finally, that humans and African apes diverged from their common ancestor about 5 million years ago.

But how could this be if all of those Miocene fossils were related to the different living hominoids? The answer was simple: These fossils were not related to living hominoids, at least in the ways in which paleontologists such as Simons and Pilbeam were suggesting. Sarich, to paraphrase a now oft-cited quote, declared that no fossil older than 5 million years—and this, of course, referred to *Ramapithecus*—could be a hominid, no matter what it looked like. Simons responded by pointing out that, if Sarich was correct, no paleontologist had ever discovered a potential ancestor of any primate group—which he found about as acceptable as assuming "that *Australopithecus* [which supposedly had evolved from *Ramapithecus*] sprang full-blown five million years ago, as Minerva did from Jupiter, from the head of a chimpanzee or a gorilla." Pilbeam was also troubled by the disagreement in dating the divergences of hominoid primates and, as late as 1972, concluded that "there is reason to believe that some of the assumptions made in arriving at the biochemical ages may not be correct or that other factors might not have been taken fully into consideration. . . . For the moment, let us assume that the fossil framework is acceptable."

Dismantling the Last Bastions of Hominoid Evolution

The 1970s were witness to parallel endeavors in sorting out primate evolutionary relationships. Morris Goodman and his group at Wayne State, and Vince Sarich and Allan Wilson, along with Jack Cronin and occasionally others at Berkeley, worked away at the molecular end of the picture. More and more molecules were analyzed, and as it became more feasible to go deeper into the molecule and assess its "anatomy"—the arrangement of its molecular units—such molecular sequences were added to the analysis. Various approaches to deciphering two different kinds of DNA molecule also were becoming more readily available.

The picture began to shift again.

It seemed that the chimpanzee alone was the most similar of the apes to humans in its molecular constitution—about 99 percent similar, to be specific. The gorilla shared a bit less of its genetic stuff with humans, and the orang a bit less again. Thus, if degree of molecular similarity reflected degree of evolutionary closeness, as was popularly assumed, then the sequence from orang, gorilla, chimp, to human represented the sequence of divergence among the large-bodied hominoids. And the date of suggested divergence among these presumed evolutionary sisters—less than 10 million years—still excluded *Ramapithecus* from the realm of human origins.

Needless to say, the breakup of the African ape sister group did not sit well with most primate paleontologists and systematists. If it was true that chimps were more closely related to humans than to their obvious look-alikes, gorillas, some explanation had to be found for how the two African apes independently had evolved knuckle-walking and all of its anatomical correlates. Or, it had to be postulated that the reason chimps and gorillas were knuckle-walkers was because the last common ancestor of humans, chimps, and gorillas had been a full-fledged knuckle-walker, and that chimps and gorillas had inherited their knuckle-walking anatomies from this ancestor. If the latter explanation was true, humans would have had to have lost all traces of knuckle-walking morphology and, in this regard, would have secondarily come to look in their bones and muscles like other, non–knuckle-walking primates.

On the paleontological side of things, there were some changes in thinking about who was related to whom, but none as radical as those happening in the molecular camp. *Ramapithecus* still headed the list of potential candidates for the ancestor of *Australopithecus*, a species of which, in turn, was thought to be ancestral to the *Homo* group. But years of new discoveries and various attempts to dethrone *Ramapithecus* had severely whittled down the number of uniquenesses in support of its relationship to hominids.

For example, more complete jaws attributed to *Ramapithecus* demonstrated that this hominoid's jaw was not broadly parabolic in shape, as it is in humans. Rather, the sides of the jaw were longer and straighter and the outline narrower in the front—sort of V-shaped. As such, the place on the original upper jaw of *Ramapithecus* that Simons had thought was part of the midline suture when he reconstructed a parabolic shape was not part of the midline suture. But while Simons erred in identifying an anatomical landmark, there also seem to have been other motivations behind accepting *Ramapithecus* as a hominid. As Roger Lewin quotes David Pilbeam's reflections during an interview in 1984 on these events: "I 'knew' *Ramapithecus*, being a hominid, would have a short face and a rounded jaw—so that's what I saw.' "

What's odd about this history of *Ramapithecus* is that, certainly by the late 1960s, it was known that not all species of *Australopithecus* had a short face, and none had a parabolic or rounded jaw—only some species of *Homo* have both. Therefore, these two features together should not have been expected to be present in a presumed ancestor of *Australopithecus*—that is, in *Ramapithecus*.

About the only feature that continued to be thought of as something shared almost exclusively by *Ramapithecus*, *Australopithecus*, and *Homo* was the development of a thick layer of enamel on the molar teeth. Thin molar enamel is by far the more common condition among primates and mammals in general, for that matter. Only three living nonhuman primates have thick molar enamel. The orang is one of them. But, because the orang was supposed to be farther away evolutionarily from humans—or hominids, in general—than were the thin-enameled African apes, thick molar enamel in orangs and hominids was interpreted as an evolutionary parallelism, a feature that arose independently in orangs and in hominids. Among Miocene hominoids, however, quite a few were found to have thick molar enamel. *Sivapithecus* was one of these. Consequently, Pilbeam argued that *Sivapithecus* and other thick-enameled Miocene hominoids, including *Ramapithecus*, constituted a group from which *Australopithecus* and *Homo* had evolved. Thus *Sivapithecus* was no longer a potential orang ancestor.

In 1980 Peter Andrews and a Turkish colleague of his, Ibrahim Tekkaya, published an article in which they argued that the morphology of the jaws and teeth attributed to *Ramapithecus* and *Sivapithecus* indicated that, at the level of the genus, these two were really one and the same hominoid. At best there should be only one genus—*Sivapithecus*, because it had been named decades before *Ramapithecus* had—which subsumed a variety of species from various Eurasian sites. Andrews and Tekkaya also announced their discovery, from late Miocene deposits of Turkey, of a portion of a lower face with its upper jaw and teeth intact.

The jaws and teeth were the jaws and teeth of *Sivapithecus*. But the face was not that of a hominid. Rather it essentially was the face of an orang-utan in many features that are otherwise unique to the orang and distinguish it from other living hominoids. Two years later Pilbeam published an article on a much more completely preserved face of *Sivapithecus* that he had found in late Miocene deposits in the Siwalik Hills of Indo-Pakistan. *Sivapithecus* was now reassociated with the orang, as a relative—but for morphological, not biogeographical, reasons this time.

The case seemed closed. If the supposedly hominid jaws and teeth belonged to the face of an orang, then the whole animal had to be an orang relative. And because orangs were not supposed to be more closely related to hominids than chimps and gorillas, whatever unique features one found in the orang, *Sivapithecus*, and hominids had to have ended up in these hominoids in one of two ways: Either they had evolved independently in an orang-*Sivapithecus* group on the one hand and a hominid group on the other, or these features had to have been retained from a common ancestor shared by all large-bodied hominoids, with chimps and gorillas subsequently losing these features. In either case, hominids no longer had a tangible, potential ancestor in the form of a Miocene hominoid. The earliest agreed-upon hominid, therefore, was *Australopithecus*, with Don Johanson's species of "Lucy," *Australopithecus afarensis*, being the oldest. But *Australopithecus* was still not older than 4 million years.

The molecular clock, it seemed, was "right" all along: Hominids had not been around longer than 5 million years, 8 million at the outside. And if the clock was correct, perhaps the relationships—orang, gorilla, chimp, human, in that order of relatedness—were also correct.

Although there were a few dissenters, most notably Elwyn Simons, most paleoanthropologists accepted the mounting morphological evidence that linked *Sivapithecus* with the orang. Eventually even Simons acceded to this interpretation. The uniquenesses shared by *Sivapithecus* and the orang, as delineated initially by Peter Andrews, ranged from features of the face, to those of the teeth, to one in particular of the palate. In terms of the palate, Andrews pointed out that *Sivapithecus* and the orang have a long, slitlike opening in the midline of the tongue or oral cavity side of the bony palate.

Pursuing Passages in the Palate

A few years after Andrews and Tekkaya's publication on *Sivapithecus* and the orang, a young colleague of Pilbeam's, Steve Ward, who is a professor of anatomy at Kent State University, and I independently pursued more detailed studies on the palates of various primates. Steve focused on the configurations and spatial relationships of the two bones that contribute to the bony palate—the premaxilla in front and the maxilla behind—and on the shape of the top of the palate, which actually constitutes the floor of the nasal cavity. In two publications, one with Bill Kimbel, who was then a graduate student at Kent State, and one with David Pilbeam, Steve suggested that there were a few definable configurations. Of these configurations, one seemed to characterize chimps and gorillas as well as, among hominids, Don Johanson's *Australopithecus afarensis*. Another palatal-nasal cavity configuration seemed to characterize *Sivapithecus* and the orang. Steve and his coauthors referred to the former configuration as an "African pattern" and the latter as an "Asian pattern." They also suggested that the respective similarities in the configuration of the floor of the nasal cavity provided further evidence that the African apes were closely related to hominids and that *Sivapithecus* and the orang were closely related to one another.

While, unknown to me, Steve was focusing his studies on the nasal cavity side of the palate, I happened to be collecting comparative data primarily on the morphology of the palate on its tongue, or oral cavity, side. I found that, on its oral cavity side, the palate of most primates is perforated near the front (just behind the upper front teeth) by a pair of relatively large openings. Most other mammals also develop a pair of openings through the palate; as I wrote about in chapter 4, these are the palatal "windows" with which a rhinarium also may be associated. These openings make it possible to pick up the skull of practically any mammal and look straight through the palate, from the oral to the nasal cavity. Humans and the great apes, however, are different. To begin with, these hominoids' palates lack the two large openings and are, as Steve also found during his studies, thicker than in other primates. Thus you cannot pick up a gorilla's skull, for instance, and easily look through the palate from the oral to the nasal cavity.

Instead of large apertures opening into the oral cavity, I found that gorillas typically have two clearly delineated canals emerging through the palate at its midline; these canals are separated from one another by a substantial bony wall. Chimps typically have two shallow canals emerging through the palate to the oral cavity; a raised hump of bone often separates these two shallow canals, which gives the impression of an hourglass lying on its side. Humans, as has been well illustrated in anatomy texts, have a large, single opening at the midline of the palate. And, as Peter Andrews pointed out, orangs have a single but long and slitlike opening at the midline of the palate.

It seemed to me that there was something significant—of potential evolutionary relevance—in all of this. If, collectively, humans and the large-bodied apes did indeed constitute an evolutionary group—and there does seem to be convincing morphological evidence of this—then the thickening of the palate and the remodeling of the two large openings typical of mammals into canals might be another feature uniting these primates as a group. Within this group, humans and orangs seemed to be even more unique in the coalescence of the two canals into one that emerges on the oral cavity side of the palate—with the orang being even more unique than humans in compressing this single canal into a long, slitlike canal.

(My research has since expanded into human fetal development—especially of the association of nerves and teeth. While writing this chapter, I got so charged up again about the palatal configurations that

I started looking at this region in the three- to five-month-old fetuses I have been studying. And just this week I found a series of specimens that illustrate perfectly in microscopic section the Y that is formed when the two canals that are separate in the floor of the nasal cavity come together to form the single opening on the oral cavity side of the palate. But back to the original study.)

When I reviewed the fossil material, I found that all hominids for which the region is preserved possess a single but large opening in the midline of the palate on the oral cavity side. Some Miocene hominoids, however—the small *Proconsul africanus* included—still retained the typical, primitive mammalian condition of two large openings, rather than the various configurations of canals seen among the living large-bodied hominoids. And, as Peter Andrews had pointed out, *Sivapithecus* did share with the orang the uniquely long, slitlike single canal. So perhaps *Sivapithecus*, the orang, and hominids did constitute a group—united by having a single opening into the oral cavity—within which there was a *Sivapithecus*-orang group and a hominid group.

Even though this conclusion flew in the face of the increasingly popular human-chimp theory of relatedness, I wrote up a brief report, which was published in the journal *Primates* at about the same time that the two articles by Steve Ward and colleagues appeared. There did not seem to be anything contradictory in what Steve had described about the morphology of the palate and the floor of the nasal cavity in hominoids and what I had found about the morphology of the palate in the oral cavity. When I thought about the details of what Steve had published, however, I could not reach the same conclusions about the evolutionary significance of what he had found. It seemed to me that what Steve called the "Asian pattern" was of significance in uniting species, in this case *Sivapithecus* and the orang. Briefly, the way in which the premaxilla overlapped the maxilla was definitely unique among fossil and living hominoids. The "African pattern," however, because it characterized the African apes and some species of *Australopithecus*, and especially because it did not characterize *Homo*—which has its own, unique configuration of the premaxilla and maxilla—could be interpreted as the ancestral condition for the entire large-bodied hominoid group, a condition from which *Homo*, on the one hand, and the ancestor of *Sivapithecus* and the orang, on the other, evolved in different ways in the configuration of their palates and the spatial relationship of their premaxillas and maxillas.

Steve and I have talked about this time and time again. We both agree on the morphologies that each of us has described for various hominoids and that our observations are completely compatible. We disagree on the interpretation of the evolutionary significance of the distribution of these morphologies among the hominoids. We have even talked about doing a joint paper—if we can ever find the time—to demonstrate our points of agreement and disagreement. This seems to be a particularly important endeavor because some of our colleagues think we have been writing about the same features—in which case we cannot both be correct in our descriptions.

By the time Steve's articles and mine appeared in print, I had become more deeply involved in the problems of the evolutionary relationships of humans and apes than I ever thought I would be. Until then most of my research in primate evolutionary studies had been on the prosimians—the lemurs, lorises, and bushbabies—and their potential fossil relatives—that is, when I wasn't on an archeological dig. But I found myself steeped in the literature (from Darwin and Huxley on) trying to learn why various theories of human-ape relatedness had been preferred over other theories, to at least find out for myself what the data being brought to bear on the problem really consisted of, and to see if the data lent themselves to alternative interpretations.

Up to My Neck in Hominoids

A reason that Steve Ward and I, or that any other paleontologist or systematist and I, might disagree on the question of "who's related to whom" is because we might employ different methods of reconstructing evolutionary relationships. I happen to subscribe to an approach that bases the reconstruction of evolutionary relationships not on species sharing similar features but on how uniquely distributed among species these features are. For example, consider the case of a single canal perforating the oral cavity side of the palate—now, that's unique.

In order to delineate uniqueness, a broad array of species must be studied so that the more commonly shared features can be sorted out from the more uniquely shared ones. The rationale for trying to delineate features of relative uniqueness is that these features probably represent evolutionary novelties that arose in the last common ancestor of the species sharing these relatively uniquely distributed features. The longstanding alternative approach to reconstructing potential evolutionary relationships relies on the delineation of the total amount of similarity shared by species. Thus the more similar species are overall, the more closely related these species are supposed to be to one another. But, especially in the last decade or so, there has been an increasing emphasis in evolutionary studies on trying to delineate potential novelties as being reflective of the evolutionary closeness of species. Looking at problems in alternative ways is, I think, healthy for a science. The problem here, of course, is that one systematist can scrutinize another's data and come to an entirely different conclusion about evolutionary relationships than the person who originally compiled the data. And that does not always sit well with colleagues.

As a starting place in my inquiries, I used a list of morphological features Peter Andrews had published in an article co-authored with molecular systematist Jack Cronin. For additional comparative data, I relied especially heavily on the work of Adolph Schultz, who had singlehandedly amassed an enormous amount of comparative anatomical data on primates and in particular on hominoid primates and who, if you will recall, had been the major force in defending the grouping together of the great apes. Upon close inspection, however, I discovered that the morphological case for Schultz's great ape group was based on little more than overall similarity: large apes with variably long arms, short legs, and a nonhuman face. Like Peter Andrews and others, I found that the African apes do indeed appear to be an evolutionary sister pair. I also found that the scheme of a human–African ape grouping did garner some morphological support. On the other hand, a human-chimp sister group could barely be justified on the basis of morphological uniquenesses shared by these two hominoids. But two hominoids—humans and orangs—emerged as sharing more unique features than I or anyone else would have imagined. An evolutionary relationship between humans and orangs had not been suggested in almost one hundred years, since the German evolutionist Ernst Haeckel proposed it on the basis of certain features of the brain.

Interestingly, fossil material does not contribute specifically to the resolution of any particular theory of closeness of relatedness among the living hominoids. In fact, many of us—for example, Peter Andrews, Terry Harrison of New York University, Lawrence Martin of Stony Brook, and I—have concluded that no *Proconsul* had any particularly close relationship to any particular living hominoid. Rather it appears that the *Proconsul* species belonged to a group including the remaining original dryopithecines plus some more recent finds that is the sister group of the living large-bodied hominoids. Darwin may have believed that fossil ancestors would be found in the same regions where living forms are found, and at one time Pilbeam may have thought he had identified them, but so far African deposits have not yielded the ancestor of either chimp or gorilla.

In my article on differences among the hominoids in the number and morphology of canals perforating the oral cavity side of the palate, I tried to deal with the consequences of humans and orangs being closely related to each—especially in terms of the molecular data, which was used to support a human-chimp relationship. I knew that I had to try to understand the molecular data and the assumptions that underlay the interpretation of the molecular data for purposes of reconstructing evolutionary relationships. I felt this was as much my responsibility as dealing with the morphological data themselves. Doing so is especially important because, in the apparent absence of fossils of any particular antiquity that could be linked directly to hominids, many paleontologists had come to accept the arrangement of hominoid relationships derived from molecular data. Had Wilson and Sarich "clocked" hominid divergence at 12 or more million years (in the middle of the Miocene), debates among and between paleontologists and molecular systematists about "who's closely related to whom" might still be going on.

While I was studying the literature on molecular analyses of evolutionary relationships, Alan Templeton, a biologist at Washington University, published an article in the journal *Evolution* in which he reanalyzed data on mitochondrial DNA that had been published elsewhere by other molecular systematists. Mitochondrial DNA had become a popular molecule to work with because it was much shorter than DNA found in the nucleus and because it was thought to be inherited only through the maternal line. Because mitochondrial DNA was supposed to be passed on only by the mother, different ways of interpreting evolution were devised.

Based on their analysis of mitochondrial DNA data, the authors of the first article Templeton reviewed—Steven Ferris, Allan Wilson, and Wes Brown, all at the time at the University of California, Berkeley— had not been able to demonstrate with statistical significance whether humans were more closely related to an African ape group or to the chimpanzee alone. Templeton, however, had devised a different set of criteria for evaluating the evolutionary signal of such DNA data and applied his approach to Ferris, Wilson, and Brown's data.

In his article, Templeton admitted that, of the six evolutionary arrangements possible for humans, chimps, gorillas, and orangs, his interpretation of the mitochondrial DNA data yielded three schemes of relatedness that were statistically indistinguishable from one another. One of these schemes (number 1 in his illustration) depicted a sequence of divergence from the orang, to humans, to an African ape sister pair. Another (number 5) reversed humans and orangs, with humans being the first of the large-bodied hominoids to diverge (the "old" human–great ape theory). And the third arrangement (number 6) linked, respectively, humans with orangs and chimps with gorillas. When Templeton evaluated other molecular data, he concluded that the human–African ape relationship was the preferred one.

I wrote to Templeton to ask questions about his article and to make certain I understood what he had done. He wrote that the "data set *cannot* distinguish between phylogenies 1, 5 or 6." And, on the basis of other data, he had "rejected phylogenies 5 and 6 in favor of 1." I had sent Templeton a copy of the manuscript I was putting together on the possible relationships of humans and orangs—which, in his reply, he reinterpreted in the context of his preferred human–African ape phylogeny—and he also generously sent me copies of the molecular data he cited in his article.

I polished the manuscript I had sent Templeton, adding a historical introduction and a section on reinterpreting the molecular data in the context of the possibility that humans and orangs are closely related to one another. Among the morphological areas that I reinterpreted was Steve Ward's data on the different configurations of the floor of the nasal cavity. In the molecular section of the manuscript, I took the same data set that Templeton had reanalyzed and, using the same approach I had applied to morphological data, gave it my best shot. As expected, some aspects of the mitochondrial DNA data set could be interpreted as uniting all the hominoids as a group. Other aspects of the data set, it seemed, united the African apes. As I had found in analyzing the morphological data, different sets of relationships among the hominoids could be hypothesized on the basis of different combinations of uniquely distributed features. Thus I did find some aspects of the mitochondrial DNA data set that united humans and the African apes as a group. But I also delineated other aspects that were shared exclusively by humans and orangs. In fact, there appeared to be more of the latter than of the former.

I ended up concluding that, of the alternative phylogenetic arrangements, it appeared that the least morphologically supported theory was that chimps are more closely related to humans than they are to gorillas and that the two most robust morphologically based hypotheses were that chimps are most closely related to gorillas and humans are most closely related to orangs. The latter phylogeny also made sense of *Sivapithecus* and of why this fossil hominoid could be hominid in aspects of its jaws and teeth and yet specifically orang in features of its facial skeleton—it was part of the larger human-orang group by virtue of being closely related to the orang. My reanalysis of the mitochondrial DNA data aside, a consequence of a morphologically based human-orang theory was that molecular similarities between humans and chimps had to be reinterpreted: Either these similarities were primitive retentions or they were parallelisms.

I sent what was by then a long manuscript to the editors of *Nature* to see if they would be interested in a shorter version. Eventually the editors wrote back that they would consider a shorter version—which, upon receipt, was sent out for peer review. As I remember, the reviews were mixed but generally favorably disposed to the manuscript getting published. One reviewer wanted a bit more discussion of the molecular, especially DNA, data, which I provided, but with my own interpretation. The revised manuscript was published in the issue of 5–11 April 1984 with a photograph I had sent of the skulls of a chimp, gorilla, human, and orang on the cover.

In the meantime, I sent the longer and more detailed manuscript off to the journal *Current Anthropology*. Eventually I heard that it would be accepted for publication and sent out for comments, which would be published together with the article, along with my responses. I continued my review of the literature, expanding into areas of research in brain morphology and reproductive physiology. Again, the morphological data lent themselves to alternative theories of who's related to whom among the hominoids. But not only was the human-orang possibility among them, this theory of relatedness emerged as the most highly corroborated of the alternatives. The comments were generally encouraging—at least in terms of thinking that my presentation and arguments would provide grist for the discussion mill. Because one commentor questioned whether the features I enumerated in the article really did demonstrate what I thought they did, I decided to include in my response the new information I had been accumulating. Another comment provoked my rethinking the chromosomal data that was being cited at the time as uniting humans with chimps.

As you might well imagine, my suggestion that humans and orangs might be closely related to one another got some noses out of joint. Vince Sarich, for instance, was one of the first publicly to express his enormous displeasure at the whole thing. At a symposium to which we were both invited the month after the *Nature* article appeared, Sarich showed a slide of the journal's cover, with the four hominoid skulls, and proclaimed that, since the article had appeared in the issue of the first week of April, it was obviously the April fool's issue.

David Pilbeam also had been invited to this symposium. His presentation represented a radically different stance from his previous position. Instead of interpreting molecular data as he had done in the past, and as I was also proposing in the context of paleontologically and morphologically based hypotheses of relatedness, Pilbeam was now strongly committed to a molecularly based orang-gorilla-chimp-human arrangement. Thus he interpreted morphology in the context of a molecularly based phylogenetic scheme and felt, for instance, that his and Steve Ward's analyses of the palatal region of hominoids supported a gorilla-chimp-human grouping. The next year, in a chapter on hominoids in an edited volume, Pilbeam and a co-author and student, Jay Kelley, further expressed their current preference for molecularly derived phylogenies and made clear their general dissatisfaction with "perspectives utilizing mostly morphological characters." They also dismissed my suggestions of possible human-orang relatedness, not by discussing the morphological characters or even my methodology but by claiming that "Schwartz . . . seriously misinterprets or cites incorrectly the work of Templeton . . . and Ward." The problem here, I think, is that of not making a distinction between data and the interpretation of data.

It happens often enough. In morphologically and molecularly oriented articles alike, the sequence of presentation usually takes the form of, first, a brief historical introduction and statement of the problem to be addressed. Then appears a statement of how the data were collected and the data themselves, a discussion of the ramifications of the data and an interpretation of them in the context of delineating evolutionary relationships, and finally, perhaps, a comment on the implications of the data and the scheme of relationships generated from them.

It sounds simple and straightforward: data in, a phylogeny out. But this is not always the case. Often, while on the way to settling on one particular phylogeny, alternative phylogenies emerge from the analysis and the interpretation of the data, and they may be identified and discussed in the text—as in the case, for instance, of Templeton reinterpreting Ferris, Wilson, and Brown's mitochondrial DNA data. But it is also the case that once a particular evolutionary scheme is accepted, for whatever reasons, as the preferred one, the alternatives tend to be forgotten, even though they may have been—and may, with other data or reinterpretation, emerge as being—logically or statistically as viable as the one chosen. Thus, and with enough repetition, what really is "data in, interpretation, alternative phylogenies out" often becomes "data in, one phylogeny out." But, in practically every one of these phylogenetically oriented articles, if you go back to the original data and the discussion of them, you will see that a choice among evolutionary schemes was made, and you also might find that reinterpretation of the data yields yet other alternative theories of relationship.

All too often, however, the data are not reexplored for alternative interpretations, and the conclusion—the author's or authors' preferred alternative—is accepted and treated as if it were data itself instead of the *interpretation* of data. Thus the reanalysis of a colleague's data and the arrival at a different conclusion using the same data can be mistaken for misrepresentation. In this light, it is relevant to note that Henry Krips, a philosopher of science and physicist, pointed out during a recent lecture that, although the philosophy of modern science emphasizes testability and falsifiability, the conclusions presented in most scientific articles are not questioned and the data are not reanalyzed. Indeed, if you were to peruse back issues of the more prominent science journals, you would find that those articles subject to questioning are those that veer too far from the mainstream.

But the human-orang theory of relatedness aside, my investigations also revealed a virtual lack of morphological support for the theory that chimps are more closely related to humans than they are to any other hominoid. Essentially, in a broad comparison among anthropoid primates of over two hundred features—based on those compiled and published by Colin Groves, a mammalian systematist at the Australian National University, and supplemented with data from other sources—humans and chimps exclusively shared only five. When I went over my analysis with Peter Andrews, he thought that perhaps I had been too generous in my assessment. His interpretation of the same data revealed only three features that he thought unambiguously supported the potential relatedness of chimps and humans. Colin, however, had interpreted the data as basically supporting two schemes of relatedness: first, humans with chimps, and, as the alternative, humans with an African ape group. Most recently, Colin co-authored an article in which a computer analysis of these characters yielded human-chimp and human–African ape groupings as the most highly corroborated alternatives. But because individual characters must first be identified as being potentially either derived (indicating closeness of relatedness) or primitive (indicating no special relationship) before the computer can generate schemes of relatedness, it is obvious that the systematist's methodological approach to determining primitive versus derived plays an important role at the very beginning of the analysis. And as Colin reiterates throughout this article, "[t]he question 'what is a character?' is a real problem."

If we are going to accept an exclusive human-chimp association, then we are going to have to accept the consequences that go along with it. The most profound consequence is, I think, that morphology has to be viewed as unrevealing when it comes to resolving the evolutionary relationships of organisms. Otherwise, the uniquenesses shared by chimps and gorillas, especially in their forearm anatomy, provide overwhelming evidence of their close evolutionary relationship. If we accept molecularly based phylogenies exclusively, and not as potential alternative hypotheses, we must reject fossils as being informative sources of data, because fossils are known only as preserved morphological entities. And, thus, because fossils cannot be placed reliably in schemes of phylogenetic relationships—that can result only from a morphological analysis—they cannot be used to provide dates from which to calibrate any evolutionary clock, molecular or otherwise.

Final Reflections

But let's return to the human-orang theory. I suggested this alternative theory of hominoid relationships on the basis of a variety of features that, through a series of comparisons, emerged as being shared uniquely by humans and orangs. And some of these apparent shared uniquenesses are rather intriguing. For instance, a group of Harvard neuroanatomists found that, compared to other primates, humans and orangs develop the greatest degree of asymmetry in two areas of the cerebral portion of the brain. Proper human fetal brain development can be monitored by assessing the level of the hormone estriol in the mother's urine. Reproductive physiologists have found that, among primates, only the great apes and humans excrete estriol. Among these four primates, humans and orangs excrete the highest levels—up to five times more than chimps and gorillas. Also tied in with brain development is the adrenal gland. And, it turns out, humans and orangs have relatively much larger fetal adrenal glands than other primates, including chimps and gorillas. To me, these features represent real uniquenesses—in addition, for example, to the lack of an estrous cycle—that humans and orangs share.

My application of the same comparative approach also revealed various uniquenesses shared by chimps and gorillas as well as by humans and the African apes together, humans and gorillas, and even humans and chimps. (For the interested reader, all of the features are spelled out in my chapter in a book I edited on orang-utan biology.) What I found (and still find) interesting about this methodological exercise is that it yielded everyone's favorite scheme of relatedness among humans and the African apes—although chimp-gorilla was more highly corroborated than chimp-human. But it also yielded a highly corroborated orang-human sister group.

Nevertheless, the broad comparison did yield sets of alternative phylogenies, which, I think, is what anyone should expect from comparative analyses. In a similar vein, Peter Andrews, for instance, has published the results of his comparative studies and come to a similar conclusion. And even though in this publication Peter disputed some of my data supporting the delineation of uniquenesses shared by humans and orangs, he still ended up conceding that humans and orangs do share some features uniquely.

Because of our similar interests and concerns about interpreting molecular and morphological data to reconstruct evolutionary relationships among the hominoids, Peter and I decided to collaborate on this endless investigation. We have been at it now for over five years, whenever I get to London. We don't agree on everything. But why should we? Peter doesn't think that humans and orangs share as many uniquenesses as my interpretation of the data yields, but that is not the point. To me, and I think I can say this for Peter as well, it is not important that any particular scheme of relatedness is "right" or "wrong." Rather, it is important that we evolutionary biologists recognize not only the limits of the data we are analyzing, but our limits of analysis and interpretation, as well. I think the human-orang theory is the most highly supported of the morphological alternative theories of hominoid relationships. But, even if this theory never becomes accepted, it is now impossible to deny that humans and orangs share some features uniquely—and, as recently as ten years ago, this was not even thought of as possible (because humans were supposed to be closely related to the African apes).

I am not, however, wedded to the hypothesis that humans and orangs are closely related to one another. On a very basic, fundamental level, I do not really care who's related to whom. What I do care about is being critical of how I or anyone else proceeds methodologically, and being aware of the consequences not only of the theories of relatedness that are generated but, especially, of the selection of one particular theory from among the alternatives that are available.

To me, what is interesting and exciting about the field of evolutionary biology that investigates the potential relationships of organisms is knowing that any one of us can discover features that add a new twist to what seems to be an open-and-shut case. The opportunity for "new" discoveries from within the "old, tried, and true" is also important for another reason: It should force us to confront and deal with inconsistencies in evolutionary schemes that derive from different kinds of data. When, for example, we embrace one particular theory of relatedness, we also are deciding that uniquenesses (or even just similarities, if that happens to be the approach) that otherwise would yield alternative theories of relatedness do no such thing—these "other" features are not, therefore, phylogenetically significant. Because we have accepted one alternative theory of relatedness, these "other" features must be interpreted as being either primitive retentions from some earlier ancestor or features that evolved in parallel with, and independently of, one another. With regard to the theory that chimps are most closely related to humans, explanations for what would otherwise be uniquenesses shared by these hominoids with other hominoids, have indeed been developed in the literature. Why not interpret things in the context of the obvious alternative theory—that, based on a suite of morphological uniquenesses, chimps are more closely related to gorillas? This, of course, would lead to a questioning of the model of molecular change upon which the chimp-human relationship is based. And that might be productive. Remember, once the preferred theory linked humans with great apes; then it linked humans with African apes; now it links humans with chimps. And now, some molecular systematists are going the other way—questioning the human-chimp theory and favoring a human–African ape theory. On the paleontological side, specific fossils were identified as ancestors of hominids, chimps, gorillas, and orangs. Now none is considered ancestral to any hominoid. Being "right" or "wrong," especially in the evolutionary sciences, is oftentimes relevant only at a certain moment in time—depending on what ideas or intellectual frameworks are popular.

There is a tendency these days to believe that the more technologically sophisticated we become—the more powerful the electron microscopes or the sequencers, or the more sophisticated the computer programs for generating schemes of relatedness—the less chance there will be for error to creep into our analyses. On one level, this belief would appear to be correct. If something is hidden, an electron microscope might reveal its presence. If things need to be counted, or if a string of DNA molecules needs to be sequenced, the appropriate computer hardware and programs can be found or created that can probably do it. But we, you and I, are still the final arbiters of the significance of what these sophisticated technological tools have revealed. This point should not be taken lightly. For example, during the very week I was putting the final touches on this chapter, an article appeared in the journal *Nature* demonstrating the inheritance of mitochondrial DNA in mice from the *paternal* line. As a consequence of this discovery, ideas of evolution based on a model of exclusive inheritance of mitochondrial DNA from the maternal line will have to be rethought. And, perhaps even more profoundly (at least in terms of the media hype it has received), Alan Templeton has reinvestigated the mitochondrial DNA "Eve," "Out of Africa" theory of modern human origins and demonstrated that the computer program used to manipulate the data and generate the evolutionary tree was not appropriate. Immediately following Templeton's article, which was published recently in the journal *Science*, was a retraction co-authored by one of the originators of the mitochondrial DNA Eve theory.

It is we who make the decisions about who is related evolutionarily to whom, about who will be recognized as a species apart from all others, about who was done in by whom or by what, or about whatever it is we think but can derive only from the reconstruction of historical or evolutionary events. As long as this is the case—and it always will be—there is no room for intolerance of ideas that run counter to the received wisdom of the time and no justification for claiming to have a stranglehold on the truth. What seems real today may very well end up in the pile of discarded truths of tomorrow.

EPILOGUE

Some months after I completed this manuscript and it was in the process of being typeset, I went to the American Museum of Natural History in New York City to give one of my semiannual workshops on human evolution for the members program. I use these visits to renew old friendships, keep abreast of new discoveries and debates, and catch-up on relevant publications.

As often happens, I spent one night at Ian Tattersall's apartment. As also often happens, we spent the evening chewing the fat about new and old projects and the state of affairs in paleoanthropological studies. Ian felt that the tide was turning, at least in terms of issues of human evolution, from the more traditional approaches to defining species and determining evolutionary relationships to those that have begun to emerge in the controversy over Neandertals. He ventured to suggest that some of my more controversial hypotheses would eventually gain wider acceptance in the field as viable alternatives. But this might take a while. Perhaps this acceptance would occur posthumously.

Fortunately—for me, anyway—the next day, when reading through recent issues of journals from the museum's library, I came across the totally unexpected. It was an article by Rajani Thiranagama, A. T. Chamberlain, and Bernard Wood on the ontogeny and comparative anatomy of the superficial veins of the forelimb in a variety of mammals, including primates. Without going through all the details, I shall quote from their concluding discussion section. (I have left in the authors's citations to the literature, some of which I had also cited in the bibliography at the end of this book; the reference to Groves [1987] is to his review of my book, *The Red Ape*):

> The phylogeny of the great apes and humans continues to evade a satisfactory resolution, although some of the morphological data and much of the biomolecular evidence appear to support a distinction between an African ape and human clade (= evolutionary group) and its sister group, the orangutan [Andrews, 1987]. However, Schwartz [1984; see also Groves, 1986, 1987] has marshalled a suite of derived character states, shared by *Homo* and *Pongo* (= the orang-utan), and has cited these character states as supporting an exclusive cladistic relationship between the two taxa. The status as synapomorphies (= shared derived character states) of some of these character states has been cogently challenged by Groves [1987] and Andrews [1987], but there are nonetheless up to 12 character states that are refractory to criticism and must be accepted as indicating a relationship (or convergence) between *Pongo* and *Homo* [Groves, 1987].

> The results of our detailed study of the forelimb superficial veins underscores the importance of ontogenetic evidence in reconstructing character phylogenies. . . . In the absence of ontogenetic data for the deveolopment of the medial forelimb superficial vein, the presence of this vein would constitute strong evidence supporting a sister group relationship between *Pongo* and *Homo*.

It's only a beginning, and there's lots more research, reanalysis, and debate over the alternative hypotheses still to be done. But, I'm not dead yet.

REFERENCES

As in all scientific publications, I have listed in the bibliography the references I consulted during the writing of this book. I have made certain to list the sources from which I have quoted post-Classical authorities. Translations and bibliographic sources for Classical authors are available in the volumes by S. Brown and P. Mosca (see listings for chapter 2).

CHAPTER 1: EVERYTHING YOU WANTED TO KNOW
ABOUT BONES (AND MORE)

Andrews, P., and J. Cook. 1987. "Natural Modifications to Bones in a Temperate Setting." *Man* 20: 675–691.

Archeological Institute of America, compiler. 1967. *Archeological Discoveries in the Holy Land.* New York: Bonanza Books.

Behrensmeyer, A. K., and A. P. Hill, eds. 1980. *Fossils in the Making:*

Vertebrate Taphonomy and Paleoecology. Chicago: University of Chicago Press.

Brain, C. K. 1981. *The Hunters or the Hunted? An Introduction to African Cave Taphonomy*. Chicago: University of Chicago Press.

Klein, R. G., and K. Cruz-Uribe. 1984. *The Analysis of Animal Bones from Archeological Sites*. Chicago: University of Chicago Press.

Magnusson, M. 1977. *BC: The Archaeology of the Bible Lands*. London: Bodley Head.

Petrie, W. M. Flinders. 1891. *Tell El Hesy (Lachish)*. London: Committee of the Palestine Exploration Fund.

Russell, M. D. 1987a. "Bone Breakage in the Krapina Hominid Collection." *American Journal of Physical Anthropology*, 72: 373–379.

———. 1987b. "Mortuary Practices at the Krapina Neandertal Site." *American Journal of Physical Anthropology* 72: 381–397.

Shipman, P. 1981. *Life History of a Fossil*. Cambridge, Mass.: Harvard University Press.

Solecki, R. S. 1971. *Shanidar: The First Flower People*. New York: Alfred A. Knopf.

Thompson, Henry O., ed. 1984. *The Answers Lie Below: Essays in Honor of Lawrence Edmund Toombs*. New York: University Press of America.

Trinkaus, E. 1975. "The Neandertals from Krapina, Northern Yugoslavia: An Inventory of the Lower Limb Remains." *Zeitschrift für Morphologie und Anthropologie* 67: 44–59.

Wheeler, M. 1954. *Archaeology from the Earth*. London: Penguin Books (1956 reprint).

White, T. D. 1986. "Cut Marks on the Bodo Cranium: A Case of Prehistoric Defleshing." *American Journal of Physical Anthropology* 69: 503–509.

CHAPTER 2: INFANTS, BURNED BONES, AND
SACRIFICE AT ANCIENT CARTHAGE

Angel, J. L. 1971. *The People of Lerna: Analysis of a Prehistoric Aegean Population*. Washington, D.C.: Smithsonian Institution Press.

Brown, S. 1990. *Late Carthaginian Child Sacrifice and Sacrificial Monuments in Their Mediterranean Context.* Sheffield, England: Sheffield Academic Press.

Glob, P. V. 1977. *The Bog People.* Ithaca, N.Y.: Cornell University Press.

Harden, D. 1963. *The Phoenicians,* 2d ed. New York: Frederick A. Praeger.

Hurst, H., and L. E. Stager. 1978. "A Metropolitan Landscape: The Late Punic Port of Carthage." *World Archaeology* 9: 334–346.

Mosca, P. G. 1975. "Child Sacrifice in Canaanite and Israelite Religion." Ph.D. diss., Harvard University.

Moscati, S. 1965. *The World of the Phoenicians.* London: Weidenfeld and Nicolson (English translation, 1968).

Pedley, J., ed. 1980. *New Light on Ancient Carthage.* Ann Arbor, Mich.: University of Michigan Press.

Schwartz, J. H. 1984. "The (Primarily) Mammalian Fauna." In *Excavations at Carthage: The British Mission,* volume 1, edited by H. R. Hurst and S. P. Roskams, pp. 229–256. Sheffield, England: University of Sheffield.

———. 1989. "The Tophet and 'Sacrifice' at Phoenician Carthage: An Osteologist's Perspective." *Terra* 28: 16–25.

Stager, L. E., and S. R. Wolff. 1984. "Child Sacrifice at Carthage: Religious Rite or Population Control?" *Biblical Archaeology Review* 10: 31–51.

Stead, I. M., J. B. Bourke, and D. Brothwell, eds. 1986. *Lindow Man: The Body in the Bog.* Ithaca, N.Y.: Cornell University Press.

Tierney, P. 1989. *On the Highest Altar: The Story of Human Sacrifice.* New York: Viking.

CHAPTER 3: BONES AND THE LAW

Black, T. K., III. 1978. "Sexual Dimorphism in the Tooth-Crown Diameters of the Deciduous Teeth." *American Journal of Physical Anthropology* 48: 77–82.

Kennedy, K. A. R. 1989. "Skeletal Markers of Occupational Stress." In *Reconstruction of Life from the Skeleton,* edited by M. Y. Iscan and K. A. R. Kennedy, pp. 129–160. New York: Alan R. Liss.

Schwartz, J. H. Forthcoming. *Human Skeletal Analysis.* New York: Oxford University Press.

CHAPTER 4: FETUSGATE

Baer, K. E. von. 1828. *Über Entwicklungsgeschicte der Thiere: Beobachtung und Reflexion.* Königsberg: Bornträger.

Cook, J. 1975. "Control of Somite Number During Morphogenesis of a Vertebrate, *Xenopus laevis.*" *Nature* 254: 196–199.

Haeckel, E. 1866. *Generelle Morphologie der Organismen.* Berlin: Georg Reimer.

Hofer, M. O. 1980. "The External Anatomy of the Oro-nasal Region of Primates." *Zeitschrift für Morphologie und Anthropologie* 73: 233–249.

Huxley, T. H. 1863. *Man's Place in Nature.* New York: D. Appleton and Company.

Meier, S. 1979. "Development of the Chick Embryo Mesoblast." *Developmental Biology* 73: 25–45.

Schultz, A. H. 1968. "The Recent Hominoid Primates." In *Perspectives on Human Evolution,* volume 1, edited by S. L. Washburn and P. C. Jay, pp. 122–195. New York: Holt, Rinehart and Winston.

Schwartz, J. H. 1984. "Supernumerary Teeth in Anthropoid Primates and Models of Tooth Development." *Archives of Oral Biology* 29: 833–842.

———. Forthcoming. *Human Skeletal Analysis.* New York: Oxford University Press.

CHAPTER 5: HUMAN EVOLUTION: DART, HUXLEY, AND DARWIN

Broom, R. 1951. *Finding the Missing Link.* London: Watts & Co.

Dart, R. A. 1925. "*Australopithecus africanus:* The Man-ape of South Africa." *Nature* 115: 195–199.

Darwin, C. 1836–1844. *Notebooks.* Transcribed and edited by P. H.

Barrett, P. J. Gautrey, S. Herbert, D. Kohn, and S. Smith, London and Ithaca, N.Y: British Museum (Natural History) and Cornell University Press, 1987.

Darwin, C. 1859. *On the Origin of Species*. Cambridge, Mass.: Harvard University Press (facsimile of the first edition, 1964).

Darwin, C. 1871. *The Descent of Man*, volume 1. London: John Murray.

Gregory, W. K. 1922. *The Origin and Evolution of the Human Dentition*. Baltimore: Williams and Wilkins.

Huxley, T. 1863. *Man's Place in Nature*. New York: D. Appleton and Company.

———. 1896. *Man's Place in Nature*. New York: D. Appleton and Company.

Leakey, L. S. B., P. V. Tobias, and J. R. Naper. 1964. "A New Species of Genus *Homo* from Olduvai Gorge." *Nature* 202: 7–9.

Spencer, F. 1986. Ecce Homo: *An Annotated Bibliography of Physical Anthropology*. New York: Greenwood Press.

CHAPTER 6: COPING WITH NEANDERTALS: THE FIRST TWELVE DECADES

Brace, C. L. 1964. "The Fate of the 'Classic' Neanderthals: A Consideration of Hominid Catastrophism." *Current Anthropology* 5: 3–43 (including replies).

Broom, R. 1937. "On Australopithecus and Its Affinities." Reprinted (1972) in *Climbing Man's Family Tree*, edited by T. D. McCown and K. A. R. Kennedy, pp. 322–327. Englewood Cliffs, N.J.: Prentice-Hall.

Busk, G. 1861. "On the Crania of the Most Ancient Races of Man.—by Professor H. Schaaffhausen, of Bonn. With Remarks, and Original Figures, Taken from a Cast of the Neanderthal Cranium." *Natural History Review* 2: 155–176.

Busk, G., and H. Falconer. 1865. "On the Fossil Contents of the Genista Cave, Gibraltar." *Quarterly Journal of the Geological Society of London* 21: 364–370.

Coon, C. S. 1962. "New Findings on the Origin of Races." *Harper's* magazine, December.

————. 1965. *The Living Races of Man*. New York: Alfred A. Knopf.

Dubois, E. 1900. "Pithecanthropus erectus—A Form from the Ancestral Stock of Mankind." *Smithsonian Report for 1889:* 445–459.

Garrod, D. A. E., and D. M. A. Bate. 1937. *The Stone Age of Mount Carmel I: Excavations at the Wady el-Mughara*. Oxford: Clarendon Press.

Gregory, W. K. 1920. "The Origin and Evolution of the Human Dentition: A Paleontological Review. Part IV. The Dentition of the Higher Primates and Their Relationships with Man." *Journal of Dental Research* 2: 607–717.

————. 1921. "The Origin and Evolution of the Human Dentition: A Paleontological Review. Part V. Later Stages in the Evolution of the Human Dentition; with a Final Summary and a Bibliography." *Journal of Dental Research* 3: 87–228.

Haeckel, E. 1876. *The Evolution of Man*, 2 vols., 3d ed. New York: H. L. Fowle.

Hrdlička, A. 1927. "The Neanderthal Phase of Man. The Huxley Memorial Lecture of 1927." *Journal of the Royal Anthropological Institute* 57: 249–273.

Keith, A. 1915. *The Antiquity of Man*. London: Williams and Norgate.

King, W. 1864. "On the Neanderthal Skull, or Reasons for Believing It to Belong to the Clydian Period and to a Species Different from that Represented by Man." *Reports, British Association for the Advancement of Science*. 81–82.

Lyell, C. 1863. *The Geological Evidences of the Antiquity of Man, with Remarks on the Theories of the Origin of Species by Variation*. London: Murray.

McCown, T. D., and A. Keith. 1939. *The Stone Age of Mount Carmel II: The Fossil Human Remains from the Levalloiso-Mousterian*. Oxford: Clarendon Press.

Montagu, M. A. F. 1964. "Reply to Brace, C. L." *Current Anthropology* 5: 28.

Osborn, H. F. 1927. "Recent Discoveries Relating to the Origin and Antiquity of Man." *Palaeobiologica* 1: 189–202.

Schmerling, P. C. 1833–34. *Recherches sur les Ossements Fossiles Décourts dans les Cavernes de la Province de Liège*, vol. 1, 2. Liège: Collardin.

Weidenreich, F. 1946. *Apes, Giants, and Man.* Chicago: University of Chicago Press.

———. 1947. "Facts and Speculations Concerning the Origin of *Homo sapiens.*" *American Anthropologist* 49: 187–203.

CHAPTER 7: STILL COPING WITH NEANDERTALS: ARE THEY ONE OF US, OR NOT?

Andrews, P. 1984. "An Alternative Interpretation of the Characters Used to Define *Homo erectus.*" *Courier Forschungsinstitüt Senckenberg* 69: 167–175.

Brothwell, D. R. 1975. "Possible Evidence of a Cultural Practice Affecting Head Growth in Some Late Pleistocene East Asian and Australian Populations." *Journal of Archaeological Science* 2: 75–77.

Clark, W. E. LeGros, K. P. Oakley, G. M. Morant, W. B. R. King, C. F. C. Hawkes, et al. 1938. "Report of the Swanscombe Committee." *Journal of the Royal Anthropological Institute* 68: 17–98.

Conroy, G. C., C. J. Jolly, D. Cramer, and J. E. Kalb. 1978. "Newly Discovered Fossil Hominid Skull from the Afar Depression, Ethiopia." *Nature* 275: 67–70.

Day, M. H., and C. B. Stringer. 1982. "A Reconsideration of the Omo Kibish Remains and the *erectus-sapiens* Transition." Premier Congresse Internationale de Palaeontologie Humaine Prétirage, Nice, vol. 2, pp. 814–846.

Eldredge, N., and I. Tattersall. 1975. "Evolutionary Models, Phylogenetic Reconstruction, and Another Look at Hominid Phylogeny." In *Approaches to Primate Paleobiology,* edited by F. S. Szalay, pp. 218–242. Basel: S. Karger.

Howells, W. W. 1973a. *Evolution of the Genus* Homo. Reading, Mass.: Addison-Wesley.

———. 1973b. "Neanderthal Man: Facts and Figures." In *Paleoanthropology, Morphology and Paleoecology,* edited by R. H. Tuttle, pp. 398–407. The Hague: Mouton Publishers.

Hublin, J.-J. 1978. "Le Torus Occipital Transverse et les Structures Associées." Master's thesis, University of Paris.

Marston, A. T. 1936. "Preliminary Note on a New Fossil Human Skull from Swanscombe, Kent." *Nature* 138: 200–201.

Rightmire, C. P. 1985. "The Tempo of Change in the Evolution of mid-Pleistocene *Homo*." In *Ancestors: The Hard Evidence*, edited by E. Delson, pp. 255–264. New York: Alan R. Liss.

Santa Luca, A. P. 1978. "A Re-examination of Presumed Neandertal-like Fossils." *Journal of Human Evolution* 7: 619–636.

———. 1980. *The Ngandong Fossil Hominids: A Comparative Study of a Far Eastern Homo erectus Group*. New Haven, Conn.: Yale University Publications in Anthropology, no. 78.

Stringer, C. B. 1976. "Some Problems of Middle and Upper Pleistocene Hominid Relationships" presented at the Sixth Congress of the International Primatological Society, University of Cambridge, August 1976.

———. 1985. "Middle Pleistocene Hominid Variability and the Origin of Late Pleistocene Humans." In *Ancestors: The Hard Evidence*, edited by E. Delson, pp. 289–295. New York: Alan R. Liss.

———. 1990. "The Emergence of Modern Humans." *Scientific American* 262: 98–104.

Stringer, C. B., and P. Andrews. 1988. "Genetic and Fossil Evidence for the Origin of Modern Humans." *Science* 239: 1263–1268.

Stringer, C. B., J.-J. Hublin, and B. Vandermeersch. 1984. "The Origin of Anatomically Modern Humans in Western Europe." In *The Origins of Modern Humans: A World Survey from the Fossil Evidence*, edited by F. Spencer and F. Smith, pp. 51–135. New York: Alan R. Liss.

Tattersall, I. 1986. "Species Recognition in Human Paleontology." *Journal of Human Evolution* 15: 165–175.

Tattersall, I., and N. Eldredge. 1977. "Fact, Theory, and Fantasy in Human Paleontology." *American Scientist* 65: 204–211.

Thorne, A. G., and P. G. Macumber. 1972. "Discoveries of Late Pleistocene Man at Kow Swamp, Australia." *Nature* 238: 316–319.

Vandermeersch, B. 1978. "Le Crâne Pré-Wurmien de Biache-Saint-Vaast (Pas de Calais)." In *Recent Advances of Primatology*, edited by D. J. Chivers and K. A. Jousey, pp. 345–418. London: Academic Press.

————. 1981. *Les Hommes Fossiles de Qafzeh (Israël)*. Paris: C.N.R.S.

Wolpoff, M. H. 1980. *Paleoanthropology*. New York: Alfred A. Knopf.

Wolpoff, M. H., X. Z. Wu, and A. G. Thorne. 1984. "Modern *Homo sapiens* Origins: A General Theory of Hominid Evolution Involving the Fossil Evidence from East Asia." In *The Origin of Modern Humans: A World Survey of the Fossil Evidence,* edited by F. H. Smith and F. Spencer, pp. 411–483. New York: Alan R. Liss.

Wood, B. 1984. "The Origin of *Homo erectus.*" *Courier Forschungsinstitüt Senckenberg* 69: 99–111.

Wymer, J. 1955. "A Further Fragment of the Swanscombe Skull." *Nature* 176: 426–427.

CHAPTER 8: FINAL REFLECTIONS

Andrews, P. 1987. "Aspects of Hominoid Phylogeny." In *Molecules and Morphology in Evolution: Conflict or Compromise,* edited by C. Patterson, pp. 21–53. Cambridge: Cambridge University Press.

Andrews, P., and J. E. Cronin. 1982. "The Relationships of *Sivapithecus* and *Ramapithecus* and the Evolution of the Orangutan." *Nature* 297: 541–546.

Andrews, P., and I. Tekkaya. 1980. "A Revision of the Turkish Miocene Hominoid *Sivapithecus meteai.*" *Palaeontology* 9: 85–95.

Goodman, M. 1962. "Immunochemistry of the Primates and Primate Evolution." *Annals of the New York Academy of Sciences* 102: 219–234.

Groves, C. P., and J. D. Paterson. 1991. "Testing Hominoid Phylogeny with the PHYLIP Programs." *Journal of Human Evolution* 20: 167–183.

Gyllensten, U., D. Wharton, A. Josefsson, and A. C. Wilson. 1991. "Paternal Inheritance of Mitochondrial DNA in Mice." *Nature* 352: 255–257.

Hedges, S. B., S. Kumar, K. Tamura, and M. Stoneking. 1992. "Technical Comments: Human Origins and Analysis of Mitochondrial DNA Sequences." *Science* 255: 737.

Kelley, J., and D. Pilbeam. 1986. "Paleobiology of Miocene Large

Hominoids." In *Comparative Primate Biology*, vol. 1, *Systematics, Evolution, and Anatomy*, edited by D. R. Swindler and J. Erwin, pp. 361–411. New York: Alan R. Liss.

Lewin, R. 1987. *Bones of Contention*. New York: Simon and Schuster.

Lewis, G. E. 1934. "Preliminary Notice of New Man-like Apes from India." *American Journal of Science* 27: 161–181.

Pilbeam, D. 1972. *The Ascent of Man*. New York: Macmillan.

———. 1984. "Hominoid Phylogeny and the Hominoid Fossil Record." Paper presented at the annual meeting of the American Association for the Advancement of Science, New York, May.

———. 1986. "Hominoid Evolution and Hominoid Origins." *American Anthropologist* 88: 295–312.

Sarich, V., and A. Wilson. 1967. "Immunological Time Scale for Hominid Evolution." *Science* 158: 1200–1203.

Schwartz, J. H. 1983. "Palatine Fenestrae, the Orangutan, and Hominoid Evolution." *Primates* 24: 231–240.

———. 1984a. "On the Evolutionary Relationships of Humans and Orangutans." *Nature* 308: 501–505.

———. 1984b. "Hominoid Evolution: A Review and a Reassessment." *Current Anthropology* 25: 655–672.

———. 1987. *The Red Ape*. Boston: Houghton Mifflin.

———. 1988. "History, Morphology, Paleontology, and Evolution." In *Orang-utan Biology*, edited by J. H. Schwartz, pp. 69–85. New York: Oxford University Press.

Simons, E. L. 1961. "The Phyletic Position of *Ramapithecus*." *Postilla*, no. 57: 1–9.

———. 1969. "The Origin and Radiation of the Primates." *Annals of the New York Academy of Sciences* 167: 319–331.

Simons, E. L., and D. Pilbeam. 1965. "Preliminary Revision of the Dryopithecinae (Pongidae, Anthropoidea)." *Folia Primatologica* 3: 81–152.

Templeton, A. 1983a. "Phylogenetic Inference from Restriction Endonuclease Cleavage Site Maps with Particular Reference to the Evolution of Human and Apes." *Evolution* 37: 221–244.

———. 1983b. Letter to author.

———. 1992. "Technical Comments: Human Origins and Analysis of Mitochondrial DNA Sequences." *Science* 255: 737.

EPILOGUE

Thiranagama, R., A. T. Chamberlain, and B. A. Wood. 1991. "Character Phylogeny of the Primate Forelimb Superficial Venous System." *Folia Primatologica* 57: 181–190.

INDEX

Teeth (*cont'd*)
  tool development and reduction of stress on, 204–5, 211
  as tools, bone remodeling and, 65–70
Tekkaya, Ibrahim, 249–50
Tell Gezer (Israel), 9, 10
Tell Hesi (Israel), 6–8
  animal bone analysis at, 8–11
  misleading historical records on, 10–11
  pottery at, 6
  state of bone preservation in, 25–26
Tells, Israeli, 9
Templeton, Alan, 256–59, 260, 265
Tertullian, 33
Thiranagama, Rajani, 268
Thorne, Alan, 231
  on culture and human evolution, 204–9
Tierra del Fuego, Charles Darwin on inhabitants of, 146–47
Tobias, Phillip, 227
Todd, T. Wingate, 78
Tools
  Cro-Magnon, 168–69. *See also* Aurignacian tool culture
  as evolutionary force, 204, 211
  Neandertal, 16. *See also* Mousterian tool culture
Tophet, 37
  Carthaginian, 40–57
Trinil (Java) skull, 159–61, 164
Trinkaus, Eric, 18

Ulna, 4
Urns, Carthaginian burial, 40–46

Vallois, Henri Victor, 194
Vandermeersch, Bernard, 223–25, 226–27
Vertebrae, lumbar, 111–12, 114
Vertebral column, ontogeny of, 109–12
Von Baer, Karl Ernst, ontogenetic stages of, 105–7
Von Linné, Karl, 123

Waechter, John D'Arthur, 196, 198
Walker, Alan, 229
Ward, Steve, 251, 253–54
Washburn, Sherwood, 203
Water, effect of, on bone preservation and fossilization, 25–27
Weather, effect of, on bone preservation, 24–25
Weigelt, Johannes, 20
W. F. Albright Institute, 6–7
Whitaker, J. I. S., 39
White, Tim, 19, 203
Wilson, Allan, 244, 246, 247
WLH 50 (Willandra Lakes Hominid) skull (Australia), 208–9
Wolpoff, Milford, on culture and human evolution, 203, 204–9, 211
Wood, Bernard, 229, 268
Woodward, Arthur Smith, 165
Wright, G. Ernest, 6, 86
Wymer, John, 196

Yordanov, Yordan, 83

Zhoukoudien cave skulls (Peking man), 178, 183
Zuttiyeh skull (Galilee), 174–75